BETWEEN CHADDOR AND THE MARKET

Female Office Workers in Lahore

Jasmin Mirza

OXFORD

UNIVERSITY PRESS

OXFORD

UNIVERSITY PRESS

Great Clarendon Street, Oxford OX2 6DP

Oxford University Press is a department of the University of Oxford.
It furthers the University's objective of excellence in research, scholarship,
and education by publishing worldwide in

Oxford New York

Auckland Bangkok Buenos Aires Cape Town Chennai
Dar es Salaam Delhi Hong Kong Istanbul Karachi Kolkata
Kuala Lumpur Madrid Melbourne Mexico City Mumbai Nairobi
São Paulo Shanghai Singapore Taipei Tokyo Toronto

and an associated company in Berlin

Oxford is a registered trade mark of Oxford University Press
in the UK and in certain other countries

© Oxford University Press 2002

The moral rights of the author have been asserted

First published 2002

ISBN 0 19 579623 3

Typeset in Times
Printed in Pakistan by
New Sketch Graphics, Karachi.
Published by
Ameena Saiyid, Oxford University Press
5-Bangalore Town, Sharae Faisal
PO Box 13033, Karachi-75350, Pakistan.

CONTENTS

FIGURES AND TABLES

ACKNOWLEDGEMENTS

Between Chaddor and the Market: Female Office Workers in Lahore is a revised version of 'Working Women between *Chaddor* and the Market: A Study of Office Workers in the Islamic Republic of Pakistan', which was accepted as a doctoral dissertation by the Faculty of Sociology, Bielefeld University, Germany, in 1999. I would like to mention a few individuals here without whom this study would not have materialized. I am particularly indebted to Prof. Dr Gudrun Lachenmann of the Faculty of Sociology, Bielefeld University, who not only motivated me to start the dissertation but who encouraged and supported me with her advice and discussions throughout the Ph.D. programme, and to Prof. Dr Dieter Timmermann, of the Education Faculty, who was also a very supportive and helpful supervisor. The Interdisciplinary Women's Research Centre (IFF), Bielefeld University, provided me with office space, computer equipment, and helped me in many other ways during crucial stages of the dissertation. I am further thankful to the Ph.D. and MA students of the Sociology of Development Research Centre, Faculty of Sociology, Bielefeld University, for sharing ideas and discussions with me.

During my field research in Lahore, Pakistan, Angela Marcks, Christiane Wauschkuhn, several teachers from the Technical Training Centre for Women (TTCW), and many women in the hostel where I stayed—without naming them here individually— provided much valuable help. I would further like to thank Dr Jamshed Tirmizi from Seer (Pvt.) Ltd., Lahore, for interesting discussions and for granting me long leave in order to complete my Ph.D. at Bielefeld University after having joined Seer in the fall of 1998 as a Social Analyst and Senior Project Coordinator.

The Federal State of North Rhine-Westphalia and the German Academic Exchange Service (DAAD) kindly granted me scholarships for my studies in Bielefeld as well as for the field research in Lahore.

Last but not least, my family, particularly Elise Mirza and Ambar Naveed, constantly supported and encouraged me during my ups and downs. Thanks to all of you.

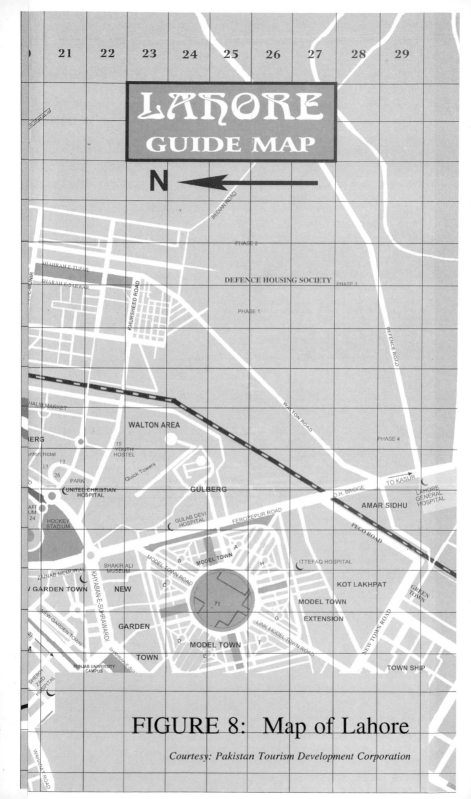

FIGURE 8: Map of Lahore

Courtesy: Pakistan Tourism Development Corporation

1
INTRODUCTION

Focus of the Study

Within the last four years so many changes have occurred in Pakistan. When I started to work at this place four years ago, very few girls could be seen in this area...and wearing the dresses we [working women] do. Now, when I come to the office there is even a bit of a rush with regard to women. Mall Road and Regal Crossing are office areas and I noticed that at the beginning women were rarely seen here. Now when I get off [the bus] at the stop I see many girls are working here. Some work in schools, some in offices....From that you can see that within only four years so much change has taken place in our culture, that the girls have started to think that 'we shouldn't be discouraged by the [societal] set-up, we ourselves have to create the set-up [in which we can work].'

(Zarka, telephone operator, 25 January 1997)

During the last decade, a new phenomenon has emerged in urban Pakistan[1] that has started to significantly change the gendered structure[2] of the urban labour market: lower-middle-class women have increasingly entered the office sector and have started to work in middle-level occupations that were regarded as exclusively 'male occupations' only a few years ago. They work as secretaries, receptionists, and telephone operators, as draftswomen, designers, and computer operators. These women still constitute a very small minority, and are hence regarded as 'strange birds' among the (male) office workers as well as among the urban lower-middle-class women in general. However, their presence in the work world has altered the working environment in offices. Female office workers have initiated, willingly or unwillingly, a process of de-segregation of the life worlds[3] of men and women, which has started at the workplace, but which might also—as the signs indicate—influence the whole social and gender order of society. Furthermore, the entry of women into the office sector has fundamentally changed the life world of these women, and it has challenged existing societal concepts of, and expectations toward, (working) women concerning their way of life, life planning, and career choices.

In Pakistan, which has a strong, patriarchal, Islamic society, this phenomenon of women entering the office sector is particularly interesting against the background of the norms of *purdah*—which include female seclusion, the gendered allocation of space, and the absence of concepts of social interaction between the sexes that pervade the social and gender order of society. The ongoing process of Islamization, too, has rather strengthened the segregation of the life worlds of men and women instead of providing concepts for mixed interaction between the sexes in all spheres of life, including the workplace. Due to the strong gender segregation in everyday life, the formal female labour force participation rate in Pakistan has always been very low, and working women have remained heavily concentrated in a few 'female' professions, for example, doctors and teachers, which are compatible with gender segregation and which are, therefore, regarded as 'respectable'. But female employment in the office sector requires the mingling of the sexes—through contact with male colleagues, and through dealing with the public—and thus de-segregation; and office jobs are, therefore, traditionally perceived as inappropriate and shameful for women.

Ironically, the women who are nowadays entering the office sector belong mainly to the lower-middle classes, which constitute the most conservative sections of Pakistani society. Klein and Nestvogel (1986: 135) describe the lower-middle classes in Pakistan as very heterogeneous. They can broadly be characterized as the sections of society that have an income above the minimum wage (as fixed by the state), that do not live in poverty according to national standards, that have adequate living conditions and can afford to educate their children at least up to tenth class. Hence, the lower-middle classes include traders, craftsmen, as well as, employees in industry and in the office sector. They constitute about 15 to 20 per cent of the urban population. Apart from this characterization, it is at least as important to consider lifestyle, and, obviously, gender constructs as an essential feature of the lower-middle classes. This section of society strictly adheres to what they perceive as the true Islamic way of life; their life world is pervaded by *purdah*, and they have been most receptive to the conservative Islamist discourses and movements in the country. Furthermore, the lower-middle classes are characterized by a constant drive to differentiate themselves from the lower sections of society, not only with regard to their ability to educate their children but also with regard to their standard of living, and the ability of the male breadwinner(s) to keep the female family members out of the labour market. For this reason, the lower-middle classes do not even consider female employment to be a possibility and there is generally no history of working women in these families. The women who are entering the labour force today are usually the first ones in their families who have been gainfully employed; thus, having working women in the family—and even in 'shameful' office jobs—is a new experience for this section of society.

I first became aware of the problems and conflicts of lower-middle-class women working in the office sector in 1992/1993. During that time I conducted a follow-up report about the market integration of former participants of a course that was offered by the Technical Training Centre for Women (TTCW), Lahore. This is a vocational training centre for lower-middle-class women that aims to provide school leavers market-oriented training for later employment in the office sector, namely Dress Designing/Dress Making (see Mirza 1992; for a revised version see Mirza 1994a: 91–9). I also worked as a research assistant for one of the local NGOs that conducted a broad survey about the socio-economic background, the employment rate, working conditions, wages, etc., of all former students of the TTCW.

For this study I interviewed about hundred women at their homes or workplaces (for the findings see Shaheed/Mumtaz 1993). Due to my involvement in these studies, and also due to my own experiences as a working woman in Pakistani society, I gained my first insights into the dilemmas and problems lower-middle-class women face when they want to take up employment in the office sector. It became clear to me that imparting skills to women for which there is a demand in the labour market was an important precondition for later employment, but that, even when they had a market-oriented education, women found it extremely difficult to bridge the gap between their life world and the world of work in the office sector, in which very different behaviour patterns and norms prevail.[4]

This study aims to analyse the process of the labour market integration of lower-middle-class women into the office sector in urban Pakistan. The focus shall be on 'engendering' the embeddedness of the market in society, by analysing the interfaces which emerge in women's life world and in the market due to women's entry into office jobs. In accordance with Norman Long, I define a social interface as 'a critical point of intersection or linkage between different social systems, fields or levels of social order, where structural discontinuities, based upon differences of normative value and social interest, are most likely to be found' (1989a: 1f). In other words, interface studies are basically concerned with the analysis of discontinuities in social life. Such discontinuities are characterized by discrepancies in values, interests, knowledge, and power. Interfaces typically occur at points where different, and often conflicting life worlds or social fields intersect. More concretely, they characterize social situations in which the interactions between actors become oriented towards devising ways of bridging, accommodating to, or struggling against each others' different social and cognitive worlds (Long 1989b: 232).[5]

The questions that shall be tackled in this study are, *inter alia*: How do these women experience their first steps into the (male-dominated) office sector? What discontinuities emerge between their own life world and the world of work, and how do women handle them? How is the office sector itself embedded in society; or, in other words, what are the interactions between the social and gender order of society on the one hand, and the office environment on the other hand? And how do they influence the access of women to employment, gender relations, and the gendered organization of work and space at the workplace? What changes have occurred—in women's lives as well as in the office sector—due to women's entry into office jobs? In this actor-oriented study the focus will be on women's logic of action, their negotiation strategies and their rooms for maneuver, and on the question regarding how these are related to their life world.

Since an understanding of the life world and gender relations of lower-middle-class women in Pakistan is a precondition for analysing the embeddedness of women's employment in their life world and in the social and gender order of society, a relatively large part of this study shall focus on discussing this issue (chapter two). An analysis of the gendered structure of the urban labour market, and the way the social and gender order of society influence women's labour force participation and career choices shall be provided in chapter three. Emphasis shall be placed on the changes that have been taking place in the gendered structure of the market, partly due to worsening economic conditions. Chapter four focuses on the market integration of lower-middle-class women into the office sector. The way women experience their new role as office workers, and the conflicts and problems arising in their life world due to their decision to become gainfully employed shall be analysed. Chapter five provides a discussion of the office sector, i.e., of the way office cultures change through women's presence at the workplace, gender relations and the gendered organization of work and space in the offices, and women's career prospects in this traditional male field of employment. Chapter six concentrates on the changes that have taken place in the life world of the working women (and their families) due to their employment. A comprehensive discussion of the results is given in chapter seven.

The Process of Field Research

The empirical data was collected with qualitative research methods; they are based on theoretical sampling and thoroughly build on the positioning of the researcher in the field.

The field research was conducted in Lahore, which is the district capital of Punjab, the largest province in Pakistan.[6] The official population figure for Lahore is approximately 5.7 million (Population Census 1998, quoted in *The News*, 31 October 1999), but according to unofficial estimations, Lahore has more than 7 million inhabitants. I chose Lahore for the collection of my empirical data for the following reasons. First, it was not possible to conduct research in Karachi, the largest city, due to the uncertain law and order situation there. Second, there are great differences between the four provinces, particularly the urban centres, with respect to the social and gender order of society. In cities like Peshawar or Quetta, female seclusion and gender segregation are observed most rigidly, and women rarely come into sight in the public sphere, and then only clad in big *chaddors* or *burqas* with a face veil (*niqab*). In contrast to this, in Karachi, the most 'modern' metropolitan city in Pakistan, many women work, and women are much more visible in the public sphere in general. Lahore is situated in-between these poles, and it, therefore, constituted a good location for my research.

Several teachers at the Technical Training Centre for Women in Lahore, who knew me because of my former temporary employment there, provided me with the addresses of former trainees. These women referred me to friends and former class fellows. I also decided to stay in a hostel for (lower-middle class) working women during the one-year field research. I had initially hoped that living in a hostel would also help me to collect empirical data, thinking I might be able to conduct some narrative interviews that would allow me to find out more about working women's lives, or that the women in the hostel might introduce me to their colleagues in their own offices, or to other working women they knew.

This, however, did not work out and for several reasons. First, nearly all working women who lived in the hostel (there were also many university and college students) were government employees, a high percentage of them being teachers, whereas I wanted to focus on women working in the private sector. I made this decision because only a small number of working women have the chance to get a prestigious government job, and because, in the ongoing process of downsizing of the public sector, the role of the state as an employer continues to lose its significance. The working conditions of women in government jobs are also quite different from those of office workers in the private sector. It is nearly impossible to get a government job in Pakistan without paying a high bribe (up to several lakhs of rupees) and/or having the right contacts, i.e., knowing high-ranking officers in public service. Thus, it is often only the relatives of government employees, particularly their children, who are able to obtain positions in the public sector. The women civil servants in the public sector did not fear losing their jobs, since government jobs are ensured, whether they work or not. It is also commonly done that the women (and particularly the men, since they are more mobile) come in the morning to confirm attendance in the register, and then leave for other private jobs, or go to the bazaar with colleagues, for example. The women are protected from harassment because they often have a male relative working in the same office (who helped them to get the job), and thus have patronage. Hence, it is important to differentiate between the public and the private sector.

Second, in the hostel, many of the working women were too well-educated to be included in my study, with some possessing university degrees. I had lived in the same hostel during 1992–93 for more than a year, and at that time the situation had been quite different. Several women who were less qualified, and who were working in secretarial jobs in the private sector, had lived in the hostel. One reason for this change in the socio-economic and educational background of the women might be the rise in the cost of living. Within three years the fees for a double room in the hostel had increased by more than 100 per cent. Despite the fact that the hostel was one of the cheapest in Lahore, only relatively well-qualified women in high-paying government jobs could afford to live there. Although I would consider the socio-economic background of most of these women to be typically lower-middle class, I decided to restrict my study to women with qualifications between a secondary school and college degree (X to XIV class), including some formal or informal skill-oriented training below university level, because I wanted to focus on office workers who worked in jobs at the middle level.

Third, the fact that I lived in the hostel and that several of the women who had been living in the hostel for years still knew me from my stay in 1992–93 was not always an advantage in the field research.[7] In 1992–93 I was a working woman like everybody else, and although the purpose of my stay was research, the women in the hostel did not really perceive my position as different. This had important ramifications for the following reasons: in the hostel the women lived together quite closely, and there were always rumours and gossip being spread around, particularly about the moral character and conduct of women. Therefore, they did not want to tell me, or other women in the hostel, personal matters or take me to their offices. They were afraid that they might become the target of gossip, as the following example indicates:

Shahnaz, a telephone operator working in a state-run bank in Lahore, had known me since 1992 when I first lived in the hostel. She had a dubious reputation in the hostel because she had had an affair with a married man, which had come to an end. Shahnaz had formerly worked as a telephone operator for a private company but was now holding a government job. When I asked her how she had managed to get this job she told me that her married boy-friend had helped her with his contacts. Later, I heard that her former friend had paid a bribe in order to get her the government job, but then their 'affair' had come to an end. Shahnaz agreed to take me to her office, but asked me not to tell anybody in the hostel or office if I might 'recognize someone or something'. I agreed, although I did not really understand what she was talking about. When we reached the office I realized that the young male telephone operator sitting next to her had visited her in the hostel several times. They remained on very formal terms at the office, and I understood that neither her office colleagues nor anyone in the hostel knew about this relationship. In the hostel everybody thought that he was a relative. For Shahnaz, it was a risk to take me to her office because I could have ruined her reputation by, intentionally or unintentionally, telling her (female) colleagues that she was dating this telephone operator, or by just greeting this man and thereby revealing that I must have seen him at the hostel before. I could also have mentioned to other women living in the hostel that the man who visited Shahnaz from time to time was not her relative but a *namaharam* man she was dating.

Like Shahnaz, many of the women in the hostel had something to 'hide', and for them it was just too risky to let me dig out their secrets. However, the fact that women move between different life worlds and present different selves according to the situation was not restricted to working women living in the hostel (though for me it was more visible there), but was a general phenomenon among many office workers. For example, the extended family and neighbours did not always know that a woman worked, because that would arouse gossip and could ruin the girl's reputation; or colleagues often did not know that a woman was divorced or separated because she feared being treated as 'prey' if this became public; or the family thought that the daughter was doing overtime, as she always said, but in reality she was secretly dating a man she had become acquainted with through her work. These facades could only be maintained as long as the women shielded their different life worlds from each other. Therefore, they were reluctant to lay open all their different roles and introduce me to all their different life worlds, since that could cause many problems to them. This made the triangulation of empirical data difficult—i.e. the analysis of a phenomenon from different perspectives and the use of different sources for the analysis of the same phenomenon (Lachenmann 1995c: 17; 1997c: 103). The experiences I had during the field research show the difficulties women face, straddling extremely gendered social spaces. However, some women did agree to show me their offices, and introduce me to their colleagues.

For the above mentioned reasons, I had to rely mainly on the teachers of the TTCW for my first contacts; as a consequence, about half of the women I selected as representative case studies are former trainees of the TTCW. I started my research by interviewing about forty women working in the office sector in secretarial and technical fields. I included large offices as well as small ones in my sample, but focused on national companies in the private sector. I decided to contact women at their workplaces because this was easier than locating their home addresses; it also enabled me, through participatory observation, to find out more about the office environment, the working conditions of the women. I phoned the women at their work places and fixed a time for a (semi-structured) interview. It was generally no problem to interview the women in their offices. I always insisted on talking to the women alone in order to have privacy during the interviews. These interviews were conducted in Urdu, and most of them were recorded.

The transcription of the interviews was done by Leila, a university graduate who lived in the hostel and worked part-time as a teacher of Fine Arts at a school. We used to discuss the interviews together and she made valuable contributions to the interpretation of the data. On the basis of her contextual knowledge, she often pointed out which of the interviewed women had obviously not told me the truth in order to protect or give a good account of themselves, and what the reasons might be for that. These discussions helped me to sort out interviews that had not made much sense, and to broach topics in subsequent interviews which I had not paid much attention to earlier.

On the basis of a first analysis of this empirical data, and of course of my own contextual knowledge, I selected twelve women working in the private sector and one woman working in a government job as typical cases for my study. I visited these thirteen women for a second semi-structured interview, which was also recorded. This was once again largely done at their workplaces, but some women preferred to be interviewed at their homes. I visited these women several times at their homes and in the offices to engage in informal conversation with them, their families and colleagues because I wanted to become acquainted with their living and working environments. I also tried to interview the employers of all these women in order to find out more about their reasons for employing female office workers, their experiences with them, and their perceptions of the changes that are taking place in the gendered structure of the labour market, and particularly in the office environments. However, a few employers refused an interview.

The selection of thirteen women representing typical cases enabled me to conduct a long-term, intensive study of individual women over a period of nearly one year.[8] This qualitative design, in which relatively much time was devoted to individual women, enabled me to understand the perspective of the women themselves, what they themselves considered important in their own life world and the problems and conflicts they faced as office workers. It also allowed me to develop analytical categories on the basis of these case studies, and to contextualize the empirical findings.[9] Apart from the thirteen case studies, several of the other interviews I conducted in the beginning of my field research will also find a special presentation in the course of this study.

Some of the office workers I interviewed did not want their real names to be mentioned in this study. Therefore, a few names have been changed in order to provide these women with the anonymity they desired. Furthermore, the names of all offices that were selected as case studies were also changed.

NOTES

1. With 34.3% of the population living in urban areas, Pakistan is the most urbanized country in South Asia. For a comparison of urbanization rates in other South Asian countries: India, 26.8%; Bangladesh, 18.3%; Nepal, 10.3%; Sri Lanka, 22.3%; Bhutan, 6% (Turner 2000).

2. The term 'gender' is understood in this study as a socially constructed phenomenon; it should not be confused with the sex of a person, which is biologically determined (for the difference between the sociological terms 'sex' and 'gender' see Abercombie et al. 1994: 180ff.).

3. In this study the term 'life world' is being used for *Lebenswelt*, a concept that has been widely used in German speaking sociology and that has, *inter alia*, heavily influenced the sociology of knowledge (*Wissenssoziologie*). Alfred Schuetz defines Lebenswelt as the structure of the common-sense world of everyday life: 'All typifications of common-sense thinking are themselves integral elements of the concrete historical socio-cultural Lebenswelt within which they prevail as taken for granted and socially approved.' (Quoted in Berger/Luckmann 1979: 28). In their book '*Strukturen der Lebenswelt*', Schuetz and Luckmann stress three characteristics of Lebenswelt. First, the naïve familiarity with a given and unproblematic background; second, the validity of an intersubjectively shared world; and third, the total and constraining and at the same time indefinite and porous character of the Lebenswelt. Situations change but the boundaries of the Lebenswelt cannot be transcended; they constitute a frame that, being itself boundless, marks boundaries (Schuetz/Luckmann 1979; see also Habermas 1981: 198ff.). Lebenswelt is thus socially constructed, and an understanding of Lebenswelt requires a phenomenological analysis of reality as it is taken for granted by the ordinary members of society in the intersubjectively meaningful conduct of their lives. It is a world that originates in their thoughts and actions, and is maintained by these. Lebenswelt differs from theoretical thought, 'ideas' and philosophical conceptions of the world (Weltanschauungen) as only a very limited group of people in any society engage in theorizing, in developing 'ideas', and in the construction of Weltanschauungen; and they can be referred to as something objective or normative. Lebenswelt, on the other hand, can not be referred to in the same manner. Actors always remain within the boundaries of their Lebenswelt; they cannot step out of it (for further explanations of the term Lebenswelt see Schuetz/Luckmann 1979; Habermas 1981; Berger/Luckmann 1979).

4. As became clear during my work at TTCW, this problem was 'solved' by many families by allowing their female family members to enroll in market-oriented training courses, but not allowing them to work after the completion of their training. This was one reason for the fact that the employment rate of the former students of TTCW was rather low. For further discussion see Mirza (1994a).

5. For a thorough discussion of the interface approach see Long (1989a; 1989b; 1993), and Long/Long (eds.) (1992).

6. The great majority of Pakistan's population live in Punjab (55.6%), followed by Sindh (23.0%), North-Western Frontier Province (13.4%)

and Balochistan, (5.0%) (Population Census 1998, quoted in *The Nation*, 9 July 1998).

7. The possibly restricting aspects of close ties on the qualitative empirical research have also been pointed out by Lachenmann (1995c: 6f). See also Fiege/Zdunnek (1993); Schulz (1993).

8. I had even known two of the women since 1992: Shaheen, who worked in the computer department of a famous private hospital in Lahore; and Aisha, who was employed at a local non-government organization. In the fall of 1992, when I worked in the TTCW, Shaheen belonged to the first batch of TTWC students who had completed a two-year course in 'Communication and Electronics'. I had also interviewed her, by chance, when I participated in a follow-up study of all former participants of the TTCW in the beginning of 1993, which was conducted by a local NGO. It was interesting to see how she had changed over a period of more than four years from a very shy and timid woman (in the TTCW) to a professional and confident office worker in 1996–97. Aisha was my colleague in 1992/1993 when I conducted the interviews of former students of TTCW for a local non-governmental organization. We conducted many of the interviews together, and I often visited her at home during that time. I became very familiar with her life world and, since I was working in the same office, with her working environment. When I came back to Lahore in the fall of 1996 to carry out field research for this study, she still worked at the same organization.

9. I am here drawing upon the grounded theory, which was originally developed as a qualitative research methodology by Anselm Strauss and Barney Glaser. A grounded theory is one that is inductively derived from the study of the phenomenon it represents. That is, it is discovered, developed, and provisionally verified through the systematic data collection and analysis of data pertaining to that phenomenon. Therefore, data collection, analysis, and theory stand in reciprocal relationship with each other. One does not begin with a theory and then prove it. Rather, one begins with an area of study, and what is relevant to that area is allowed to emerge. For further details about the grounded theory see Strauss/Corbin (1990); Strauss (1987); Strauss (1994).

2

LOWER-MIDDLE-CLASS WOMEN IN PAKISTAN: LIFE WORLD AND GENDER RELATIONS

Purdah and its Meaning for the Gender Order in Pakistani Muslim Culture

An analysis of the life world of women cannot be adequately carried out without taking into account the crucial importance of *purdah* as a constant element in everyday life in Pakistani Muslim culture.[1] Processes of societal change, and the way they affect women's lives, the spaces women have and the strategies they use to act in the societal context, as well as gender relations, have to be explicated within the context of Pakistan as a purdah-society:

> ...in Pakistan, purdah is such a critical factor in women's lives, and one that is normally ignored, particularly in development-related research (Shaheed 1989: 18).

Before focusing on the life world and gender relations of lower-middle-class women in Pakistan, it is first necessary to take a closer look at the institution of purdah. Here, the following questions arise: How can purdah be defined as a social phenomenon? How is purdah legitimized, i.e. which values and moral concepts build the foundation of purdah? What are the objectives of the purdah-system? And, finally, how does purdah shape the perception of and behaviour towards the other sex, i.e. gender relations, as well as the gender order of society?

One of the most striking phenomena in Pakistan—as in many other Muslim countries—is the absence of women from public life. Men, on the other hand, are everywhere. Unhurriedly, they stroll down the roads or stand together in groups in front of their houses, in the streets and bazaars. They sit in public parks and on the grass at the roadside to spend their leisure time with friends, chatting and exchanging the latest news. And they are omnipresent in the world of work, in the markets, the offices and shops. Women, particularly younger ones, are rarely seen. Clad in a burqa, a chaddor or a dupatta, their heads bowed and their eyes cast down, they walk quickly, even hastily, through the streets, while everybody's eyes follow them until they are out of sight again. Commonly they are seen in pairs, small groups, or accompanied by a man, or they are pillion riding in the side-saddle style on a bicycle or motorbike with a man sitting on the front seat.

These street scenes of everyday life have often lead to a misinterpretation of the meaning of purdah. A differentiation of society into a public and a private sphere is assumed, whereby the private interior space (i.e. the family and the household) is associated with women and the public exterior world is ascribed to men (for Pakistan, e.g. Ibraz 1993: 105 and 115ff; Shaheed 1990: 24; Shaheed 1989: 18 and 90; Mandelbaum 1988: 100). However, as it will be shown in the course of this chapter, defining purdah in terms of a simplistic division between the private (female) and the public (male) sphere is misleading.[2] Women are present and take part in public life although the spaces they occupy and the ways in which they enter the public sphere are quite different from, and not as visible as those of the men. Women do not have access to the public sphere to the same extent men have, but reducing women's lives to the private sphere blurs the fact that their spaces in public do exist and are—particularly during processes of societal transformation— constantly redefined and renegotiated. Transformation processes can even lead to the creation of new spaces for women outside their private realm, and the extension of already existing ones.

Definitions of purdah (literally meaning 'curtain' in Urdu) commonly refer to the practice of gender segregation and the seclusion of women and girls, as well as their veiling in public (for example, Balchin 1996: 178; Shaheed/Mumtaz n.d.: 75). Terms like 'segregation' and 'seclusion', which are usually associated with purdah, make clear that the 'crucial characteristic of purdah observance is the limitation of interaction between women and men outside certain well-defined categories' (Papanek 1971: 519). Therefore, purdah certainly aims at the 'creation of "separate worlds" of men and women' (Papanek 1971: 528):

... one of the most defining features of Muslim purdah is that social intercourse between men and women is delimited by the criterion of kinship. In this respect, social access and interaction between men and women is possible only if they are related ... (Ibraz 1993: 105).

In other words, the only men and women between whom social interaction is permitted are those between whom marriage is prohibited: they are said to be *maharam* to each other. Maharam is the legal term denoting a relationship by blood, milk, marriage or sexual union that makes marriage between persons so related forbidden. The term is also used in the sense that maharam persons are those with whom one can mix freely and be on informal terms. Familiar behaviour, however, is unacceptable towards *na-maharam* persons. Na-maharam literally denotes any person of the opposite sex whose kinship does not represent an impediment for marriage (Khatib-Chahidi 1993: 114). Na-maharam also includes cousins and other distant relatives between whom marriage is permitted according to Islamic law.

This restriction of interaction between na-maharam men and women is often attributed in the literature to what Vagt names the 'Islamic Theory of Sexuality and Sexual Behaviour of Men and Women' (Vagt 1992: 35). The Moroccan Sociologist, Fatima Mernissi (1987) is probably the best-known social scientist with regard to the analysis of the Muslim understanding of sexuality, and many studies which follow her line of argumentation have been published during the last few years (e.g. Sabbah 1988: 25–43; Heller/Mosbahi 1993: 66–82; Gerani 1996; Dahl 1997). Although not all these publications are necessarily coherent—they are marked by different, even contradictory statements and interpretations—the central points the analyses are based on are nevertheless quite similar. In short, the main idea is that, according to the Muslim concept of sexuality, women's sexuality is regarded as active and therefore dangerous for the social order.[3] The overwhelming sexual desires of the woman are so strong that they can hardly be kept under control; and since they have to be satisfied by the man, a situation arises in which the woman becomes the hunter and the man the prey.[4] At the same time it is insinuated that the woman exerts a dreadful attraction which breaks the willpower of the man and makes him helpless and unable to withstand the temptations that emanate from her (Vagt 1992: 35f; also Guenther 1993: 67):

> Such an interpretation of sexuality presents woman as the cause and man as the victim. The woman has desire, beauty, and power of attraction, thus presenting a disturbing danger for men. In order to protect men, women should, therefore, be controlled and kept separate—or chaos may be the result (Dahl 1997: 134).

Segregation of na-maharam men and women becomes a precondition for safeguarding the passive man who cannot control himself sexually in the presence of lust-inducing women (Mernissi 1987: 142). Therefore, 'for the devout Moslem any sharing of space with namaharam persons is to be avoided, as it could lead to illegal sexual intercourse outside the bonds of marriage, which is forbidden to all Moslems' (Khatib-Chahidi 1993: 114).

It becomes clear that in this concept of sexuality, men and women are primarily seen as sexual agents (Pahnke 1992: 11; Mernissi 1985: 220). The constant drive of women for tempting men is not regarded as an individual deviation, but as a dangerous collective phenomenon (Heller 1993: 69) that has to be tackled on a global level, i.e. through gender segregation. In this context the veiling of women in public, where segregation between na-maharam men and women cannot be maintained, serves two purposes. On the one hand, it shields women from men so that they do not come into contact with each other; on the other hand, it covers the women's sexual attractions which the men would otherwise not be able to resist, and they would become all too easily victims of their own desires. In Islamic literature it is emphasized that the main purpose of veiling is the protection of the family, because veiling is assumed to prevent extramarital sexual encounters (Darwisch/Liebl 1991: 7; see also Sherif 1987: 151).[5]

Veiling as a behaviour code imposed on women in order to reduce sexual tension in public places presents a good example of the fact that within the purdah-system it is basically the women—not the men—who are made responsible for maintaining gender segregation:

> They [the women] are expected to conform to certain codes/ideals of modesty, certain behaviour restrictions, especially in terms of their visibility in the public domain and in their interaction with un-related males. The need for restricting women's mobility arises because, relatively, there are no restrictions on the mobility of men. So that the two sexes will remain segregated and not freely interact, it is the mobility of women that must be restricted...(Ibraz 1993: 115).

Due to the alleged absence of internal control on the part of the men, men are removed from the individual responsibility of self-control and temperance (Reece 1996: 40). It is the women who must conduct themselves in a modest manner, and who have to be careful not to attract the attention of men. When they leave their homes, they must not wear tight clothes that reveal their figures, use fragrance, or display excessive make-up (Rahman in Reece 1996: 38f; also Sherif 1987: 159)—only to name a few preventive measures that would eradicate sexual attraction. Even a handshake between na-maharam men and women is unimaginable—a touch could elicit excitement or pleasure (Sherif 1987: 163).

Thus, the social order in Muslim societies is pervaded by notions concerning (female) sexuality and by concepts of how sexuality can best be organized and controlled.[6] This worldview is simply there, operating between people more or less unconsciously as a part of everyday life (Dahl 1997: 104/134; also Mernissi 1987: 45). The outcome is a gender order whose main characteristic is gender segregation.

Paradoxically, veiling and gender segregation actually have the opposite effect of what they intend—they enhance the sexual character in the interaction between men and women:

> Sexual segregation...fuels, and is fuelled by, the conflicts that it is supposed to avoid between men and women. Or better, sexual segregation intensifies what it is supposed to eliminate: the sexualization of human relations (Mernissi 1987: 140; see also Guenther 1993: 67; Heller/Mosbahi 1993: 191).

In fact, the sexual aspect becomes so omnipotent in any heterosexual interaction that a man can rarely imagine a relationship with a na-maharam woman that is not a sexual one (Minces 1992: 49). Thus, the woman is reduced to a 'woman-as-body', a sexual being, that is perceived as 'exclusively physical' (Sabbah 1988: 25).

Gender Relations outside Kinship: Men's and Women's Worlds Apart

A strong sexualization of gender relations in Pakistan is manifest, first of all, in the public sphere where women, particularly younger ones, are constantly stared at. As soon as a woman leaves her house and walks down the street the men raise their heads to stare at her, even turn around when she has already passed by, and jog to their friends to make them aware of her presence. Under these conditions women feel uncomfortable in public, and generally very few women are seen in public life. Many women I talked to during my field research commented on this situation jokingly, but also in anger that 'the men stare at us as if it is the first time they have seen a woman in their lives'; 'they think that a woman is something that has fallen from heaven. This is why their eyes almost pop out of their heads when they see one'; 'I don't know why they have to stare all the time. Don't they have sisters in their own home? Don't they know what a woman is?'[7]

The close link between purdah and the sexualization of gender relations is very visible in Pakistani society. In Pakistan's lower-middle class, everyday life is dominated by purdah restrictions, which lead to a far-reaching segregation between the life worlds of men and women without many interfaces for social intercourse. The whole organization of social life is geared towards shielding women from men, protecting women from men gazing at them. In the *mohalle*, the residential areas, the houses are constructed in a way that they shield the female inhabitants from strangers. The small lanes and pathways of the mohalle are marked by high walls on both sides. Commonly two doors lead into a house: one door is used by the family members, and opens the way directly into the house or to a little courtyard which is used by the female inhabitants to sit outside while doing household chores or just to chat or sleep at night during the long and hot summers, and at the same time be shielded from passing strangers. The other door is for visitors and leads to a visitors' room—which, however, is also used by the family during the absence of guests—from which neither the courtyard nor any other part of the house can be seen. Even in houses with no courtyard or only one entrance door there is always some kind of room for visitors. Windows commonly lead to the courtyard, but in case they can be seen from the street they are covered with curtains. Young women are not supposed to open the door and let a stranger in; this task is performed by a man, a boy or an older woman. Male visitors who are na-maharam or do not belong to the inner family circle are not allowed beyond the visitors' room. Even tea and snacks, which are commonly served to visitors, are not brought in by a woman but by a man or child, or food is placed on a tray outside the visitors' room and then taken inside by the man who is entertaining the guests. It rarely happens that couples who are not immediate kin visit together, but if that is the case the woman is led to the female family members inside the house or in the courtyard. Visitors for women are mainly restricted to female relatives, who visit each other quite frequently. But even when other women drop in, for example, neighbours who just want to chat or exchange the latest gossip, they are often allowed to go beyond the visitors' room and sit together with the women of the family. Men, on the other hand, are supposed to spend their leisure time outside. When men spend too much time inside the house they even run the danger of being ridiculed that they are not men, but women, because they stay at home all the time. Therefore, as far as the private realm of the houses is concerned, the purdah rules for men are much stricter. Men who belong to the same *mohalla* often stand together in groups in front of their houses or go to one of the small teashops or snackbars nearby when they want to meet and talk. They are not really supposed to bring friends into the house, because that would mean exposing 'their' women to na-maharam strangers.[8]

When girls reach the age of seven or eight, they are not allowed to go outside, even to play, any longer. They stay in the house with the women. Girls of the lower-middle class nowadays attend school at least up to Matriculation (X grade). They even study up to FA/F.Sc. (XII grade) or BA/B.Sc. (XIV grade). However, since all educational institutions up to college level (BA/B.Sc.) are gender segregated[9] (except in primary school), girls do not come into contact with males.[10] Students as well as teachers are female. Even transport to school/college is organized through a rickshaw or a mini-bus that picks up the girls from their own neighbourhood in the morning and brings them back home when school/college has finished, or a male relative takes them and brings them home by motorbike or bicycle. The shuttle service for school and college girls has, in fact, become a lucrative business in Pakistan. When colleges and schools close, dozens of vehicles wait in front of the educational institutions and—together with the private cars, motorbikes and bicycles—pick up the great majority of the girls. The reason for this is the inefficient public transportation system for women and the ubiquitous harassment of girls and women in public. Once the girls have completed their education they stay at home until they get married. The marriage is, in most cases, arranged by the parents.

The men of the family make the daily purchases, or a boy from the neighbourhood is sent to the shop or bazaar to buy urgently needed items. Doing all outside work is regarded as the duty of the men. Women just give the orders to their brothers, fathers, sons, etc. and get the things delivered. Women do not even go to the *tandoors* in their own mohalle, where the *rotis*, the loops of bread that are eaten with every meal, are baked and sold. If no male relative is available, the women stand in the half-opened doors of their houses until some child from the neighbourhood comes into sight, who is then sent to the tandoor. Women avoid going there because around the tandoors there are also, usually, small snackbars where men sit and have their meals. Buying the roti herself would mean that the woman has to wait in front of the tandoor until her rotis are baked, while the men sitting around stare at her in an indecent manner.

When, during 1992–93, I was working for several months at the TTCW, we offered counseling to women who were interested in getting admission to the TTCW, to help them find the right course that would match their qualifications and interests. However, we failed to consider that the women would not come down to the centre to get information about the courses. Only a few women came on their own, either with a girlfriend or with their mothers. In the majority of the cases, a brother or the father came to get the prospectus and the application form which the women would fill out at home and send back again via a male family member.

Social events, like weddings or engagements, also funerals, take place separately in different rooms. Recreational activities, which men seek outside the house, are brought into the home for the women, for example, women do not go to the cinema but from time to time a video player is rented so that they can watch a movie at home. Snacks, which are sold at every corner and which are eaten outside by the men, are packed and then carried home for the women. It is not only unthinkable for women to sit down at the tables and chairs that are often placed around these snack vendors and eat the food there, most women also feel ashamed, for example, to buy snacks on the street and eat them while continuing on their way. 'It doesn't look nice when you eat on the street because everybody will stare at you and the food will stick in your throat anyway. So, it's better to get the things packed and eat them at home.'

Even within their own mohalle the girls are shielded from men so that they remain unknown to the male inhabitants of the area. Whenever I wanted to visit women at their homes during my research, they drew a map for me so that I would be able to find them (street and house numbers are nearly impossible to locate). They would always write down the names of the brothers, father or husband, so that I could ask in the mohalla for the respective person. However, they never expected me to take their own name. A typical comment was that 'people don't know my name here, but if you take my brother's name they will show you our house.'

I had a similar experience when, in 1993, I was working as a field worker in Lahore, collecting interviews of women who had been enrolled in the TTCW. Together with the other field workers, I had only copied the names and addresses of the girls from the school's old application forms. We did not write down the fathers' names which were also on the application forms. Since it was quite difficult to find the houses in the small, winding lanes and pathways, we often asked the young men who were standing around in the mohalle. But they would always ask us for the name of a male resident. They would even shake their heads in ignorance when the girl we were looking for lived right next door. The Pakistani woman who was leading the field research later even became a bit worried that we always had to take the girls' names for inquiries. She feared that the families might become annoyed with us, because, as she said, 'the people here don't keep their daughters in purdah that we walk around and shout out their names up to the main road to any guy standing around.'

Shielding women from men even goes beyond the basic physical level. Once, I was sitting in the visitors' room of one of the working women I had interviewed earlier, when the mother proudly showed me the photographs of her sons which were hanging on the walls. When I asked her why she had not hung her daughters' snaps on the walls she answered that 'you know, here in Pakistan the set-up is not like that. Sometimes visitors come to meet my sons and then they sit in this room. It would not be proper if I exposed my daughters' photos so that they could see them. I have snaps of my daughters, too, but they are in the other rooms of the house, not here.'

It becomes clear that women spend the greatest part of their time inside the house and due to purdah do not have much exposure to male strangers. A confrontation with the 'male world' is therefore a traumatic experience they find difficult to face (Shaheed 1990: 26). Most women have never been alone to a bank, a government office, or even to a bookshop. Irshad, a student of economics who lived with me in the hostel, once asked me to accompany her to a bookshop. Her family lived in Quetta but she had some relatives in Lahore whom she always contacted when she needed to get things done, like shopping or purchase of items she needed. The book, however, was an urgent matter because her exams were due within a couple of days. When I went with her into the first bookshop, I advised her to directly ask the salesman because there were several shelves with books about economics and it would be quite time-consuming to look through all the shelves. She turned down my suggestion and went to the shelves to search through the titles of the books. When she could not find the one she was looking for, I repeated my suggestion. But she insisted on going to the next bookstore and quickly left the shop. In the second bookstore the same happened. When I then insisted that she should ask the salesman she agreed, but wanted me to go to him. So, I went to the counter and asked him for the book. I had expected her to follow me in case the book was not available and a book order was necessary; but she had already stepped back even further from the counter. So, when the salesman asked me if I wanted to order the book, I had to walk across the bookstore to ask her and then go back to the counter to answer the man's question. At first I could not really understand her behaviour but then I realized that she was just too shy to question a strange man. Additionally, both bookshops were full of men, and she felt very uncomfortable being stared at. Approaching the salesman would have meant that everybody's eyes would turn towards her, and this would have been more than she could cope with. I witnessed similar scenes quite frequently. Particularly if young women are alone and outside their familiar mohalla, they cannot even manage to go to a PCO (Public Call Office) alone or to a grocery store to buy some goods. They become confused and irritated because they are not familiar with addressing and speaking to male strangers.

The inability to interact with male strangers is closely intertwined with the purdah-system, which again is based on the absence of concepts for mixed social interaction. Islamic law, in fact, does not have any concepts for social intercourse between na-maharam men and women. It lays down regulations for interaction within the family and community, but not for interaction between men and women who are not related to each other. Any uncontrolled contact between na-maharam men and women is simply forbidden because it could lead to a sexual encounter, which is prohibited according to Islamic law (Mernissi 1987: 137; see also Guenther 1993: 72f). Consequently, relationships between na-maharam men and women are perceived as predominantly sexual ones. The latter also finds its expression in the fact that social behaviour—particularly that of women—is commonly judged and interpreted in sexual terms. Every contact of a woman with a na-maharam man is instantly interpreted in terms of immoral or sexually-inviting behaviour, or even a sexual encounter or affair. It brings into question the 'moral character' of the woman, and it is generally assumed that a man and a woman who meet each other alone only have one thing on their minds.[11] Shamza, a 20-year-old BA student who lived with me in the hostel, once complained to me about the dilemma she had to face because she studied in a co-educational college:

> When we stand even for one minute outside the class with one of our [male] class-fellows, the members of the Jamaat-e-Islami [a conservative political party that also has students' wings at the university and college campuses] come and harass us. Sometimes you just need the notes from a student, and then you have to ask him. In the beginning it also felt very strange to go to a co-educational institute, but I said to myself that these are my colleagues, my class-fellows, and I should not worry. After a time you become used to that. But the students of Jamaat-e-Islami say that 'there is nothing to say between men and women. They must be having an affair, otherwise they would not stand together and talk', and then they cause problems.

A similar incident also happened to me on a trip to the museum with my brother. When we went inside people no longer looked at the exhibits, but turned their attention towards us instead. Indeed, there was no mixed couple to be seen: the visitors consisted of men in small groups or families with children and several adults. There were a number of guards in the halls and when we entered a small doorless room that was attached to one of the exhibition halls, one of the guards suddenly jumped up and hurriedly followed us. He then remained standing at the door and observed us until we had left the room again. At first I thought that this was some kind of safety measure, but this did not seem to be necessary when men or families entered the room. Then I understood that the guard had categorized us as a 'couple' and therefore did not want to leave us alone in a room because this might have caused temptation for 'indecent' behaviour.

Gossip that very quickly takes on the overtones of sexual misbehaviour is a constant threat to a woman's reputation. In the mohalle with their narrow lanes and the houses standing wall to wall, rumours spread at an incredible speed. Nothing remains unseen or unheard by the women who, behind the windows or slightly opened doors of their houses, observe what is happening in the mohalla. This can best be illustrated by the following incident that was related to me by Aneela, the 21-year-old neighbour and friend of Tasneem, a draftswoman I visited many times at her home as well as in her office. Aneela had just finished her B. Com. in a co-educational institution and was able, together with other female class fellows, to successfully push through her application for admission into a Master's course in economics, in a private institution that had not accepted female students before:

> Some time ago there was a trip to Murree that was organized by our College. It was planned that we should leave Lahore very early in the morning and come back late in the evening. Although all the boys from our College also participated in the trip, my parents gave me permission. They trust me, so they said that 'o.k., if you are so eager to take part, then we won't forbid the trip.' We came back from Murree quite late, at about midnight. The College-bus stopped at the main road and I, together with another girl who lives in my area, got off. Of course, we could not go home alone at night, and therefore a teacher and a boy from my class brought us to our houses. Someone in my mohalla must have seen that and the rumours spread like wildfire: 'Aneela has been moving around at night with two men.' And my parents were approached during the next days: 'You let your daughter move around at night with men?' People here are afraid of such gossip because it ruins the girl's reputation. This is why they don't let their daughters out of the house.

Gender Relations within Kinship: Women's Behaviour as the Embodiment of the Family's *Izzat* (Honour)

For both men and women the family constitutes the centre of social life and, therefore, plays an essential role throughout their lives (Weiss 1994: 132; also Vagt 1992: 131; Laudowicz 1992: 32; Minai 1992: 209). Men and women commonly live with their parents until they get married, and even after marriage the women continue to live within the joint family system, i.e. with the husband's family.[12] Yet, the institution of the family plays a much more crucial role for women. With the exception of very few hostels in urban areas for working women, which constitute a small niche in which women can live relatively independently, women cannot live alone without male protection (see also Alavi 1991: 125). Widows—and divorced or abandoned women, particularly with young sons—usually return to their original homes to live with their parents or a brother. But even in joint families a woman (especially a young, unmarried woman or girl) is usually never left alone in her own home, a fact that runs counter to the general ascription of the private realm to women. The practice of not leaving a woman alone at home is also partly in recognition of the fact that the home is not necessarily a safe place for women. Therefore, even a small boy or another woman may act as a chaperon while the other household members are out (Balchin 1996: 180).

The norms of purdah also pervade gender relations within the family and the organization of family life. Due to the strong gender segregation in public life, women spend a great deal of their time within their family and home, and rarely go out. Spending time and money on recreational activities outside the home, like going to the theatre or dining in restaurants, or pursuing hobbies, for example, sports, is quite common in the more Westernized and wealthier upper and upper-middle classes, but not among the lower-middle class. Therefore, women neither have much exposure to men nor to women outside their own extended family. The friendship ties among women of one family, however, are strong, and female relatives visit each other in their homes frequently. Heine and Heine (1993) even use the terms 'visiting cultures' (145) and 'visiting rituals' for this phenomenon of women visiting each other within the family circle. Contrary to this, behaviour towards the other sex is rather reserved. Even close relatives avoid any kind of body contact between the sexes, for example, a brother will not sit next to his sister or a father next to his daughter, not to speak of more distant relatives.

A clear division of labour in which all reproductive tasks[13] that are performed inside the house are ascribed to women and all outside tasks—which do not only cover employment, but also reproductive work like purchasing daily goods from the market, shopping, etc.—are done by men, as well as a hierarchical family structure in which age, and particularly gender play an important role for the position each member occupies within the family hierarchy, does not leave much room for social interaction among the individual family members, especially among men and women. Parental authority is not called into question. Although different generations live together, conflicts between the generations as they occur in Western societies are not known as everybody adheres to the traditional family structure. Social interaction within the family often takes the form of either requests and pleas, or orders, permission, and prohibition, depending on the lower or higher position the respective person occupies in the family hierarchy (Laudowicz 1992: 33). Even disputes between daughters-in-law and mothers-in-law are conflicts that do not really threaten the equilibrium of the family (Minces 1992: 23). Weiss describes the family life of working women in the informal sector in the Walled City of Lahore as follows:

Of course, women would interact with closely related men often throughout the day. Their relationship, however, was one of servitude: women were to ensure a clean home, tasty cooked food, obedient children, and maintain social relations. Maintenance of social relations included attending the many [gender segregated] functions associated with marriage, birth, death and performing certain rites identified with Islam, and expected from a woman in that particular family (Weiss 1994a: 132).

The gender hierarchy and the absence of concepts for a mixed social life even within the family can best be illustrated with the relationship between husband and wife. The term *majazi khuda* (imaginary god) for the husband already indicates his culturally superior position. It is further strengthened through his unconditioned legal rights for polygamy, divorce and child custody, and the absence of any financial liabilities with respect to his wife in case of separation or divorce. The clear division of tasks performed by men and women within the family, and the limited interfaces between the life worlds of men and women in general, further reinforce the belief that the relationship between husband and wife is not conceived in terms of companionship or partnership (Tirmizi 1989: 43). Mandelbaum writes about family life saying that 'men have different social networks and meeting places than do women. Men spend their free time with work colleagues, friends, and kinsmen. They meet in teashops, coffeehouses, or restaurants. When a man visits the home of a friend or kinsman he rarely takes his wife along. He and his host stay in the sitting-room, the housewife rarely joins them, and she sends in refreshments with a child. A woman has her own network of kin and friendly neighbours and visits with them in the early afternoon' (Mandelbaum 1988: 40).

The behaviour of women is closely observed and guarded by the male family members. A sister is considered the joint responsibility of all her brothers and personifies the izzat (honour) of their household (Tirmizi 1989: 40f). Thus, the negative conduct of a woman not only affects her own izzat; it also has consequences for the reputation of the whole family, particularly her (unmarried) sisters, whose moral characters will also be brought into question. The behaviour of men and women, therefore, is judged differently, because 'if a man should violate a social norm, it may raise some concern, but if a woman violates virtually any social norm, it becomes a calamitous event for her family with disastrous results for the woman's future' (Weiss 1994a: 132; also Pastner 1990: 250). For this reason, from an early age the socialization of a boy is geared towards protecting his sisters against any kind of exposure to, or relationship with, an unrelated male (Tirmizi 1989: 40f). Talking to a stranger, coming home after dark, leaving one's home too often, or standing in the mohalla and chatting with the neighbour's son are all behaviour patterns which are interpreted as indicators of a loose moral character of the woman.[14]

Preserving one's own and the family's izzat is also important for the women themselves. I was often told by the women I talked to that 'there is nothing more important than your own izzat', or 'the izzat of a girl is as fragile as glass. You only need to talk to someone and it will affect your izzat. So, you have to be very careful.' Any plans a woman has for her life, for example, going to a co-educational college, enrolling in a market-oriented vocational training school, or taking up employment, are choices that are first considered by the family in the context of respectability and their effects on the izzat of the woman and the whole family. Women are not supposed to make such decisions on their own. So, when I asked women why they had not chosen to learn a marketable skill or why they did not start working after completing their education, quite common answers were, 'my family did not give me permission', 'my brothers were against it', or 'in my family women don't work'.

Women in the Islamic State: Towards *Chaddor aur Chardivari*

Although politics in Pakistan has always revolved around religion,[15] and every ruler has employed and interpreted Islam arbitrarily in consonance with individual political objectives (Kaushik 1993: IIX), the major setback for women started in the 1970s, when Ziaul Haq, in search of a basis for the legitimacy of his military rule, launched an Islamization campaign unparalleled in the modern history of Islam in South Asia (Weiss 1994: 417). It is a common phenomenon that gender policies are at the centre of Islamist movements, where women assume the onerous burden of a largely male-defined tradition, and are cast as the embodiment of cultural identity and the custodians of cultural values (Moghadam 1994: 9).[16] Similarly, women were the primary target of Zia's decade of Islamization (1977–88).

During this period, women's legal rights were reduced through the laws that were passed, like the Hudood Ordinance in 1979, or the Law of Evidence in 1984. According to the Law of Evidence, in certain cases two male witnesses, and in the absence of two male witnesses, one male and two females, are required for proving a crime (Shaheed/Mumtaz 1987: 109); thus the worth of a woman's evidence is reduced to half of that of a man. The Hudood Ordinance makes, among others, rape, fornication, and adultery punishable (fornication and adultery were not regarded as crimes in Pakistan before 1979). In order to prove a rape either the rapist's confession is needed, or at least four Muslim adult male witnesses of good moral character who must confirm to having seen the actual penetration during the act of intercourse. Women and non-Muslims are not accepted as witnesses, neither is the victim's own evidence, medical evidence or expert opinion. In addition to these strict standards of proof which provide very little possibility that punishment is inflicted on a rapist, by making fornication/adultery a crime, the ordinance has created further hardship for women because the law confuses the issue of rape with fornication/adultery. The demarcation line between the two offenses is extremely thin in practice (the distinction between consensual sex and rape is very difficult to define in most cases, because non-consent is so difficult to establish legally). Therefore, when a woman comes into court in a case of rape, there is a possibility that she might herself be convicted of fornication/adultery, because of lack of evidence to prove the case of rape. The onus of providing proof in a rape case rests with the woman herself. If she is unable to prove her allegation, then this is considered equivalent to a confession of sexual intercourse without lawful marriage. In this case, the woman runs in danger of being punished with a maximum prison sentence of ten years, thirty lashes, and a fine while the accused man is released for lack of evidence. Therefore, the ordinance has created a situation in which women victims of rape dare not even complain about sexual violence against them for fear of penalties that they themselves invite under this iniquitous law, while the culprits go scot free because of its extraordinary provisions (Alavi 1991: 137; for more detailed information see also Mehdi 1990; Jahangir/Jilani 1990).

Apart from these backlashes in the legal system, Ziaul Haq also tried to impose new standards of morality on society, particularly on women. The government launched a general campaign in the media, extolling people to be more Islamic in their lives and to ensure that their neighbours were also (Shaheed/Mumtaz 1987: 71). In the name of a fight against 'obscenity' and 'pornography', several directives targeting women and women's conduct were issued. Female television announcers had to appear on the air with their heads covered by a dupatta and in full-sleeved dress. This order was extended to women teachers and government employees who had to wear the chaddor over their clothes and cover their heads. Women were not allowed to compete in various athletic events, ostensibly so as not to risk immodest exposure (Goodwin 1995: 55; Human Rights Watch 1992: 35; Weiss 1994: 424). Female models were not to appear in commercials for more than 25 per cent of the allotted time, and newspapers had to reduce the number of photographs of women (Shaheed/Mumtaz 1987: 82)—only to name few directives that, directly or indirectly, affected the everyday lives of women.

Female visibility was generally regarded as synonymous with obscenity, but women being harassed for example, by virtually naked men dressed only in shalwars rolled up to their thighs all along the canal road in Lahore was not considered obscene. A woman's appearance on television with an uncovered head was obscene, but obese wrestlers in loin cloth were deemed decent. While the cause of segregation was espoused everywhere, the women's section in public transport was invaded by men who harassed female passengers at will, and no member of the public rose to defend the women. Television programmes depicted women as the root cause of corruption, as those who forced poor men into accepting bribes, smuggling or pilfering funds, all in order to satisfy the insatiable female desire for clothes and jewelry. If women were harassed, killed or raped in the streets, or at home, it was because women had provoked these attacks by their speech, action, or just by their very presence (Shaheed/ Mumtaz 1987: 82). Thus, the process of the so-called Islamization reinforced the already deep-rooted and staunch notions of male domination in Pakistani society, and it generated:

> an atmosphere...in the country in which attacks against women became commonplace, legitimated in the name of religion. Such campaigns were led by mullahs, the custodians of ignorance, and by criminals and mischief-makers in general, who all seem to derive a kind of perverted psychic pleasure from molesting women under the pretext of enforcing morality....Violence against women increased behind the cloak of 'Islamization' (Alavi 1991: 136).

The Zia government idealized the image of women faithful to chaddor aur chardivari—remaining veiled and within the confines of the four walls of one's home[17] (Weiss 1994: 417), and blamed in particular working women for the (real and visible, rampant) moral ills of society, and the disintegration of values in the family (Shaheed 1995: 87). Yet, it was during the very decade of Islamization in which women became more integrated in the public domain than ever, as says the sociologist and women's rights activist Farida Shaheed:

> There is no doubt that this decade was the most retrogressive for Pakistan's women, marked by state-sponsored legislation, directives, and campaigns seeking to reduce women's rights, to curtail their access to economic resources, and to restrict both their mobility and visibility. Yet, ironically enough, in this same decade the largest number of women were recruited into the formal labour market and the number of women in the informal sector also grew, female applicants for higher education increased, as did the number of technical training institutes for women; and, in urban areas, even as dress codes became more uniform, an unprecedented number and new class of women started appearing in public places of leisure such as parks and restaurants (Shaheed 1995: 89).

The process of Islamization did not come to an end in 1988, when, with Benazir Bhutto, for the first time in history a woman became a Prime Minister of a Muslim State. Benazir Bhutto did not modify the existing policies toward women, neither did her successor, Mian Nawaz Sharif. On the contrary, with the declaration of the Sharia, the Islamic law, as the legal code of Pakistan in 1991, Nawaz Sharif continued to promote the process of Islamization in the country.[18]

Islamic politics as a whole had a growing appeal for the emerging middle and lower-middle classes, particularly in urban areas (Kaushik 1993: 183; Rashid 1996: 65). Ziaul Haq's promises to protect the sanctity of the chaddor aur chardivari touched the vital chord of the conservative lower-middle-class values (Jalal 1991: 101). Also economically, the lower-middle class greatly benefited from Zia's Islamization programme. This class obtained lucrative job opportunities in the oil-rich gulf countries (Kaushik 1993: 183); starting in 1974, a constant stream of migrants flowed into the Middle East, and by the early 1980s, nearly three million migrant workers lived in the Gulf states. In effect, at some point during the 1970s and 1980s, at least one in ten Pakistani households had a (male) wage earner in the Middle East. These (lower and lower-middle class) migrants could save up more money in a few years than families would ordinarily have been able to accumulate in a lifetime (Burki 1994: 279f; Addledon 1992: 137), and—through the transfer of money—could easily keep their women within the chaddor aur chardivari.

It is also this section of society that has been most susceptible to religiously-oriented political parties, for example, the Jamaat-e-Islami. This party, because of its highly organized and well-knit structure and the influence of the writings of its founder-ideologue, Maulana Abu A'la Maududi (1903–1979), is perhaps the most significant of all religiously defined political parties in the country (Mahmood 1995: 303; Mumtaz 1994: 23). The Jamaat-e-Islami is the strongest Islamic movement in Pakistan (Davis 1997: 282). Maududi is one of the central figures of modern Islamist thinking in the entire Muslim world whose ideas have had a profound influence on Islamist thinkers everywhere, and he has unquestionably been the primary Islamist figure in Pakistan over the last several decades (Fuller 1991: 7; Davis 1997: 282f; also Hassan 1991a: 50). His book entitled *Purdah and the Status of Women in Islam* (1987), that has appeared in numerous reprints to date, intends to help people to 'understand clearly the nature of the correct relationship between man and woman in social life' (VI). Maududi's perception of gender relations as predominantly sexual ones, and his primary concern with female sexuality and its control is typical of the Muslim understanding of sexuality. He furthers the need for a society based on gender segregation and female seclusion. In a chapter titled 'Laws of Nature', Maududi writes:

> ...man has been endowed with this (sexual, J.M.) urge in a liberal, unparalleled measure, knowing no discipline whatever. Man knows no restriction of time and clime and there is no discipline that may control him sexually. Man and woman have a perpetual appeal for each other. They have been endowed with a powerful urge for sexual love, with an unlimited capacity to attract and be attracted sexually. Their physical constitution, its proportions and shape, its complexion, even its contiguity and touch, have a strange spell for the opposite sex. Their voice, their gait, their manner and appearance, each has a magnetic power. On top of that, the world around them abounds in factors that perpetually arouse their sexual impulse and makes one inclined to the other. The soft murmuring breeze, running water, the natural hues of vegetation, the sweet smell of flowers, the chirping of birds, the dark clouds, the charms of the moon-lit night, in short, all the beauties and all the graces of nature, stimulate directly or indirectly the sexual urge between the male and female (Maududi 1987: 84).

Since, according to Maududi, the sexual attraction between men and women seems to be omnipresent and uncontrollable, the free intermingling of the sexes would inevitably lead to 'a flood of obscenity, licentiousness and sexual perversion, which ruin the morals of the whole community'. Therefore, 'the object of Islam is to establish a social order that segregates the spheres of activity of the male and the female, discourages and controls the free intermingling of the sexes...'. Maududi further suggests that 'social life should be so organized that it becomes really difficult for a person to commit a crime', that 'sex stimulants should be eradicated from social life', and that 'such checks should be imposed on the relations between men and women that the inclination among them for illicit relations is curbed by strong social barriers'. For Maududi, it is the woman's sexual attraction that is a threat to the social order, and for this reason it is the woman who has to behave in a manner that does not attract men:

Neither should she wear glamorous clothes that attract the attention, nor should she cherish the desire to display the charms of the face and the hand, nor should she walk in a manner as may invite the attention of others (201).

Being a supporter of a strict gender segregation, Maududi strongly opposed 'that the sexes should freely mix in schools and colleges, offices and factories, parks and places of entertainment, theatres and cinemas, and cafes and ballrooms as and when they please' (209).

The Jamaat-e-Islami's idea of an Islamic society and Islamic ethics can also be gleaned from the following statement that its Central Committee made in the mid-1980s:

Open violation of Islamic ethics, rebellion from Islamic teachings has now reached an alarming point in our society. The public media organizations, with the connivance of certain corrupt officers, are bent upon converting our society into a mixed and shameless one. Vulgar songs, semi-nude and immoral advertisements, programmes of dance and music, encouragement of mixed gatherings on television, particular unreserved [sic] dialogue delivered by boys and girls, the colour editions of newspapers full of huge coloured pictures of women and feminine beauty are only a few examples of this condemnable conspiracy. This dangerous wave of vulgarity has now gripped the country. Performances by foreign troupés attended by certain very important government officials, fancy dress shows, vulgar stage plays in the name of art, mixed gatherings, country-wide virus of VCR, dancing and musical programmes, printing of girls' pictures in the newspapers in the name of sports, mixed education, employment of women in certain government departments to make them attractive and the day-by-day rising process of seating men and women under one roof in government and business offices and even in local councils are all 'red' signs of dangers against the society and Islamic ethics. This meeting condemns all these things very strongly and demands to the government that it should take immediate steps to stop such shameless, vulgar, and obscene activities and fulfill its promised safety of chaddar and chardiwari (quoted in Saeed 1994: 83).

Although the Jamaat-e-Islami (JI), as well as other religious political parties, have never been able to win enough votes to form a government on their own, their role in politics and society should not be underestimated. The JI (and other politico-religious parties) have often been in a position to help tilt the balance between the two major political parties and therefore have been able to exert great pressure on the government for what they consider to be an Islamic state[19] (Rashid 1996: 75; Saeed 1994: 98). Furthermore, the JI constitutes a powerful social force in Pakistan (Davis 1997: 280) that has been very successful in acquiring a following among the conservative lower-middle class (Rashid 1996: 60; Mahmood 1995: 297; Fuller 1991: 6). Through its well-organized members it tries, even violently, to impose its own moral standards on society as a whole, for example, through the harassment of what the members of JI consider as na-maharam 'couples' in public or through publicly forbidding and violently disturbing celebrations and parties they consider un-Islamic. It was, for example, announced before New Year's Eve, in December of 1997, that the JI would not tolerate any New Year celebration and that, if they came to know about any private party, they would interrupt the party and bring it to an end, if necessary, violently.

But even the general public religious discourse is limited to a very conservative one, in which the society that existed at the dawn of Islam in the Middle East fourteen hundred years ago is held up as an example to model the present society on. Saeed writes about everyday religious life in Pakistan:

In almost every mosque of the country there is a paid imam (prayer leader). Imams of the main mosques everywhere also act as preachers and deliver sermons on Fridays and lectures on special occasions. These prayer leaders usually belong to the lower working class with a rural background, though some come from the urban lower middle class. They graduate from religious studies institutions which are generally private and financially endowed or supported by religious institutions....Courses of instruction at these institutions are antiquated and are based on the syllabus created in the 18th century, which in turn is based on the literature belonging to the medieval period....Modern subjects and literature are completely shunned, with the result that the graduates of these institutions are out of touch with reality and the modern world (Saeed 1994: 98).

Acting on the Quran is promoted as the solution to all problems of society, also by politicians,[20] and particularly the strict adherence to the concept of gender segregation and purdah is promulgated. Three passages from articles that appeared in the daily press are worth quoting here:

Islam forbids free intermixing of men and women and commands pardah for women. A number of Ayaat and Ahadith advise women not to exhibit their adornment and garb themselves in such a manner that the contours of their body do not provoke the sexual passions of the opposite sex and ultimately society does not tread the path of immorality. This Islamic injunction confers a dignity on [the] fair sex and endows her with a noble place in society. Modesty is the most precious ornament of a woman and pardah gives it protection. It shields her against the lustful looks of the lewd profligate (Concept of pardah in Islam, *The Nation,* 26 May 1995).

It is not permissible for a man and a woman to be alone in a closed room if they are not related (Islamic Codes and Conduct, *US-Magazine for the Young,* 11 April 1997).

Allah has very clearly ordained womenfolk that they should neither go and display their adornments to men other than their husbands, nor to gaze upon other men, except their husbands and sons, and fathers or husbands' fathers or brothers and brothers' sons and sisters' sons....Muslim women should never go to parties or gatherings where the participants are male members....if necessary, a woman can go in execution of some work unaccompanied, having concealed her adornments, with proper clothes and allowing her face and palms only [to be] visible to others. Going of women to gatherings, consisting of 'na-maharam', is strictly prohibited and transgressions of the commandments of Allah and this transgression is punishable by Allah, as revealed in verse 140 Surah 'An-Nisa' (The Women), (Participation of Muslim women in mixed gatherings, *The News*, 16 January 1998).

Such behaviour rules based on Islamic principles can be read in the press over and over again. They mirror the failure of public religious discourse to provide women (and men) with behaviour codes for mixed social interaction, and to legitimize and support women's access to and participation in the public sphere in general. The narrowness of public religious discourse and its inability to integrate new concepts for social intercourse between na-maharam men and women leads to its persistence in gender segregation and purdah as the fundament of a society based on Islamic principles.

Public religious discourse, therefore, turns a blind eye to the reality of social life. This is determined by the increasing participation of women in the public sphere, particularly the labour market, into which women have been pushed out of dire economic need and where they have started to work in professions in which gender segregation can no longer be maintained. It ignores this trend, which is linked to a growing interaction between na-maharam men and women, and fails to provide women (and men) with guidance for the development of behaviour patterns for this new phenomenon of mixed interaction that, especially for working women, is becoming an ever greater part of everyday life, and that both, men and women, find difficult to cope with. Women and men are not being given any guidance and orientation for this process of de-segregation that is happening in the urban areas. Interpretations of the Quran and Sunna in the light of the present processes of societal transformation or feminist reinterpretations of Islamic scriptures are still in a very early stage, if one can even say that they have started at all.[21]

Directives that have been issued by the government or government officials during recent years indicate that the government follows the line of public religious discourse; it therefore seems very unlikely that it will promote new role models and behaviour patterns for women (and men) that acknowledge and facilitate the changes in gender relations that are taking place in the public sphere, and women's increased participation in mixed social gatherings and in public life in general. In 1992, the Ministry of Education, Punjab, issued a directive to all the principals of women's colleges, government girls' higher secondary schools, and government girls' high schools, division Faisalabad, to advise the female students to observe purdah, particularly while going to school and back home. This was regarded as a step 'to eradicate "obscenity" and "pornography" from female educational institutions in Division Faisalabad by asserting the observance of purdah at these institutions' (*Frontier Post*, 2 November 1992). The Punjab Government also made it compulsory for girl students above VII Class in government schools in Khanewal District to wear a burqa (*The Nation*, 17 March 1998)—obviously for similar reasons. The increasing (sexual) violence against women and rape in police custody became an issue in the mid-90s,[22] and separate police stations only for women and with female staff were set up in the major cities in order to tackle this problem (*Taz*, 3 June 1994). Similarly, it was announced that, due to the harassment of women in public, buses for women only would be added to the public transportation system (*Taz*, 15 September 1995).[23] In November 1997, several restrictions were imposed on the state-run TV channel, Pakistan Television (PTV). In advertising spots, images of women tossing their hair to promote shampoo and smiling seductively to sell tooth paste have been banned as politicians have bowed to pressure from the mullahs. Advertisers have been told that commercials should instead be 'simple and congruous with the Islamic values and culture. Ladies projected in TV commercials should wear full national dress...(and) unnecessary featuring of females should be avoided' (*The Friday Times*, 21–7 November 1997). Men and women are also barred from co-hosting light entertainment shows, and scenes from foreign films, and even cartoons have been censored, for example, a scene was cut from 'Tom and Jerry' in which a cat kissed a dog. In August 1998, the first (gender segregated) university for women was inaugurated in Quetta; one month later, another women's university was opened in Islamabad.

The nomination of Rafiq Tarar, politically close to, though not a member of, the Jamaat-e-Islami, as the candidate for the presidency by the ruling party (the Muslim League) and his election as president of Pakistan in January 1998 further indicates that an enforcement of more purdah and more gender segregation, in order to build up what the conservative religious right considers a true Islamic society, are likely to occur in the near future. Indeed, in August 1998, [former] Prime Minister Nawaz Sharif, in his ongoing attempts to Islamize the country, declared his intention to promulgate the Sharia, the Islamic law, as the sole jurisdiction in Pakistan. He thus tried to remove the (still existing) 1973 Constitution which gave women more rights than any other constitution that Pakistan has had; for example, stipulating that there is to be no discrimination on the basis of sex (Shaheed/Mumtaz 1987: 63). The Sharia Bill was passed in the National Assembly, but still has to be approved by the Senate, where the governing party, the Muslim League, does not have the majority of seats, and it is, therefore, pending.

The receptiveness of the lower-middle class to this conservative public religious discourse should not be underestimated; for this class, Islam represents 'native culture' much more than the Western 'foreign culture' the elite identifies with (Fuller 1991: 16). Religion is very much embedded in the lower-middle class's life world, not only as far as religious duties like praying or fasting are concerned, but also behaviour patterns of everyday life are constantly discussed and judged in terms of their compatibility with Islam and Islamic values. When, in 1992, I was for about four months a resident of a hostel in Lahore in which mostly working women and students from the upper and upper-middle class lived, women also wore jeans and T-shirts inside the hostel. They changed their dress into shalwar-kameez and dupatta when they went outside because, as they stated, 'our culture is not so far developed yet' or 'people are very narrow-minded here, so we have to wear shalwar-kameez outside'. The hostel where I lived later on (i.e. in 1992/93) for more than a year and again in 1996/97 during my field research, was a typical hostel for lower-middle-class women, and wearing Western clothes was out of the question. On the contrary, I was told that shalwar-kameez was a very good dress for the maintenance of purdah because it was loose fitting and would not display the contours of a woman's body. Once, in a discussion with Tasneem, a draftswoman I interviewed and visited in her office and home several times, she said she was against women wearing jeans because 'our religion forbids women to wear men's clothes.'[24] When I then commented that if women were not allowed to wear clothes men use, then they should not wear shalwar-kameez either because shalwar-kameez is also a traditional dress for men, she became confused because she had not considered this point earlier. We had long discussions about the appropriate dress codes and behaviour codes of women according to Islam, for example, whether it was appropriate for women in the hostel to go to the hostel's kitchen without wearing the dupatta (which some women indeed did). Most women considered this indecent behaviour, because by not covering themselves with a dupatta, the women would display their body contours to the male servants who also had access to the kitchen. Comments from women working in the office sector like 'according to Islam, women should not work at all; they should remain in chaddor aur chardivari', or 'our religion is very strict; Islam demands that women be veiled, that not even a wisp of hair be visible', and 'they are not allowed to sit next to a man either', indicate that although lower-middle class women are increasingly participating in the public sphere, particularly in the educational system and the labour market, the lower-middle classes still remain one of the most conservative sections of Pakistani society.

Transgressions of Purdah Restrictions: Male Agency

'One afternoon when I was going with my class-fellow to the tuition centre we regularly studied at, a man riding on a bicycle passed by. We were walking down a small deserted lane, and, as usual, no other people were in sight. When the man was about 10 or 15 meters ahead he stopped, descended and knelt down at one side of his bike. We did not really notice all this consciously, and I thought that maybe the chain of his bicycle had jumped off. So, we were coming nearer and when we were passing by, we just cast a glance at him because he was still kneeling there, in the middle of the road. At this moment he pulled down his shalwar so that his private parts became visible, looked at us and said some very obscene things. It was very clear that he was asking us to have sex with him. We were shocked and, when after a second we came to grips with ourselves again, started running until after a short while some people came into sight. Then we felt safer. I never talked to anybody about this. Whom could I have approached anyway? The men on the street? Obviously not. And my parents or brothers? They would not let me out of the house again after hearing such a story.' (Shumeïla)

'I came from the office and got off the bus at the bus stop to go to the hostel. Already at the bus stop I felt that somebody is following me and I turned around and saw a young guy, maybe 17 or 18, walking behind me. Maybe he had been travelling in the same bus, I don't know. I started slowing down my speed so that he could pass by, but he didn't. I then had to cross a broad traffic road, using a little bridge. I did not know if the guy was still following me because I did not want to encourage him by turning around and making him feel that I was interested in him. However, he was still there and since only very few people were on the bridge he used his chance and passed by, and while passing by came very near to me and said something like 'good girl, you are a very nice girl, I love you'. He kept his face straight, so that nobody could see that he was talking to me. He descended the stairs of the bridge on the other side of the road and waited for me there. I did not know what to do and so I ignored him and continued on my way. I then had to enter a small lane that directly leads to the hostel. There are high walls on both sides and commonly not many people are to be seen. He also realized that and attacked me by coming near me, touching me and saying some obscene things. I shouted at him and even tried to slap him but he just kept following me by keeping a distance of 4 or 5 meters. I felt that if I now enter the hostel and show him that I live here he will feel encouraged and might come back any day and wait for me. Therefore, I passed the hostel and rang at the door of one of the next houses. Thank God that I did this because he now thought that I live there and became afraid. So, he quickly ran away.' (Rubina)

'After I started working, I enrolled in a computer course which took place in the afternoons at a college in another part of the city. You won't believe me how often, when I was standing at the bus stop there, cars would stop and the men sitting inside would say to me, "get into the car, I will drop you off", or "can I take you somewhere?" Society has become so corrupted. In the past there were certain places for prostitutes and the men knew them and could go there. But when Ziaul Haq came to power he closed down all these places, and now these women can be found everywhere, at places where normal women also go, even in good areas like Liberty or Pace [shopping areas for the upper and upper-middle classes]. Some wear burqas and wait for the cars of clients to pick them up. And the men move around outside and harass the common women because they think they might be prostitutes. Society is so depraved. Even our neighbours who live nearby do not send their daughter to our house alone. She is about 8 or 9 years old and learns the Quran from my brother. Her brother, who is only one year older than her, brings her to our house and picks her up again. Her parents say that nowadays you cannot trust anyone and even the children are not safe. And they are right.' (Andeela)

These are only three incidents of daily harassment picked out from uncountable occurrences that were told to me by working women and women in the hostel where I lived. Staring at and touching women, passing remarks or verbally abusing women, and trying to talk to them are common forms of harassment. What is even worse is when cars and motorbikes stop in front of women with the purpose of enticing them into the car or onto the motorbike by offering them a lift, and the fact that women are followed on foot, on motorbikes and even in cars. This can last for hours and it makes women afraid because they do not know the intentions of the person(s) following them. The fact that the newspapers are full of cases of rape and abduction where girls and young women are dragged into cars or trapped by men following them, additionally increases the fear women experience, even when they are only harassed or followed by 'harmless' culprits.[25] A recent survey conducted by an English language newspaper (*The Frontier Post*, 14 March 1994) reveals that harassment is a common part of everyday life for women. All the women questioned in the survey (100%) had already experienced harassment, and nearly two out of three (62%), were afraid to go out alone.

When I discussed the reasons for harassment of women in the public sphere with the working women or the women who lived in the hostel, which I often did because all the women, including myself, were confronted with this problem so frequently, the answers I got were very similar. On the one hand, I was told by many women that the people in Pakistan were uneducated and therefore did not know how to behave properly. With the rising of the educational standard of the people, men would stop harassing women. On the other hand, mis-conduct by men was often—at least partially—understood to be a reaction to the inappropriate behaviour of women. In this way men were in fact freed from any responsibility for their own behaviour. As I was told by Ghazala, a student who herself wore a burqa whenever she left her house, and whose sister, Shagufta worked in an office as a software developer, 'of course, the men do stare when they see a beautiful woman. When I see a pretty woman on the street I also look at her. Men definitely do the same. With a burqa the attraction of the woman is covered and men are not urged to look at her. I avoid this by wearing a burqa, and I feel that I am much more respected since I do so.' Similarly Naghma, a 20-year-old student of Islamic Studies, told me when I asked her why she had adopted wearing the burqa with niqab, 'the woman has to cover her body contours. If she doesn't do so, then she shouldn't be surprised that men stare at her. Burqa and chaddor protect a woman. She protects herself with it from the bad gazes of men and from her surroundings.' But even working women in the hostel would relate the misbehaviour of men to the inappropriate conduct of the women themselves. 'Do the girls in the hostel have to go to the grocer's in the evening after darkness?' Kishwer, a government employee who worked at the flight inquiry at Lahore airport complained once, 'When they go outside at that time, the men will definitely think that they are indecent girls and tease them.'[26]

Both of these arguments are however, more than questionable for the following reasons: first, harassment is not only restricted to poor, uneducated men. Women are also harassed by men driving cars and motorbikes pointing to a certain degree of wealth and at places like theatres or public libraries, which are commonly not visited by the uneducated sections of society. It cannot be ignored that there is a difference between upper-class and lower-middle/lower-class areas. If a woman goes to an upper-class shopping centre she will not have any problems with the men there, but if she goes to a common bazaar, not only the men who are walking and standing around, but also the salesmen, will drop their work and stare at her (see also *Jang*, 11 August 1997). However, I would not attribute this different environment primarily to a different class background of the men in the respective areas. Instead it is based on the fact that the bazaars with their small lanes and little shops are very crowded and offer optimal conditions for harassment (for example, touching or following women) without a great risk of being identified as the culprit. Upper-class shopping areas, on the other hand, are marked by broader roads with big shops where it is not as easy to harass women while remaining unidentified. Furthermore, the small shops in the bazaars are usually family-owned, i.e. the men working there are also the shop-owners and therefore can afford to stare at women. Contrary to this, the salesmen in the upper-class shopping centres are commonly employees who fear losing their jobs if they show any indecent behaviour toward female customers. The argument that harassment is caused by a lack of education also fails to explain why attacks on women have substantially increased after the country was 'Islamized' at the beginning of the 1980s (Goodwin 1995: 52), and why violence against women has continued to rise till to date (*Dawn*, 19 July 1999; *The Sun*, 25 January 2000)

Second, it seems that harassment of a woman does not so much depend on her own (wrong) conduct and outward appearance, as it is often assumed, but on the chance men have to harass her, and that men indeed go out in search of such opportunities. It is no secret in Pakistan that men intentionally go 'hunting' for girls to watch and tease, particularly in crowded areas like bus stops during rush hours, or bazaars, or where they have the chance to stare at a girl or a young woman unobserved near girls' colleges and schools, and near women's hostels. According to the above mentioned survey (*The Frontier Post*, 24 March 1994), nearly half of the men questioned (45%) openly admitted that they had teased girls (it is not unrealistic to suggest that the real figure is much higher), and only a small minority (10%) said that they harassed women in response to assumed signals of enticement. The majority of the boys harassed girls just for fun (60%) or as a result of their frustration (30%).

The hostel for lower-middle-class women where I lived in 1992–93 was very popular with young men who were looking for some fun. They would circle around the hostel in their cars, motorbikes and bicycles and harass, particularly touch, the women passing in or out. The hostel was not situated in a mohalla but in a small lane with high walls on both sides. All the women living in the hostel had to go through this lane and therefore could easily be harassed. A woman walking alone on this lane was very probably one living in the hostel, and once I saw that even a woman clad in a burqa, who was not living in our hostel, was harassed in this lane by two young men on a motorbike. The women of the hostel later shifted to another area, a mohalla, where they rented a bigger house. Interestingly, I was told by a woman living in the street where the hostel was first situated that after the hostel had shifted, the harassment of women in that lane had also come to an end. The men who had regularly passed through that street only in search of women they could harass, found out after a while that the women had gone and, therefore, had no reason to come to that place any longer. The women of the hostel then decided that they would not hang up the board with the hostel's name at the new place in order to remain unidentified and not 'attract' men again. It is worth mentioning here that there were not nearly as many problems of that sort in the hostel where the wealthier women lived, simply for the reason that they did not need to walk on the streets; they could afford to travel by rickshaw, and some of them even had their own car. In this way, the women could not solve the general problem of harassment, but they could avoid it to a great extent.

To sum up, harassment of women is not restricted to a certain (uneducated) class of men, neither is it caused by the women's own behaviour, but it primarily mirrors gender relations and the way men and women perceive each other:

We are living in a closed society. A woman is a mystery for men in this highly segregated society and vice versa. As the two genders confront each other under whatever circumstances, they just don't know how to react and where to stop. The men are brought up in a milieu where a very subtle form of male dominance expresses itself in the form of physical violence on women. The natural reaction of women is fear. Inflated egos amongst men and fear in women prevents a healthy and rational approach in either of the two sexes. But for all practical purposes women turn out to be the worst sufferers in a male's paradise ... there is an immense amount of fear being poured into the psyche of women through what men think

[of] as innocuous eveteasing which does not come under the
purview of any law (*The Frontier Post*, 14 March 1994).

The majority of women do not react to harassment (in the
above mentioned survey, 90 per cent of the women stated that
they ignore harassment) and herewith unintentionally further
encourage the miscreants who do not have to fear any
consequences. The passive behaviour of women is certainly
linked to the absence of any legal means for prosecution,[27] but
also to the fear of further harassment from the culprit for publicly
discrediting him. Particularly when women use a certain route
regularly, for instance, to college or work they are afraid that
the miscreant might—together with his friends—come back and
take revenge. Cases where young men threw acid into the faces
of women who had publicly scolded them for harassing girls
have also been reported in the press (see *Dawn*, 4 January 2000;
Balchin 1996: 226).

What is even more important is the indifferent behaviour of
the public. Two men on a motorbike harassed a burqa-clad
woman and although our *chaukidar* saw the incident he did not
intervene. During another incident, I was sitting in a public van
when I saw a woman shouting at a man standing next to her on
the street. It was obvious that he had harassed her. No one else
was to be seen. The driver slowed down to see what was going
on. After he had passed, he jokingly said, 'haha, the bibi has
become quite angry', a comment for which he earned some
grins from the male passengers sitting in the van. No one
suggested they stop to assist her.

The belief that a woman who has been harassed must have
encouraged the culprit, i.e. that she has, in some way or the
other, provoked the incident herself, is deeply embedded in the
minds of Pakistani society. In her study of sexual violence
against women in Pakistan, Hussein (1991: 3) concludes that
'the fault...was always on the woman's side, sometimes because
of her mental inability, sometimes because of her
irresponsibility, and sometimes due to her own cowardice which
had prevented her from taking care of herself. The essence of

the conversation was always that if she had remained in her house then nothing would have happened to her. This attitude was prevalent everywhere: doctors, police officers, and the common people...' (translation by author). Indeed, the very presence of a woman in public arouses suspicion because it symbolizes transgression of purdah restrictions:

It is always the woman's fault for bringing it upon herself, whether she is a journalist, stewardess, beautician or a char woman. In a manner of speaking, women do bring it upon themselves by merely being 'female' in a society whose morality is deeply ingrained in sex—the common perception of a woman who steps outside the household hearth is that of a 'badmaash'—a slut who not only is willing to brave into a man's world but is brazen enough to do so (*The Nation*, 11 November 1995).

To conclude, the harassment of women is closely linked to the strong sexualization of gender relations in Pakistani society, and the absence of concepts for social interaction between na-maharam men and women, particularly in public life. It is, therefore, an intrinsic part of the gender order of society. I often observed men's inability to communicate with women in any other way than through teasing. Staring at, whistling behind or touching women are the only forms of communication many men know. When, during my research I went towards small groups of young men standing around in the mohalle or bazaars and staring at me from afar, for instance, to ask them for an address I was looking for, I was often surprised how stunned and confused they suddenly became just because they were not used to a woman addressing them so directly and boldly.

It is more than questionable whether the enforcement of more gender segregation and purdah, as proposed by public religious discourse and the government will reduce the problem of harassment of women in the public and change existing gender relations so that new patterns of interaction can emerge. These are urgently necessary for both men and women in order to cope with the mixed social interactions that are increasingly becoming an inevitable part of public life.

Women at the Interface: Strategies to Enter Male Territory

The fact that the gendered organization of space defines the public space as a traditionally male space, which a woman has no legitimacy to enter because this would mean violating the purdah-rules on her side, does not mean that women are not present in the public. On the contrary, women are developing many strategies that are enabling them to enter and claim public space. They are redefining parts of public male space as women's space or shifting the purdah-rules from physical to symbolic purdah. Another strategy is to redefine gender relations from na-maharam to maharam, i.e. from being a foe to being a protégé through the integration of male strangers into a fictitious kinship system. Other ways to enter male space and at the same time remain protected and safe from harassment and gossip regarding one's moral character also exist.

Women's Spaces in the Public Sphere

When taking a closer look at the public sphere, a lot of spaces for women become visible which segregate women from men but at the same time enable them to take part in public life. Lachenmann (1993) describes these spaces as 'parallel structures' (18), 'women's spaces' (7), a 'women's world' (7), and 'female social spaces' (1997b: 33). Minces (1992: 55f) uses the terms 'parallel culture' of women and an 'autonomous women's world', and Vagt speaks about a 'dual public' (1992: 50). Spaces for women in the public are even a precondition for the maintenance of gender segregation, particularly schools and colleges for girls with female staff and surgeries and hospitals with female doctors to treat female patients. But other spaces for women also exist in everyday life, for example, at celebrations like weddings, engagements and religious ceremonies, or at funerals, where separate rooms for women enable their participation. It is even a custom that the first day of a wedding ceremony (that usually lasts for at least three days), the *mehndi*, is only celebrated by the women of both the bride's and the groom's family, and by other female guests. The women meet at the house of the bride (and on another day at the house of the groom), play the *dholak*, a traditional small drum, sing traditional wedding songs, dance, and have a lot of fun. Then they put *mehndi* (henna) on the hand of the bride/groom. All this is believed to bring luck to the future couple; and I have always considered the female-only mehndis to be the most exciting and enjoyable part of the weddings.

In some restaurants, ice-cream parlours and snackbars a corner of the room is often separated by a curtain or partition, and reserved for women only. In the public transportation system two seats in the buses, the front seats adjacent to and behind the driver, that can be reached through a separate door, are reserved for women. The public libraries offer segregated areas for women where they can sit and study. New spaces for women that enable them access to places and fields that are normally restricted to men have been developed during recent years, like the first public parks for women in Rawalpindi (*Dawn*, 21 September 1999) and in the town of Sobhodero (Der Spiegel 40/1993), and the Olympic Games for Muslim Women, which took place for the first time in 1993 with the exclusion of men (FAZ, 3 June 1994).

Yet, compared to other countries of the Islamic world, Pakistan lags far behind in providing spaces for women in the public. The women's section in mosques and the *hamaams*, the famous bathhouses that exist in many Muslim countries, are public spaces for women that are not only important meeting places; they also form an intrinsic, and socially accepted, part of public life. However, in Pakistan, women do not have access to mosques[28] and hamaams are not known in the country.

The participation of women in public life in Saudi Arabia clearly shows that a strict enforcement of gender segregation should not be confused with the exclusion of women from public life. Heine and Heine (1993: 206f) point out the existence of so-called women's markets in Saudi Arabia and some other Gulf countries, in which the customers as well as the traders are all women. In addition to the female traders and customers, many more women are involved in these women's markets: women who live near the markets and prepare sweets and snacks at home, which are then sold to women traders for the market, and female money lenders who give loans to women traders. The opening of banks, libraries, shopping centres, fitness centres, and hospitals for women, and the setting up of separate office hours at some local government offices during the last few years have led to the development of a 'dual structure of public institutions' (Vagt 1992: 43). They have also initiated what Lachenmann (1994: 2) calls a 'women's public sphere', Vagt names a 'dual labour market' (1992: 158), and Heine/Heine describe as an 'economic niche' for women (1993: 213). Since men and women are not allowed to work together in one office, and mixing of men and women is strictly prohibited, all these segregated spaces for women necessarily have female staff only (on the gendered nature of the labour market in Saudi Arabia and the Arab world, see also Minai 1991: 221–40).

In Pakistan such spaces for women in the labour market and public institutions hardly exist. In Lahore, there are no shops or shopping centres only for women, with female staff. Even typical female items like jewelry or underwear are commonly sold—and often bought—by men.[29]

Where no spaces for women exist in public life women are virtually excluded, for example, from going to a cinema, taking part in local festivals or pop concerts. Theoretically, no law forbids women to watch a movie at a cinema, but the absence of segregated seats or a segregated area for women in the cinema hall practically enforces it. I went to the cinema only once, with a male relative, to see a movie. Lots of provisions had to be made in order to prevent any kind of 'problems'. The tickets had to be booked and picked up from the ticket office in advance—of course, not by me. I would have had to stand in the male crowd which would very probably have made me the target of harassment. In the cinema hall itself we had to find a seat in a corner so that only my relative could sit next to me. The cinema hall was quite large and very crowded with young men. I could only see two other women in the whole hall, one European couple that seemed to be tourists, and another young couple that looked as if they belonged to the upper class and who were perhaps dating secretly. Women visiting the cinema alone, i.e. without any male company, was out of the question. During the film there were a lot of catcalls, particularly when women were shown on the screen. The film had been censored anyway and all 'indecent scenes' had been cut out. But when a woman was shown undressed to shoulder height only, under a shower, the whole crowd started roaring and whistling. When the film was over, we had to remain seated until most of the visitors had left the hall, another safety measure in order to circumvent mingling with the crowd, and being touched or pinched in the rush.

During recent years, however, and concomitant with the increasing presence of women in public life, lots of new spaces for women in the public have been created. Attracting women as customers has become a market-niche, so to say, that has been detected, for example, by the small snackbars in the bazaars and shopping areas which increasingly offer segregated spaces for women. Although food and beverages are served by men, the shops advertise their special provisions on signs stating 'women only' or 'special space for women inside'. Particularly the lower-middle class, who cannot afford to go to the expensive, Westernized restaurants in which gender segregation is not usually observed, take advantage of these provisions.

In the private co-educational colleges, too, that are mushrooming nowadays due to deteriorating educational standards in the public educational institutions, and that compete with each other for students, special provisions for female students are being made. Women commonly have a separate room to relax during breaks, the 'women's room'—which they directly approach as soon as they reach the college before and between classes. During the lectures they sit in the first two or three front rows that are reserved for them. While the male students spend their breaks and free time between the lectures relaxing in the courtyard and building, the women remain in their 'women's room' and only come out, usually in groups, to attend the classes.

The decision of a famous local pop group in the summer of 1997 to give a concert only for women in a women's college in Lahore provided a rare chance for women to take part in such an event. It also indicates that women are increasingly being 'discovered' as lucrative clientele. The reasons for organizing a women's concert were certainly not only altruistic ones—the tickets were expensive and priced at Rs 200 each, and they were completely sold out.

The provision of spaces for women in the public for economic profit has definitely opened new avenues for women during recent years, although there have also been backlashes. A shoe company that has numerous branches in Lahore had started a pilot project and opened a branch for women only in one of the bazaars in Lahore. The sales manager and the sales staff were all women and had been trained by the company. It turned out that men would enter the shop in the company of women or would pretend that they wanted to buy shoes for a female relative, and they would then harass the saleswomen. 'What could we do?' asked a male sales manager who had been involved in setting up this branch, 'The men came in only to watch the women and to tease them. They were not interested in buying shoes. We could not post someone with a stick in front of the shop to keep the men out. The only shops exclusively for women that are successful are beauty parlours and dressmakers; apart from that they do not work. We had to close the branch and dismiss the saleswomen.'

It is, of course, much more problematic to establish women's spaces in fields where no economic, or other, benefit can be obtained or where even a financial loss might be involved. Women face such problems, for example, in the public transportation system. The buses are run privately, and the government only regulates the different routes and fares. Merely two seats in the whole bus, the ones near the driver, are reserved for women. Even this space for women is not always acknowledged, either by the male passengers or by the drivers and conductors. It is a common phenomenon that during rush hours men occupy the front seats as well, without consideration for female passengers. When travelling long distances, women are often forced to pay for any unoccupied seats, otherwise reserved for women, to ensure that these seats are not taken by male passengers, with the connivance of the conductor and driver. The drivers would never dare to behave in such a manner if single women passengers were accompanied by men. Yet, these behaviour patterns further indicate that women's spaces are not respected as an intrinsic part of public life—be it for economic or other reasons, and always have to be defended against male monopolization.

Veiling and Symbolic Purdah

Despite the gendered allocation of space in everyday life, men's and women's spaces do not exist side by side as clearly defined units that are fenced off from each other. There are many interfaces between men's and women's spaces, and it is a normal occurrence that women enter male space and vice versa. Furthermore, spaces for women often simply do not exist in the public sphere, and in such cases other mechanisms are necessary to enable women to use (male) public space. Where the sharing of space between na-maharam men and women is unavoidable, the strong internalization of the concept of purdah is manifest in the avoidance of eye contact with men through looking towards the ground or behind them (*nazar ka purdah*), or in lowering the voice when women talk to men or when there are men nearby (*awaaz ka purdah*) in order to maintain social distance (Shaheed 1990: 25). A woman in the public sphere moves quickly and with determination, looking neither right or left. She makes sure that there is always enough space between herself and men, not only when men pass by in the streets but also when she stands at crowded places like bus stops, or in shops. When she has to wait or take a seat at places with no segregated areas for women, like in public institutions, she will try to find a free corner of the room or a bench that is not occupied by men. In case she has to sit down somewhere she will be careful that at least the two immediate seats to her left and right remain unoccupied by men. In one of the best hotels in Lahore I even observed that a woman did not enter the elevator because she would have been the only woman in it, and only when I moved in did she follow me into the lift. Behaviour patterns like standing or strolling around in public, looking a man straight in the eye, or talking to him, have to be avoided at all costs because they are interpreted as slatternly and 'inviting' behaviour and might result in teasing or harassment.

Another way of protecting oneself in the public sphere is the practice of veiling. One form being the wearing of a dupatta, a piece of cloth, about 2.5 meters long, that is wrapped around the shoulders to cover the upper part of the woman's body and is also mostly drawn over the head and worn with the shalwar-kameez. The chaddor is significantly larger and usually covers the woman's head and body down to the knees. Women sometimes also cover the face, with the exception of the eyes, with a corner of the chaddor that is fixed behind one ear with a safety pin. The burqa, a long, often black coat with sleeves, reaches down to the ankles and wrists and is worn either with or without a face veil (niqab). All women must at least wear a dupatta if not a chaddor or burqa in public. Although the veil is not enforced on women as it is in countries like Iran or Saudi Arabia,[30] it is nevertheless unthinkable for a woman to enter a public space without wearing a dupatta for fear of harassment.

By using the veil women try to protect themselves from suggestive behaviour or offensive remarks they may face during their presence in the public sphere. When they are alone in public places, they generally cover their heads with the dupatta, although they might not do so if accompanied by their brother or mother. Women who do not otherwise cover their heads with the dupatta will definitely do so in crowded places like bus stops, in buses or in the bazaars, because here the danger of being harassed or touched is greater than in other places. Women living in the city dress in a burqa with niqab when they visit their families in the villages, because appearing unveiled is not acceptable in many parts of Pakistan, particularly in the rural areas. Even women who were strong supporters of the burqa moved around in the hostel—and in front of male servants—without a dupatta. They went to the neighbourhood bazaar clad only in a chaddor because, as I was told, it was not far, 'just around the corner', and it would be too tiring to always dress in the burqa just for short trips like shopping or making phone calls from the Public Call Office. None of the teachers who always came to the TTCW in a burqa and niqab were seen dressed like this in Murree, a tourist resort. They all moved around in Murree in chaddors or even just the dupatte and, contrary to their behaviour in Lahore, most of the teachers did not even consider it necessary to cover their heads there. In Murree, a tourist resort affected by the casual attire of many local and foreign tourists who come from the urban areas and the West, an atmosphere has been created in which women can sit in the snackbars and stroll around in the bazaars and the public without fear of being harassed.

The fact that women very often practice different forms of veiling indicates that they do not perceive purdah as a fixed set of rules. It is rather a broad set of behaviour patterns that can be employed flexibly and that enable them to adjust the degree of purdah observance to their surroundings and the respective situation. The motivations of the women in Pakistan for veiling, therefore, are very similar to those of the 'new Islamic women' (Zuhur 1992: 109) in North Africa (maghreb)[31] where women re-veil as a personal strategy to provide themselves with legitimate public space (Reece 1996: 36; Watson 1994: 141). Reece, analysing the symbolism of dress among Muslim women, differentiates between veiling as a self-definition and veiling as a reflection of societal roles and perceptions (Reece 1996:36). She comes to the conclusion that for women veiling is not so much related to a self-definition; instead it primarily has a liberating aspect because it helps them to extend their spaces of action and gain access to the public sphere:

> The current situations in specific countries such as Iran, Saudi Arabia, and Egypt document various attempts by young women to carve out a legitimate public space, to protect themselves from abuse, and to satisfy their cultures' expectations (Reece 1996: 35).

Contrary to this, veiling in Pakistan is much more part of the Muslim culture; movements of unveiling or re-veiling as known in some North African and other countries have never occurred. The dupattas are part of the national dress, the shalwar-kameez, and it is very fashionable and traditional to wear matching and colourful dupatte with which women cover their heads and bodies.

Development of Fictive Kinship

Particularly in the mohalle, the residential areas with the small lanes and houses standing side by side, everyday life does not seem to be marked by much contact between na-maharam men and women at first glance. A closer look behind the scenes, however, reveals a different picture. The postman, the newspaperman, the milkman, the fruit and vegetable sellers, who move daily through the little lanes are all, strictly speaking, na-maharam men. Yet, they are known to people of a mohalla and not really regarded as strangers. Women communicate with these men daily, sometimes even talk about personal matters or scold them for their high prices, without considering this to be inappropriate behaviour.

Men and women from the same mohalla also frequently come into contact with each other. Often two or more families share one house or courtyard; therefore social intercourse can not be completely avoided. Neighbours, predominantly, but not only women, drop in for small errands, such as using the telephone, the freezer (for ice), etc. Women also regularly send, via a son or any other (male) relative, some food or sweets they have prepared to the house of a neighbour or friend as a neighbourly gesture, particularly on special occasions; or people just drop in because they want to borrow this or that item, be it an umbrella, the VCR, or some spices.

Women do not come into contact with total strangers—strangers are not invited beyond the visitors' room anyway—but they do interact with people from the mohalla and other regular visitors who are not kin but have been known by the family for a long time. Since there is no concept of friendship or acquaintance in Pakistan where the other sex is concerned, such relationships between na-maharam men and women are redefined through the use of kinship terms which integrate unrelated persons into a fictive kinship system. The use of terms like *beta* (son), *bhai* (elder brother), *chacha* (father's younger brother), *baba* (old man) or the English term 'uncle' are very common when women address unrelated (and of course related) men. Women are addressed as *beti* (daughter), *baji* (elder sister), *bhabhi* (elder brother's wife), *khala* (mother's sister), *phuphi* (father's sister) or simply as 'aunty'.

The members, particularly the women, of one's own family are respected and protected through the use of kinship terms which indicate that a man respects the woman he is addressing the way he respects the women in his own family. For women, the use of kinship terms makes them feel safer when in contact with na-maharam men. Addressing someone as 'bhai' or 'uncle' creates responsibilities for the man in terms of respecting and safeguarding the woman, who has shown that she perceives him as a (fictive) family member. It is not uncommon, particularly in the mohalle, that the fictive bhai drops off or picks up his fictive baji from the bus stop, or that he gets some urgent items from the store for his fictive bhabhi if no male of their own family is available to perform these tasks.

Very close friendship ties between two families often result in the use of kinship terms, and for outsiders it is difficult to differentiate which relatives are real ones and which are fictive ones. This often came up during the interviews I conducted. When I talked to Sadaf, a woman working in a state-owned insurance company, she told me that her uncle had helped her to get a job in the company she was now working for. Before she started to work she had, together with her cousin, completed a computer course at a private institute. When asked if these were her real relatives (*sage rishtedar*), she told me that they were not, that her uncle was a good friend of her father and her cousin was a neighbour's son who had grown up with her in the same mohalla. Such facts only surface when they are particularly asked for. They indicate how flexible the concept of maharam and na-maharam is in reality, and how it can be manipulated and extended in order to include non-family members into the family system. This point has also been illustrated by Khatib-Chahidi (1993) in her study about recognized procedures for making na-maharam persons maharam in the Islamic Republic of Iran. This is achieved by fictive and temporary marriages that are legal according to Shia law and remain unconsummated. Marrying, for example, a new servant to one of the little children in the house—even if the 'marriage partner' is not mature, and may not even know that he or she is married—makes this person legally maharam for all family members. It, therefore, permits persons of the opposite sex to share the same physical space. Such marriages are, however, subject to strictly controlled terms and conditions.

Yet, the use of fictive kinship is not always a successful means to be treated respectfully in the public sphere, particularly as far as more casual acquaintances are concerned. Women in public also address total strangers as 'bhai' or 'uncle', but men do not always respond positively to their attempts to manipulate male conduct and ensure that women are treated respectfully.

Creation of Other Mechanisms for Protection and Social Control

'When you go to the bus stop, don't take the main road because then you will have to walk through the market, and the people there are ill-mannered. Go through the little lanes of the mohalla and you avoid all kinds of problems', I was advised by a male relative. When I asked what the difference was, because the men who could be seen in the little market that was just a bit ahead of the house were the same who lived in the mohalla, I was told laughingly, 'yes, the men are the same, but when you meet them in their own mohalla they cannot afford to behave improperly; this is why you should choose the way through the mohalla and not through the market.'

The fact that the behaviour of men cannot be labelled as good or ill-mannered in general, but is rather related to a specific situation, was an experience I often had. Once a small group of young men saw me turning into a lane alone. One of them quickly gave his friends a jog with his elbow to initiate some mischief. Then they stared at me as I came nearer. As I passed by they started singing love songs and tried to get my attention by loudly greeting me—a very common way of teasing. My friend who lived in the mohalla was really surprised because she had never experienced any kind of teasing or harassment in her area. 'The guys here don't misbehave in our presence because my family has lived in this area since this abadi was built nearly thirty years ago. Everybody knows us here. If something like that happened to me or my sister then my parents would go to that house and put these people down in front of everybody, and they know that. But they did not know you, and that you were coming here to visit me.' Similarly, I often went to visit Asieh, a woman who worked as a designer in a small advertising agency. Whenever I walked down the street I felt that everybody was staring at me. But when both of us walked down that street together, I did not feel that we were being stared at, although she had not even covered her head with her dupatta. I asked her why and she answered that 'my husband was born in this area. Everybody knows him, and that I am his wife. So, how can they stare at me? And now you are with me, so how can they stare at you, either?'

Women know that as long as there is some kind of social control they can safely enter the public sphere. For instance, they can move around relatively safely in their own mohalla and they can also go alone to the general store nearby, because everybody in the area knows their family,[32] but a woman from another area could probably not do the same. When I lived in the hostel and had to buy things from the store or make phone calls from the PCO, the men there would try to talk to me, ask unnecessary questions, even go so far as to offer me tea or cold drinks. When I complained to Kauser, a teacher who also lived in the hostel, she told me that 'it does not matter where you go, this will happen every place. This is the corruption in society. Don't go there alone. Either send the servant or ask some woman from the hostel to accompany you. Then they won't do anything.' And she was right. But in another area of the city, where I lived later I could go to the stores alone without any problems. The difference was not that the men in the new mohalla were nicer than those in the old one, but that the family I was living with was well-known in the area, and I made sure that, from time to time, I was accompanied by a male family member.

In cases where a woman is not known in a certain area or mohalla or when she does not have any male family member she becomes vulnerable. In the hostel where I lived we had, for example, a problem with a small agency located opposite our main entrance door. The whole day men, probably the owners and their friends, were seen sitting or standing in front of the agency, staring in the direction of the hostel. Whenever a woman left or entered the hostel, which indeed happened quite frequently, all the men from the other side of the street would turn their heads and stare at her. One of the older women, a teacher, about 55 years old, who had spent most of her life in the hostel, went to the agency and complained about the disrespectful behaviour. She was told that 'we are standing on our own property and on our property we can do whatever we want', a comment that would have been unthinkable if a family with male family members had inhabited our place.

When women leave their mohalle, they look for other mechanisms for protection (apart from women's spaces, veiling and symbolic purdah, and fictive kinship). The first—and safest—is the company of a male relative. Men spend a great part of their free time accompanying their sisters, daughters, wives, and other female family members, dropping them off at their school, the tuition centre, a girl-friend's or relative's house, the bus stop, etc., and picking them up again later. Women also go in small groups or in pairs, or they even take a child to accompany them.

Brothers, Cousins and Telephone Friends: Transformations of Gender Relations

The strict enforcement of gender segregation in everyday life and the negative effects that any contact between an unrelated man and woman have on the reputation of the woman easily leads to the assumption that friendships do not exist between the sexes. However, this is not true. Since the chance to meet and become acquainted with someone of the opposite sex is very rarely available, young people become very creative in developing strategies through which they can come into contact with each other discreetly, i.e. without making themselves the target of public gossip and putting their own, particularly the woman's, reputation at stake. A popular way to become acquainted with someone of the other sex is through the telephone. A number is dialed arbitrarily by a man, and when a woman picks up the phone he tries to involve her in a conversation. It is then up to the woman to let him continue or not. If a conversation starts, the person might phone again and some kind of telephone friendship develops. It rarely, if ever, comes to a real meeting; both remain anonymous and therefore feel safe talking to each other.

Although the majority of such calls are made by men, women are not totally innocent. Many phone calls were received by a relative of mine, from young women, mostly at night. When I or other women in the family picked up the phone, the caller just put down the receiver and phoned again after a few minutes, hoping that this time they would get the right person on the phone. When his brother answered the phone, they even tried to involve him in small talk that was peppered with sexual allusions. Such conversations would be unthinkable in face to face situations, but the anonymity of the telephone enables men and women to behave in an unconstrained manner they otherwise would not dare to.

Since it is not acceptable for women to phone strange men they find ways in spite of societal restrictions. A favourable time is in the middle of the night when everybody is sleeping. Women also ask young men to dial a number for them (at the PCO) and ask for a certain male person. When the person asked for is on the phone they give the receiver back to the woman. Men also ask women (their relatives, colleagues, etc.) to phone their girlfriends, and get them on the phone.

Secret meetings also take place, but they are much more exceptional than telephone friendships. Even when some kind of friendship develops, a woman would never dare to introduce her boyfriend as such; instead, she would always address him as her 'bhai' or 'cousin' in front of others in order to legitimize the relationship. Cousins are na-maharam, but purdah is not observed so strictly in front of male cousins, and meeting or being accompanied by a cousin is not really perceived as a violation of purdah. Several women who lived in the hostel had some kind of 'bhai' or 'cousin' who came to visit them daily. They were often ridiculed by other inhabitants, behind their backs, of course, for having such nice and attentive brothers who would visit their sisters daily for hours and bring them presents.

There are only a few places where couples can meet secretly, for example, in one of the public parks. Once I went to a public park in Lahore on a Saturday afternoon and was astonished to see so many couples sitting on the grass, behind trees or bushes, and generally away from the footpaths and benches in order to get some privacy. All kinds of women could be seen, women with dupatte, chaddors and even women with burqas. These secret meetings, however, are risky. Not only does the woman remain in constant fear of being seen by her relatives or acquaintances—because it is her reputation that is at risk—but the police also arrest couples, even when they may be simply talking to each other and sitting openly in a public place, who cannot prove the legitimacy of their relationship, for example, through their marriage contract (*nikahnama*). The true motive for this is to frighten the couple and get a bribe for setting them free.

Such friendships rarely result in marriage—with the possible exception of those couples who happen to belong to the same family or biradari—because many families do not agree to their children marrying outside their own family or biradari. Marrying against the will of the family, however, is usually considered unthinkable and when it does happen, it can lead to the repudiation of the 'miscreants' by their families. Love marriages have a bad reputation as against marriages arranged by the families, and couples who marry for love are often reluctant to admit this later. A love marriage implies that the woman has been meeting secretly with a na-maharam man before her wedding, a fact that not only questions her own moral character but also that of her (unmarried) sisters.

NOTES

1. I am restricting myself in this study to the Muslim majority of Pakistani society. Among non-Muslim minorities, for example, the Christians, who according to their own estimations form about 6–7 per cent of the population, purdah does not play such a significant role in everyday life. Although elements of purdah are also found among Christians, many facets of purdah which can be observed among the Muslim majority and which are commonly regarded as part of their Muslim identity are practiced to a much lesser extent or do not exist at all among Pakistani Christians. Taking into consideration non-Muslim minorities could not be done within the scope of this study. Therefore, the use of terms such as 'Pakistani culture', 'Pakistani society', 'Pakistani women', etc. in this study always refers to the Muslim majority.
2. It is worth mentioning here that the projection of concepts like the public/ private differentiation which are actually derived from Western societies on the life world of women in non-Western societies has been criticized

within the ethnological and anthropological feminist discourse (Fazwi El Solh/Mabro 1994: 14; Lachenmann 1993: 7; Lenz 1988a: 171; Moore 1988: 49). It has been pointed out that due to the dichotomization of non-Western societies into public/private-male/female-women's spaces in the public, which do not exist in this way in European societies, have been ignored and during processes of socio-economic transformation even destroyed (Lachenmann 1993: 7).

3. This concept of an active female sexuality stands in fundamental contradiction to the Western perception of women's sexuality as a passive one (Gerani 1996: 5; Laudowicz 1992: 34f).

4. Heller/Mosbahi (1993: 76) point out a significant inconsistency that underlies Muslim sexual morals: on the one hand the institutions of polygamy and concubinage that grant men the right to have several sexual partners at the same time are justified by his allegedly stronger sexual drive. On the other hand, it is particularly the supposedly insatiable sexual desires of the woman, her uncontrollable libido, which builds the foundation of the Islamic understanding of female sexuality and which is believed to be controllable only through the institution of purdah.

5. However, the practice of veiling in everyday life does not necessarily mean subordination as it is often interpreted in Western discourse (Vagt 1992: 63f). For the individual woman, veiling can also be used strategically as a means for broadening her space of action, for instance, for gaining access to the public sphere that would otherwise be denied to her.

6. A number of academics do not agree on the point that the perception of female sexuality as active and dangerous for the social order constitutes an inherent feature of Islam. These notions of female sexuality have been traced back, for example, to pre-Islamic traditions which later became interwoven with Islam (see Chabel 1995; Ahmed 1992: part 9–38; Mernissi 1991: part 72f; also Hassan 1991a; Sherif 1987: 157f). Since it is particularly the Hadiths in which the woman is presented as uncontrollable and full of sexual desires (Minces 1992: 76), another field of research consists of feminist reinterpretations of the Quran and the Hadiths that have strongly questioned the authenticity of many of the misogynic Hadiths on which notions of the woman and her sexuality are based (see for example Roded 1999: 48–57; Heller/Mosbahi 1993: 118ff; Mernissi 1991: part 49–85; Hassan 1991a, 1991b, 1987). Furthermore, it has been shown that the women's cause also fell prey to necessary political alliances at the dawn of Islam which had to be made under pressure of a strong patriarchal opposition, and which for the sake of the expansion of Islam led to the enforcement of more and more misogynic directives against women (see Heller/Mosbahi 1993: 112ff). And, finally, it has been argued that the extreme dualistic perception of the sexes, combined with notions of an active female sexuality, is not a specific

Islamic phenomenon, but can also be found in other religions (Riesenbrodt 1990). Tracing back the origins of the concept of female sexuality, however, is not of primary importance in the context of this study. What is interesting for us here is how attitudes of (female) sexuality and its control, as well as the purdah system itself and the practice of veiling (which are all deeply embedded in Pakistani Muslim society, and which are perceived by the members of Pakistani society as inextricable features of their religion) affect women's lives and shape their spaces and strategies for acting in their societal context, as well as the ways in which access to (public) space is (re)negotiated, particularly during processes of societal transformation.

7. In Urdu there are different words for the English term 'woman'. The women I talked to generally did not use the Urdu equivalent to 'woman', which would be *aurat* but referred to themselves as *larkian* (which means young, particularly unmarried, women) and to the men not as *admi* or *mard*, i.e. 'men', but as *larke*, which means young, particularly unmarried, men.

8. For an interesting account of the gendered division of space in selected residential areas in Lahore, see also Weiss 1998.

9. Only a few (private) colleges, particularly in the field of commerce, economics, medicine, and engineering, etc., are co-educational. Otherwise only at university level do men and women study together.

10. There are higher standard private schools in Pakistan which are co-educational and where the language of instruction is commonly English. The lower-middle class, however, cannot afford these expensive schools, and children are sent to the segregated (state-run) Urdu-language schools. Despite this, as Weiss (1994: 35) has pointed out, the increase in female education should not be underestimated in terms of its effect on women. It may not be what is actually learned in school but the experience of leaving one's home after puberty and attending classes that exposes a woman to other students and teachers and, in effect, to the larger society from which she was once hidden and uninformed.

11. The saying that when a man and a woman are alone in a room then *shaitan* (the devil) will be the third person present, is quite common in Pakistan. This saying seems to be known in Arabic countries too (see Dahl 1997: 97).

12. All the married women I interviewed lived in a joint family: with the husband, the husband's parents, his brothers and, if married, their families, and the husband's unmarried sisters. Only two women had—after living in the husband's family for many years—set up their own nuclear family, and one separated woman lived with her children in her parents' home.

13. 'Reproductive work' is understood in this study as an antonym of 'productive (i.e. paid) work'. Contrary to the rather narrow term 'housework', which has been used frequently in sociology, particularly

gender studies, 'reproductive work' includes a broader spectrum of activities such as housework, raising children, caring for the elderly, maintaining social relations, and subsistence production (e.g. growing vegetables and other food for home consumption).

14. The embodiment of the family's izzat in the (sexual) behaviour of the women is a common phenomenon in traditional Islamic societies. A woman who behaves shamelessly puts to shame the whole family (Bauer 1994: 32). I do not agree with Weiss who states that the notion of what is accepted as respectable and what is not in the women's behaviour is not tied to matters of sexuality (Weiss 1994: 134). According to my point of view, negative conduct is very closely identified with violating the purdah-rules. Purdah, as it has been pointed out earlier is an institution based on notions of (female) sexuality and sexual behaviour and its control. Therefore, the judgement of women's behaviour as decent or not always has a more or less strong sexual connotation. For the interrelationship between purdah observance and izzat, see also Mandelbaum (1988: 24 and 105).

15. Pakistan is the only modern country created on the basis of religion. The very idea of Pakistan emerged from the theocratic commitment of the Muslim community of the Indian subcontinent. Pakistan thus cannot disassociate its character and identity from religion—Islam is its very raison d'être (Fuller 1991: 1; also Kaushik 1993: ix).

16. In her analysis of the relationship between Islam, the state and the position of women in modern nation states of the Middle East and South Asia, Deniz Kaniyoti (1991) points out that the 'woman's question' has been, and still is, hotly contested ideological terrain for both secular and Islamic movements; it is instrumentalized to legitimize and support new forms of state power. In Turkey, for example, the secularization of the family code and the enfranchizing of women were part of a broader struggle toward secularization to liquidate the theocratic institutions of the Ottoman state and to create a new legitimizing state ideology. For an interesting collection of articles about the instrumentalization of the 'woman's question' by secular and Islamic states in the Muslim world see Kandiyoti (ed.), (1991).

17. Chaddor aur chardivari literally means 'shawl and four walls'. It is also an alliterate allusion to the concept of women's seclusion originally given currency after the promulgation of martial law by General Ziaul Haq (Farukhi 1987: 60).

18. A more complex elaboration of the process of Islamization in Pakistan is provided by Shaheed/ Mumtaz (1987: 71–122) and Rashid (1996). For a historical analysis of the impact of state policies on women since the creation of Pakistan, see Jalal (1991).

19. A good historical analysis of the role of the Jamaat-e-Islami in the process of Islamization is provided by Rashid (1996). On the historical development and ideology of JI, see Mahmood (1995).

20. See 'Mould lives according to Islam': Tarar, *The News*, 21 November 1999; Tarar urges women to adopt Islamic values, *The News*, 15 November 1998; Islamization solution to all problems: PM, *The Nation*, 30 August 1998; Acting on Quran can resolve Muslims' problems, *The News*, 9 April 1997; Hazrat Fatima role model for women of all ages, *The Muslim*, 14 November 1996.

21. There are gradual changes in the position of the religious right, for example, the Jamaat-e-Islami, who are no longer able to shut their eyes to the economic realities in the country. While it was considered an invitation to immorality in the beginning of the 1980s for women to step out of the confines of their houses, over the years it has become acceptable for women to go out 'if and when absolutely necessary'. Where earlier paid employment was considered a male activity, women's right to work 'in times of necessity' is now promoted (Mumtaz 1994: 235).

22. More than 70 per cent of women in police custody experience physical or sexual abuse (Human Rights Watch 1992: 2; see also Taz, 3 June 1992; Goodwin 1995: 49f).

23. To my knowledge this has not been accomplished so far.

24. These opinions clearly reflect the conservative religious discourse in Pakistan. While it has become common for men to wear jeans and T-shirts, i.e. Western clothes, women are prevented from doing so on the grounds of religion. Under the heading 'Dresses for Muslim women', a newspaper article states: 'The dress of a Muslim woman should not be such that manifests the...curves of her body.... Now-a-days it has become a trend of the ultra-modern society that the girls wear trousers and jeans which are normally worn by male members (sic!). In this connection there is a Hadith which clearly prohibits the female members, wearing dresses like those of the male members' (*The News*, 16 January 1998).

25. For more information and case studies about sexual violence against women see Human Rights Commission of Pakistan (1999: 215–23); Human Rights Watch (1999); Goodwin (1995); Human Rights Watch (1992); Haeri (1995); *The News*, 22 April 1997.

26. The opinion that women are themselves responsible for the misbehaviour of men is also commonly heard at the discussion forums organized by local newspapers from time to time. The suggestions that are put forward, even by women, to eradicate harassment of women clearly mirror the Muslim understanding of sexuality, namely, that men harass women because they feel tempted by women's innate seductiveness, and because they cannot control themselves sexually in the presence of women. It has, for example, been proposed that women should keep their appearance and dress decent, and that they should appear modest in public (*Jang*,

11 August 1997). It has further been suggested to ban satellite programmes showing Western films (that expose men to scenes that arouse sexual desires), and to get men married at an early age (obviously to fulfill their sexual desires), (*Jang*, 16 October 1995)—although harassment is not only accomplished by unmarried men, and elderly men are also known to be a 'dangerous species' (see *Frontier Post*, 14 March 1994). Furthermore, it has been suggested that women should also wear a face veil in order to protect themselves (*Jang*, 9 October 1995), i.e. not to attract men by their outward appearance.

27. In Pakistan no law that covers harassment exists. Additionally, sexual abuse and harassment of women in police stations in Pakistan is a common phenomenon and therefore a woman would hardly address a policeman in case of harassment for fear that she might be taken to a police station to give a statement about the happening.

28. Islamic education, particularly praying and memorizing the Quran and Ahadith, is given to children, both boys and girls, through the maulvis in the mosques and madrassas. Islamic education is also omnipresent in schools and colleges; 'Islamic Studies' is a compulsory subject, from primary school up to college level, but also other subjects like 'Urdu', 'Pakistan Studies' or 'English', which are all compulsory up to BA/B.Sc., abound with texts about Islamic history, Islam in Pakistan, and the life and sayings of the Prophet Muhammad (PBUH).

29. Yet, there is a bazaar called Meena Bazaar, for women in Karachi, and a bazaar for women craftsmen was opened in Islamabad recently by a local NGO (*Dawn*, 27 October 1998).

30. In Iran, women are controlled in the streets to assure that they adhere to the Islamic dress code. The use of nail polish and make-up, and wearing of high-heeled shoes are also prohibited (Bassiri 1992: 68). Similarly, in Saudi Arabia, the religious police (*Mutawin*) often stop women in the streets if strands of hair show from under their head coverings or if their ankles are visible beneath their long black robes (Reece 1996: 45).

31. Several studies about re-veiling in North Africa have been published during the 1990s. See for Egypt, Zuhur (1992), Werner (1997), Maclead (1992), Watson (1994); for Jordan, Darwisch/Liebl (1991); for Algeria, Kebir (1992); for Turkey, Göle (1996).

32. Very often, however, young unmarried women are not allowed to go to the stores in their own mohalla, particularly when they are alone. When I asked the mothers why they did not let their daughters go there the answer I generally got was that 'it does not look nice' (*achha nehin lagta*).

3
WOMEN IN THE URBAN LABOUR MARKET

The Embedded Market

In his famous article 'Economic Action and Social Structure: The Problem of Embeddedness' that appeared during the mid-eighties, the sociologist Mark Granovetter argued that:

...the majority view among sociologists, anthropologists, political scientists and historians...sees the economy as an increasingly separate, differentiated sphere in modern society, with economic transactions defined no longer by the social or kinship obligations of those transacting but by rational calculation of individual gain. It is sometimes further argued that the traditional situation is reversed: instead of economic life being submerged in social relations, these relations become an epiphenomen of the market (1992 [1985]: 53).

The perception of the market as a domain autonomous from the wider society (not only by economists but also by social scientists) resulted in its being widely neglected in the social sciences for several decades; thus, studies of the market were nearly entirely left to the economists. During the period 1950–70 almost no sociological analyses of the market appeared, and in the 1970s only a few articles on this subject were published. In one of these studies, Mark Granovetter pioneered a networks approach to markets by looking at the role that acquaintances and friends play in job searches (Granovetter 1974).[1] Only since the 1980s has the 'sociological invasion of the market' Zelizer (1988: 616) boomed[2] and led to the emergence of a 'New Economic Sociology'.[3]

New Economic Sociology calls into question the image of the economy as an autonomous entity (Block 1990: 293). While for neoclassical analysts, rationally motivated exchange dominates economic life, New Economic Sociology stresses the social and cultural embeddedness of economic processes and institutions.[4] Thus, with the approach of New Economic Sociology the concept of the 'embedded economy' that was already developed in the 1940s and 1950s by the anthropologist Karl Polanyi (1978 [1944]; 1992 [1957]), and that implies a fundamental critique of the dominant neoclassical 'disembedded' economic theory, is experiencing a significant revival.

Polanyi was inspired by two major themes: the birth and development of a market-dominated society in the nineteenth and twentieth century, and the relationship between economy and society in primitive societies (Smelser/Swedberg 1994: 14). He saw his work as an attempt to develop a new type of economics in which the economy was firmly subordinated to society as a whole and, as a consequence, could not be defined in abstraction from the wider society (Swedberg 1994: 266; Holton 1992: 19). In his article 'The Economy as Instituted Process', Polanyi states:

> The human economy is...embedded and enmeshed in institutions, economic and noneconomic. The inclusion of the noneconomic is vital. For religion or government may be as important for the structure and functioning of the economy as monetary institutions or the availability of tools and machines themselves that lighten the toil of labour (Polanyi 1992 [1957]: 34).

In his works Polanyi never questioned the 'disembeddedness' of the economy in market societies, nor the adequacy of classical economic theory for analysing market economies;[5] he only rejected the application of the classical and neoclassical economic theory to traditional societies, i.e. societies before the 'Great Transformation' and the emergence of the self-regulated market (Schrader 1995: 2). Hence, in new sociological studies of the market his dichotomization into embedded (traditional) and disembedded (market) economies has been widely criticized (for example, Schrader 1995: 9; Evers 1995: 6; Swedberg/Granovetter 1992: 10; Prattis 1987: 18; Granovetter 1992). It is now stressed that, not only in traditional but also in market economies, the market is embedded in society and that it therefore cannot be analysed in separation from its societal context.

Numerous studies of markets that have been conducted in Western societies in the course of the resurgence of economic sociology, have pointed out the social and cultural embeddedness of economic action and processes; however, only a few analyses concerning the embeddeness of markets in non-Western societies exist so far. One of them is the study of Evers and Schrader (1994) titled 'The Moral Economy of Trade', in which the authors analyse the strategies that traders in moral economies of agrarian societies develop to avoid the 'traders' dilemma', the dilemma that, on the one hand they have to make profit and accumulate money, but on the other hand they have the moral obligation to redistribute their profits among the community. While sociological studies often stress the discrimination and ethnic isolation of the traders, Evers and Schrader focus on the perspective of the traders themselves. With this actor-oriented perspective they regard, for example, petty trade, which leaves the profit margin so small that a redistribution becomes virtually impossible, or the ethnic or cultural differentiation of the traders, which enables them to distance themselves from the moral-economic demands of their social surrounding, as strategies of the traders to solve the problems they face due to their structural position in society.[6]

A few more market studies have been published during the 1990s that stress the embeddedness of economic action in non-Western societies, such as Dore's study about the sentiments of friendship and the sense of personal obligations which accrue between economic actors in Japan and their effects on the structure of the economy (1994); Hamilton/Biggart's historical-comparative analysis of the structure of the economies in Japan, Taiwan and South Korea, in which they point out the importance of culture and the state for the constitution of the economy

(1992); and Fukuyama's analysis of the economic structures of different Western and Asian societies within their ethical, moral and cultural contexts (1995). However, a sociological theory of the market is still underdeveloped within development sociology, and it remains concentrated on the analysis of the structures of market trade (Evers 1995: 2f). Similarly, not much attention has yet been given to the gender-specific aspects of embeddedness; these have remained absent from, or at best marginal to, the literature.

It is true that there is no lack of market studies on women in development sociology to date. On the contrary, in the course of economic restructuring that has been taking place since the beginning of the 1980s in the countries of the South, an increasing number of women have become integrated into the labour market, especially into industrial labour. Economic restructuring through Structural Adjustment Policies refers to the process by which many developing nations are reshaping their economies to be more free-market oriented. This involves policies to promote a greater export orientation, deregulation of the economy, and reductions in the size of budget expenditures and the scope of intervention in the economy (Cagatay et al. 1995: 1834). Many developing countries do that more or less involuntarily, as a condition for receiving new loans from foreign commercial banks and/or multilateral institutions such as the International Monetary Fund (IMF) and the World Bank (for more information about Structural Adjustment see Sparr 1994a). This economic restructuring is closely linked to the emergence of a 'global assembly line' (Bakker 1994: 2) i.e. the flexibilization of work and the relocation of labour-intensive production, particularly of export-oriented industries (like manufacturing and electronics), from countries of the North to those of the South, and the filling of these new (formerly male) jobs with women. Thus, a huge number of empirical studies, focusing particularly on female factory workers in export-oriented industries, have been published since the 1980s.[7]

However, these studies, dealing primarily with the life and working conditions of women in export-oriented industries, have tended to discuss the effects of economic restructuring on women in too narrow a way, namely in the form of the advantages and disadvantages that women's entry into paid employment, i.e. into factory work in export-oriented industries, has brought for women (Lachenmann 1997a: 16; Pearson 1996: 175f). On the one hand, employment of women in export-oriented industries is seen as another proof of their deteriorating living conditions. The low wages, no prospects for advancement in the jobs and also the observed appropriation of the income by male family members, all indicate a negative impact of female employment on the women. On the other hand, it is argued that the women's own income, apart from the actual amount and its final use, positively influences the self-perception of the women, enhances their independence and status, and increases their mobility outside their families (Mirza 1994a: 28). Furthermore, in the hitherto existing studies not much attention has been given to other fields of employment, in which women have also become more and more integrated, for example, the office sector.[8]

It is only in recent feminist works on economic restructuring, particularly (and interestingly enough) in economics, that the importance of analysing the market as a gendered structure is being stressed, and the first steps towards adding a gender perspective to the concept of embeddedness of economic action are being made. Thus, instead of showing the negative 'impact' of Structural Adjustment Policies (SAP) on women's lives, as has been done since the 1980s (see Elson 1991; Sparr 1994b; Harcourt 1994; Mukhopadhyay 1994), one focus is now being shifted to the relevance of 'gender' for macroeconomic analysis and to the connection between gender relations and macroeconomic outcomes (Lachenmann 1997a: 28):[9]

> Instead of thinking of the economy as something external that has an impact on women, we can think of the economy as a gendered structure, and economic change as a gendered process. Gender relations condition all the operations of the economy. That is, economic institutions and processes must be perceived as permeated

by gender, even though at first sight they may appear to be gender neutral (Elson/McGee 1995: 1991; for similar statements see Elson 1993a; Elson 1995: 1863; Bakkar 1994: 5).

It has been pointed out by feminist economists that gender relations (and gender inequalities) are reflected in the market and influence the way economic processes take place (Gagatay 1995: 1827f; Elson 1993a: 545; Elson 1995: 1864). Furthermore, women's responsibility for the social reproduction of the family, which is often ignored in economic analyses (for example, in SAP), leads to different economic behaviours of women as compared to those of men. For instance, female heads of households in rural areas may not adopt export crops (as desired by SAP) to the same degree men do, because they have greater direct responsibility for the well-being of their children, and for this reason prefer risk aversion (Elson 1995: 1881). Elson therefore stresses the importance of looking at the economy *'from the standpoint of women's lives*, in which much time is devoted to unpaid work in social reproduction as well as to paid work in production; and that we recognize unequal gender relations as an intervening variable that structures economic processes at macro, meso and micro levels' (Elson 1995: 1863, my italics).

Despite this—nevertheless progressive—approach within economics towards gender-sensitive analyses of the economy, Lachenmann (1997a: 30) argues that, within feminist economics, instead of looking at the interrelationships and interactions between subsistence production and market production[10] which characterizes the everyday lives of women, the primary responsibility of women for subsistence production is perceived as a mere 'constraint' that hinders women's entry into the market (e.g. Palmer 1995: 1982). Similarly, unequal gender relations are perceived as 'barriers' to the 'most effective and productive use of human resources' (Elson 1995: 1856), and to the 'achievement of the macroeconomic objectives of adjustment policies' (Cagatay et al. 1995: 1828; also Elson/McGee 1995: 1991; Walters 1997: 49). Here, the starting point is the complete removal of gender differences that would, as it is implicitly assumed, lead to equal economic activities of men and women. This conception neither considers the social realities of women's lives, nor perceptions of gender differences in other societies (which are not necessarily hierarchical), (Lachenmann 1997a: 38ff).

Picking up the thread of this feminist discourse in economics that, though not always explicitly stated, aims at analysing the social embeddedness of the economy from a gender perspective, Lachenmann suggests joining feminist works in the social sciences with findings of the New Economic Sociology. She introduces the term 'women's economy' (Lachenmann 1997a: 14ff/41) for the gender-specific embeddedness of the economy in society ('gendered embeddedness'). According to Lachenmann the crucial characteristics of the 'women's economy' are that women's employment interacts with and is complementary to their life world (which also includes their responsibility for subsistence production), (Lachenmann 1998: 298; also 1994b: 5). As a consequence, an understanding of the 'women's economy' requires the analysis and contextualization of women's work in their life world:

...the focus is on the analysis of the interfaces and interactions between economy and society on various levels from a women- and gender-specific perspective. In this action-oriented approach, the focus is on intersections and spheres of action.... I refer to these as women's economy (Lachenmann 1995a: 16, transl. by author).

'Teaching is a Respectable Profession'—Attitudes toward Working Women

A purdah society, which is based on the segregation of the sexes, cannot function without working women. Men cannot teach in girls' colleges and schools, only to name one example. Therefore, in Pakistan female employment has never been condemned in principle; approval or disapproval rather depends on the compatibility of an occupation with gender segregation, i.e. on the ability to perform a job in a female working environment. Furthermore, attitudes concerning female employment also vary among the different socio-economic classes.

The most negative attitude toward female employment can be found among the lower-middle classes (Shaheed 1989: 18; Marker 1987a: 3) for several reasons: first, the life world of this section of society is pervaded by the norms of purdah. Second, most jobs that can be attached to the middle range of the occupational spectrum are nearly exclusively performed by men. These include work in shops and offices, in hotels and restaurants, and in the bazaars, in industries and handicraft. Working in such middle-level occupations, in which mingling with men cannot be avoided, would clearly result in a loss of social status for the respective women and their families. Doing home-based work in the informal sector, a field of employment that is often chosen by unskilled and uneducated women from the lower classes who have to work in order to make ends meet, but who prefer to work in a gender segregated environment, would be considered to be below the standards of women from the lower-middle classes. The few occupations that can be performed within a female working environment, like teaching (in the female-only educational institutes) and practicing medicine (for the treatment of female patients), need a high educational background that is normally above that of lower-middle-class women, and are, therefore, mainly occupied by women from the upper and upper-middle classes. Due to this structural position, female employment in the lower-middle classes is closely identified with economic need, and the inability of the male family members to provide for their family. Therefore, observance of purdah and keeping the women of the family out of the market is not only a religious obligation but it has also become a social status symbol.[11]

When I asked women office workers what they thought the societal attitudes towards women working in offices was, the answers clearly mirrored a negative image. Answers like 'people think that they are not good women', or 'they think that these women have a bad moral character' were common. Asieh, a woman working in a small advertizing agency, brought the public attitude to the point:

> Regarding offices, people think that the boss has his own room and the secretary is like this [i.e. is a bit of a tart]. They think that she has some private [i.e. sexual] affair with the boss. That is the view here, although every office environment is different. They think that all offices are the same, that there are two rooms, and the boss sits in one room and outside the woman. And she goes into the room of the boss to meet him and to have an affair. People imagine that this happens. And the boss has a secretary and 'God knows what he does with his secretary'. That is the point. They don't see that there are other people also in the office.

The following quotation from the daily press also illustrates the public attitude that there is no general disapproval of female employment but that it has to remain in accordance with purdah. As usual, questions are not raised regarding how more jobs that can be performed in an all-female environment can be created, particularly middle-range jobs, and how the increasing numbers of (lower-middle-class) women entering the market can be channeled into jobs that do not require any contact with men:

> In an Islamic country, though the opportunities are boundless, the people are not totally free to choose any economic activity to conduct in any manner they like. Ethical and moral requirements of Sharia have to be kept in view in this process. This point is even more relevant to female employment. As observed earlier, female labour force participation is steadily increasing over time. If this job search is not guided properly, this could lead to serious social and moral implications for the society. Therefore, efforts have to be made to design projects and institutions where those females who, for various reasons, have to do a wage-based job could find employment in a decent and morally acceptable environment (*The News*, 25 June 1994).

It is worth mentioning here that, although it is generally stressed that female employment is acceptable in an Islamic society but it should not violate the norms of gender segregation, it does not seem to be against the purdah rules to have men working in typically female professions such as gynaecology. One of the best private hospitals in the field of obstetrics and gynaecology in Pakistan, situated in Lahore, belongs to a male gynaecologist. Furthermore, during my field research it became a matter of public interest that a male gynaecologist had been appointed as Assistant Professor at the gynaecological ward of one of the government hospitals in Lahore, ignoring two senior female gynaecologists. This aroused vehement criticism by different medical associations (*The News*, 11 November 1996b; 19 November 1996a).

Attitudes toward female employment are quite different in the wealthier and more Westernized upper and upper-middle classes. Particularly, highly educated women like teachers and doctors are needed for maintaining gender segregation, and this demand has had a positive influence on the employment of highly educated women in these fields. Due to the compatibility of these professions with gender segregation, and the high educational background which they require, they are associated with a high social status, and highly qualified women are still mainly concentrated in these two professions: one quarter of all doctors and one-third of all teachers in Pakistan are women (Government of Pakistan 1989b). Contrary to this, there are only a few women at policy and administrative levels in the Directorates and Ministry of Education because there has been a continuous policy to give preference to men (Patel 1991: 74). Furthermore, women in the medical profession generally do not study beyond the level of the general practitioner. There is an acute shortage of women doctors in specialized ('unfeminine') fields such as general surgery, heart surgery, neuro surgery, radiology, and neuro physiology (*Jang*, 26 November 1991).

During the last two decades, though, changes in the occupational choice of working women from the upper-middle and upper class can be observed. Women have taken up occupations that were formerly regarded as exclusively 'men's jobs'. This trend of women entering new, so-called 'male', professions has definitely been influenced by the freezing of public-sector employment since the 1980s, which, due to women's concentration in the public educational and public health system (teachers, doctors), has disproportionately affected women's career options. In the beginning of the 1990s, there was a total freeze on further recruitment in the public sector for about two years, and this made women, particularly academics who would formerly have found (and probably preferred) employment in the traditional women's professions, switch to other fields of employment.[12]

While, for example, only twenty years ago no women were employed in banks in Lahore (Nestvogel/Klein 1986: 161/168), nowadays many banks have female employees. Women deal with the (increasing) female clientele or they are assigned tasks that do not require contact with male customers. Although women still form only about 3 per cent of the employees in banks (Government of Pakistan 1989b), their share is very likely to increase in the future. The establishment of the 'First Women's Bank' in 1990, which already has several branches in major cities, has definitely made the entry of qualified women into banking much easier than it was before.

Journalism is another typical example of a formerly 'male profession' which women have managed to enter in considerable numbers. The number of women journalists has increased steadily during the last years. Women work for women's journals and magazines, for the women's page of newspapers, or they write on women's issues in general. This development has found its counterpart in the increasing recognition of women as an important clientele in the (daily) press. While, for example, the Urdu newspaper, *Jang*, which is widely read in Pakistan, formerly only included a women's page once a week, now, in every edition, i.e. daily, there is a women's page (or half a page) that deals specifically with women's issues. These are not restricted to articles about fashion and cooking but cover a wide range of topics like harassment of women in public, female employment, marriage and dowry, and women's health.

It can be argued that in many of the new fields of employment the concept of gender segregation—though it is now managed a bit more flexibly—has remained more or less intact. Yet, highly-qualified women from the upper and upper-middle class have also entered professions that require a considerable degree of mingling of the sexes. There are women architects and designers who have been working in the office sector for more than ten years. More and more women are also choosing law as an academic discipline, and starting to work as lawyers after their graduation (even if they often take cases dealing with women's issues only, like divorce or child custody). Similarly, women have entered disciplines like 'economics' and 'business administration' in higher education, and they work in higher administrative positions in the government and private sector.[13] When highly-qualified women push open a door to a profession that has formerly been exclusively male, then this is often documented by the daily press.[14]

It is true that until now highly-qualified women are still heavily concentrated in teaching and medicine—in the beginning of the 1990s, about 60 per cent of all professional working women were teachers (Mohiuddin 1991: 972)—and that they still constitute only a small minority in unconventional professions. Nevertheless, they seem to have considerable possibilities as far as their career choices are concerned. One reason for this phenomenon might be the fact that the observance of purdah (and the sexualization of the life worlds of men and women) is not as strong among the upper (middle) classes as among the lower-middle classes. Children of the upper and upper-middle classes are mainly sent to elite, private English-language (and often co-educational) schools and colleges, and even go abroad to Western countries like the US or the UK for higher education. Among this section of society, female employment is not uncommon; working women can even be found among the older generation, though they commonly work (or worked) in 'female' professions (teaching, medicine).

Maskiell's study of female college graduates in Lahore between 1919 and 1960 points out that, although teaching was considered the only completely respectable employment for women during that period of time, the high demand for female teachers made it possible that nearly all college graduates (who wanted to work) could teach in women's colleges. Therefore, many women took up employment in this 'female' profession (Maskiell 1985). In addition, employment in the upper sections of Pakistani society is identified with career aspirations and not with economic need.[15]

Zubta, a 25-year-old upper-middle-class woman, had done her Master's in Business Administration and worked as an export manager for a company producing quilts. Although she was the first woman from her family to work in a 'male' profession, she told me that even her grandmother had been a working woman, the headmistress of a girls' school. When I asked her why she had chosen this profession she told me, in fluent English, that it had just been the novelty appeal. Since all the women of her family were teachers or doctors, she just wanted to try something nobody had done so far. Zubta earned about Rs 14,000, a considerable salary, and her occupation required extensive travelling within and outside Pakistan—a fact that would be unthinkable for a woman from the lower-middle class. Such irregular working times and overnight stays in hotels would arouse wild speculations and gossip about the woman's moral character in the mohalla and extended family that would definitely ruin her reputation (and that of her family).

The Structure of Female Employment

According to official figures, the female participation rate in the labour force in Pakistan is one of the lowest worldwide. Although in the latest Labour Force Survey 1996–97, informal sector activities have been included for the first time, the crude labour force participation rate for women in urban areas is only 5.9 per cent,[16] with 55.3 per cent of the urban female workforce—or 3per cent of all urban women engaged in informal sector activities (Government of Pakistan 1998b).

Contrary to the low female labour force participation rate in official statistics, the World Bank (1989) names a much higher figure. It is estimated that in urban areas, apart from 4.7 per cent[17] women working in the formal sector of the economy, 20.3 per cent women work in the informal sector, in which about 69 per cent of the urban work force are engaged:

> Evidence from micro-level studies, combined with deductions from the official statistics and more informal research and analyses, suggest a conservative estimate of about 20-30% of the female urban population working in the formal and informal sectors combined ... Altogether it is likely that the total female work force in the urban sector (formal and informal) is just under 2.5 million women (full-time equivalents), including about 2 million in the formal sector (World Bank 1989: 29; for similar estimates see Shah 1986: 270; Akhter 1986: 59; *Jang*, 27 November 1997).

In other words, less than one-fourth of the urban working women are recorded in the official statistics (the Labour Force Survey 1996–97). In what follows, therefore, the gendered structure of the urban labour market as presented in the official statistics shall be analysed and special emphasis shall be placed on the informal sector, in which the greatest part of the female workforce is concentrated, but which largely remains unrecognized to date.

The Formal and Informal Sector

A closer look at the distribution of women among the different occupational groups shows a clear gender-specific segmentation of the labour market. Figure two illustrates that nine out of ten women are concentrated in four out of eight occupational groups: among the 'professionals, technicians and associate professionals', the 'service workers and shop and market sales workers', the 'crafts and related trades workers', and 'elementary (unskilled) occupations', whereas only 62.8 per cent of the male workers can be found among these four occupational groups. Barely 5.6 per cent of the working women are employed as administrative or clerical workers (legislators, senior officials, managers, clerks), as against nearly one-fourth of the men.

FIGURE 2

Distribution of Employed Persons in the Urban Labour Market by Occupational Groups and Sex, 1996–97

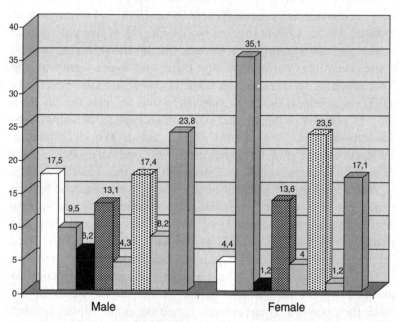

□ Legislators, senior officials, managers
▨ Professionals, technicians and associate professionals
■ Clerks
▨ Service workers and shop and market sales workers
□ Skilled agricultural and fishery workers
▨ Craft and related trades workers
□ Plant & machine operators and assemblers
▨ Elementary (unskilled) occupations

Source: Government of Pakistan 1998b.

The fact that about 35 per cent of the women belong to the category of the 'professionals, technicians and associate professionals', as against only 9.5 per cent of the men, is remarkable, and it offers evidence to support the assumption raised above; namely, that highly-educated women have considerable possibilities to take up employment and pursue a professional career. Indeed, the percentage of women among the 'professionals, technicians and associate professionals' has steadily increased since the beginning of the 1970s; it rose from 9 per cent in 1970 to 15 per cent in 1981, to 19.4 per cent in 1993/94, and it is 21.1 per cent[18] according to the latest figures (Kazi 1990: 3; Government of Pakistan 1995a, 1998d). In other words, one out of five professional workers in the country is a woman. In the urban areas, women even constitute more than one-third (33.5 per cent) of the 'professionals, technicians and associate professionals' (see figure 3). These are high figures if one takes into account that in 1998 only 14 per cent of the 15-year-old women (and 41 per cent of the 15-year-old men) were literate (The State of World Population 1998, quoted in *Dawn*, 05 September 1998), and barely 0.8 per cent of the female population have a university degree (Thiel 1994: 82).

Apart from the 35 per cent of the working women who belong to the category of the 'professionals, technicians and associate professionals', the categories of 'service workers and shop and market sales workers', 'craft and related trades workers', and 'elementary (unskilled) occupations' include about 55 per cent of the female workforce. These workers stand in sharp contrast to the professional workers as far as the social status of the tasks they perform is concerned. It can be assumed that women in 'elementary (unskilled) occupations' and female 'craft and related trades workers' are heavily concentrated in the informal sector, where they perform home-based and low-paying piece-rate work, which also includes craftswork like sewing, crochet, and embroidery. Female 'service workers and shop and market sales workers' seem to be concentrated among the service workers, where they are employed as cooks, maids, sweepers, washerwomen, street cleaners, hairdressers, etc. This assumption is sustained by the Labour Force Survey, 1993–94, in which

FIGURE 3
Percentage of Female Workers in Different Occupational Groups in the Urban Labour Market, 1996–97

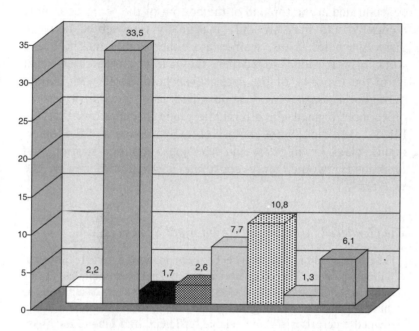

☐ Legislators, senior officials, managers

▨ Professionals, technicians and associate professionals

■ Clerks

▨ Service workers and shop and market sales workers

☐ Skilled agricultural and fishery workers

▨ Craft and related trades workers

☐ Plant & machine operators and assemblers

☐ Elementary (unskilled) occupations

Source: Government of Pakistan 1998b.

'Service Workers' and 'Sales Workers' appear as separate occupational groups, with 14 per cent of the female urban workforce being categorized as 'service workers' but only 7.9 per cent as 'sales workers'. Furthermore, according to the Labour Force Survey, 1993–94, about 15 per cent of the 'service workers' are women, whereas only 2.5 per cent of the 'sales workers' are female. (Government of Pakistan 1995a).

To conclude, women in the urban economy are heavily concentrated at the top and at the bottom of the socio-economic hierarchy, and they are only marginally represented between these two poles. Thus, women are either highly qualified and work in professional jobs where they can pursue a career (that is, in the majority of the cases, even compatible with gender segregation), or they work in unskilled, low-status positions out of economic need. In all middle-range occupations that are filled—even though not exclusively—by members of the lower-middle class, i.e. in office and sales jobs, in administration, and in industry, women only constitute a small minority of the workers.

The Gendered Structure of the Informal Sector

There is a distinct difference between male and female informal labour markets. The male labour market spectrum includes, at one end, unskilled, marginal workers subsisting in such casual jobs as hawking and car washing and, at the other end, small-scale, family-owned enterprises that are viable, efficient, and labour intensive. The informal female labour market is organized along different lines, because women's choice of activity is determined by the norms of female seclusion....

Work in which contact with males cannot be avoided is associated with loss of respect and diminished marriage prospects for single girls. Thus, Pakistan's urban informal labour market is highly segregated, even for a Muslim country. The workers, street vendors, market sellers, carpenters, mechanics, and barbers are almost exclusively male. Women are confined to being domestic servants (who work in a home when the master of the house is away at work and have dealings only with the mistress) or home-based workers (who stitch clothes, make lace, weave baskets, embroider, make food products and 'bidis' [home made cigarettes], for sale by male family members or middlemen), (World Bank 1989: 55f).

According to the World Bank, 77–83 per cent of women working in the urban informal sector—and 53 per cent of all urban working women—are home-based workers. About half of these women work on a piece-rate basis for middlemen or factories; the other half are self-employed. None of them have any financial or job security, and they work for minimum wages. Between 17 per cent and 23 per cent of the women in the informal sector work outside their houses. The great majority of these women (77 per cent), again, work in other people's houses as charwomen, cooks, and *ayas* (babysitters); and according to a recent survey every third household in Lahore employs a full or part-time female domestic (*Jang*, 4 July 1997). Only very few women, the poorest ones with the lowest socio-economic background, work in the public as road workers, labourers in brickyards and in quarries (for a study of women construction workers see *Jang*, 2 October 1995).

In her study of poor (lower-class) working women in the Old City of Lahore, one of the poorest residential areas in Lahore, Weiss, too, stresses the importance of the compatibility of the norms of purdah with the economic activities performed by the women. Figure 4 shows that out of a group of 33 women, 26 (78 per cent) worked either at home or in a female profession (teaching). But even the remaining seven women (21 per cent), who worked outside their own homes, avoided mixing with men: two women worked as domestics in other peoples' houses, one worked in a factory with only female employees, one was employed in the female section of a beauty parlour, and two older women worked as traders, though they were assisted by their sons or other male family members (for example, when they had to travel).

FIGURE 4
Type of Work Performed by Working Women in the Old City of Lahore

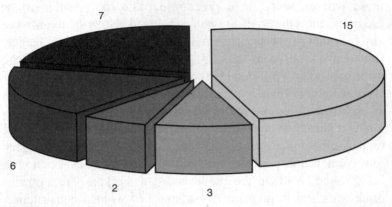

Piece work at home
Family work at home
Other work within the home
Teaching
Work outside of the home, not teaching

Source: Weiss, 1992.

Weiss points out that women in the informal sector do essentially the same kind of small-scale manufacturing that men do in the bazaars, but they do it at home and for significantly less remuneration. The high level of exploitation of home-based work is also caused by the dependency of women on middlemen since the women cannot market the products themselves and need someone to deliver the raw materials and pick up the finished products later. The women had chosen economic activities that could be performed at home because they feared gossip and a loss of respectability and social status that the mingling with the other sex would cause [for studies of women in the informal sector see Weiss (1992); Khan (1990); Hussein (1983); Shaheed/Mumtaz (n.d.)].

To sum up, while the informal sector includes a broad spectrum of economic activities with very different skill levels and incomes, women are concentrated in unskilled and semi-skilled fields of employment with the lowest remuneration and social status.

As in the formal sector, in recent years there have also been small changes with regard to the gendered structure of the informal sector. Women have, for example, started selling exotic fruits in certain areas in Lahore that are commonly not available at ordinary fruit stalls in the bazaars. These women do not have their own fixed stalls as is common in the bazaars, but sit on the roadside with one or two baskets filled with fruit like mulberries or strawberries. Once I asked a friend of mine, why they could sell the fruit there but were not present in the bazaars. In the bazaars, she told me, 'a lot of men hang around and women fear being teased. But this is a through road; it does not have any shops on either side, and there is not even a footpath. People don't hang around here, they just pass through on their motorbikes or in their cars. Most of them will only stop if they really want to buy some fruit.'

Similarly, I saw women and girls selling vegetables alongwith the male traders in the *jumma* (Friday) bazaars, markets that differ from the ordinary bazaars in so far as they only take place once a week on the public holiday,[19] under large tents that are temporarily erected. It was obvious that the male and female sellers who were sitting side by side were acquainted with each other.

This illustrates that women in the informal sector do work in a mixed environment where remuneration would be higher than for home-based work. Yet, there is still a great dearth of sociological studies regarding how women in purdah societies manage to embed such unconventional occupations into their life world despite the norms of gender segregation and seclusion. One exception which is worth mentioning here are the studies of Lessinger (1989; 1990) on female market traders in Madras, India. Lessinger analyses how women manage to overcome the strong purdah norms in Indian society and work in an occupation that requires extensive public dealing with unrelated men. She states that the women traders redefine the marketplace through fictive kinship, and thus manage to treat the marketplace as if it were an extension of their home or neighbourhood. As a consequence, the male traders are protective and courteous, and they can even be instrumentalized for 'social chaperonage', i.e. they can vouch for the innocence of the interactions with male strangers. Furthermore, women rely on male relatives for tasks that have to be performed outside the marketplace, like travelling or purchasing goods at the pre-dawn wholesale markets.

Lower-Middle-Class Women in the Market

Middle class women are frequently not gainfully employed. More usually, they take care of the household and children, often without the assistance of servants and perform income-saving activities such as sewing, knitting, stitching, crochet or other work (Klein/ Nestvogel 1986: 135).

This situation remains valid for the great majority of lower-middle-class families. However, although women and their families desire that the women remain at home (and consider it a status symbol), significant changes in female employment at the middle level have come to light since the mid-1980s. Teaching in the numerous low-standard private Urdu-language primary and secondary schools remains one important field of employment for women from this class. The increase in female education, particularly in the urban areas, and the worsening economic conditions combined with the lack of other 'respectable' employment alternatives, have led to an increasing supply of women looking for teaching positions. These schools, though, can only absorb a small percentage of women that are looking for work, and the competition between semi-qualified job seekers has led to very low salaries, between Rs 500 and 1000 per month—that actually do not amount to much more than pocket money. The totally inadequate financial remuneration may be one reason for lower-middle-class women taking up new, unconventional—and better paying—occupations that were regarded as shameful for women only a few years ago.[20]

One example is factory work, which until recently was a traditionally male domain. Although the lower-middle classes frowned upon women working in industrial labour, in the mid-1980s, 8 per cent of the workers in industries were already women (Hafeez 1983: 8). A nationwide study of female factory workers points out that the 'average' female worker does not belong to the uneducated lower class, but has finished secondary school. Women holding 89 per cent of the jobs in the cosmetics industry, 83 per cent in the pharmaceutical industry, and 80 per cent in the electronics industry have at least finished secondary school. Even in the garment factories, one-fourth of the female workers have studied up to tenth class or beyond (Government of Pakistan 1990). Further, the 'average' female factory worker is single, and below the age of 30 (*Dawn*, 7 January 1990; for similar results see *The News*, 28 January 1994). The wages of the women stand in marked contrast to their educational background. In 1990, 60 per cent of the female factory workers earned less than Rs 1000, which was the official minimum wage at that time (*Dawn*, 7 January 1990). In the cosmetics industry 69 per cent of the women, in the pharmaceutical industry 52.2 per cent, in the electronics industry 86 per cent, and in the garment industry 84.5 per cent, earned Rs 1000 or less (Government of Pakistan 1990). 80 per cent of the factories were not registered, and were, therefore, situated in a grey area between the formal and the informal sector. Only 20 per cent of the female factory workers, but 50 per cent of the men, had permanent employment status with paid holidays, medical and maternity leave (for women only), and right to increments (Mumtaz 1985: 50; Mumtaz 1987: 21; Hafeez 1983: 8).[21] In order to attract female workers several factories have already organized different working hours for male and female workers so that gender segregation can be maintained in the factory. However, a hierarchical gender-specific division of labour seems to be more common, in which women are assigned to unskilled tasks with the lowest remuneration and no chances for upward mobility like packing, sorting, and cleaning, and/or they are (unskilled) operators, whereas supervisors, cutters and master tailors are men (Kazi 1990: 9; Khan 1989: 8; Mumtaz 1986: 11; Mohiuddin

1991: 970). In addition, evidence indicates that the expansion of women's work in industries, particularly in (export oriented) manufacturing, has to a great extent taken place outside the regular factory workforce and mainly in the form of temporary and contract (home) work (Kazi/Raza 1990: 4). This development was already pointed out by Maria Mies at the beginning of the 1980s in her study of the lace makers of Narzapur, India. Women produce goods in their own homes that are either sold in the urban centres of their own countries or on the world market. The atomization of the homeworkers and their social definition as housewives make their extreme exploitation possible. And even here a feminization of labour-intensive home production can be observed while the better paid tasks such as the trade and sale of the products are dominated by men (Mies 1991). Nevertheless, women working in industries earn considerably more than homeworkers in the informal sector do or (probably equally or even higher-qualified) teachers in low-standard private schools.

Women have also increasingly entered the office sector. Between 1980 and 1990 their numbers increased twelve times.[22] At the beginning of the 1990s they still formed only about 3 per cent of the office workers, and although no up-to-date statistics are available, women have become much more visible in offices during the last few years.

The increasing demand for employment among lower-middle-class women has also become evident in the nursing profession. In contrast to the high status that is attached to being a 'lady doctor' who treats female patients, nursing is a profession that is looked down upon because it requires close physical contact with male patients. Although nurses receive a relatively good income and their employment in the civil service is almost guaranteed (together with all benefits like pension and health insurance, life-long employment, paid holidays, medical and maternity leave, etc.), nursing has traditionally been dominated by the Christian minority. Only a few years ago the hospitals could barely scrap together enough women for their four-year programmes in nursing because very few wanted to work in what was considered a demeaning occupation. Nowadays, the demand for seats in the training programmes for nursing has increased to such an extent that applicants also have to be rejected (Mirza 1994c: 69). The Christian minority has been, due to the increasing demand for training and employment in the field of nursing among the Muslim majority, largely pushed out of this profession, and now only about 5 per cent of the nurses are Christian.[23]

The job search among women from the lower-middle class, particularly school leavers, is great in the urban areas. According to the labour exchange in Lahore, the majority of the women looking for employment are young, i.e., below the age of twenty-five and have completed secondary school, but do not have any job-specific skills (Klein/Nestvogel 1986: 166f). Ms Nusrat, a lady working in an employment exchange only for women, that is coordinated by one of the local women's NGOs in Lahore, said that women do contact the employment exchange of the NGO, including uneducated domestics as well as highly educated women, but the majority of the women have qualifications between Matriculation (X Class) and a college degree, and are, therefore, looking for employment at the middle level of the occupational spectrum.

There is a sharp rising trend in educated and youth unemployment in Pakistan (*The News*, 22 December 1995; *Dawn*, 6 September 1994). The official unemployment rate is about 6 per cent—it was 5.37 per cent in 1997–98 (Government of Pakistan 1998b)—but unofficial figures which include underemployment and decrease in overseas employment estimate the unemployment rate to be about 25–30 per cent (*The News*, 6 January 1996; *The News*, 22 December 1995; *Dawn*, 6 September 1994). 1.1 million young people were added to the job market during 1998, of which less than half found any form of gainful employment. One half of the unemployed were among the educated (Human Rights Commission 1999: 239). This trend is increasing with the privatization of the economy. The public sector has not only ceased to absorb a significant number of young (educated) job seekers, but the downsizing of the public sector also means that government employees are increasingly pushed out of the civil service with a 'golden handshake' and thus further contribute to the rise of unemployed workers in the private sector.[24]

Ironically, despite this trend there is a shortage of skilled middle-level white-collar workers like receptionists, secretaries, office workers, laboratory assistants, and workers in the fields of computer science, tailoring, drafting, printing, electronic repairing, etc., but also of blue-collar workers like masons, carpenters, ironsmiths, painters, and electricians (*The Nation*, 27 September 1992; Kazi 1990: 20; Klein/Nestvogel 1986:176). This demand for skilled workers might be, at least partially, traced back to the changes in the occupational composition of Pakistani migrant workers in the Gulf countries. In the 1970s, the demand for unskilled workers, particularly for the transport and construction sectors (but also for semi-skilled craftsmen like masons, painters, steal fitters, carpenters, etc.), was high. However, since the 1980s, a new demand for all types of skills for the service sector has tended to replace that for unskilled construction workers (Zingel 1994: 28ff; Addledon 1992: 64; Cameron/Irfan 1991: 16) and has led to the migration of significant numbers of skilled (male) workers to the Gulf region.

Structural Adjustment and Economic Change: Recent Developments

When I returned to Lahore in October 1996 I was stunned by the increase in the prices of basic commodities like food and utilities which had increased enormously since 1993, and were still rising almost daily.

FIGURE 5
Price Indices: 1990/91–1998/99
(Base 1990/91 = 100)

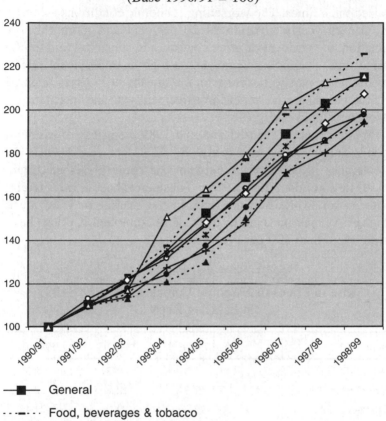

—■— General

· · ·—· · · Food, beverages & tobacco

—○— Apparel, textile & footwear

—◇— House rent

· · ·✳· · · Fuel & lighting

—●— Household furniture, equipment, etc.

—+— Transport & communication

· · ·▲· · · Recreation, entertainment & education

—△— Medicine

Source: Government of Pakistan 1999a.

Over a period of three months during 1997 the daily newspaper, *The News*, published thirty announcements of price increases of one or more basic goods,[25] and bus fares were raised three times. The worsening economic conditions—caused by a high yearly inflation of 20 per cent and more,[26] heavy taxation, the removal of price controls and subsidies, and (at the same time) stagnating wages and a high unemployment rate— were due in part to the Structural Adjustment Policies adopted by the Pakistan government in agreement with the International Monetary Fund (IMF).[27]

While between 1984/85 and mid-1989 the prices of essential goods and services rose 'only' by 82.30 per cent (*Dawn*, 29 September 1989), Table 1 explains the rising prices of certain essential goods since 1990. These are based on official information while actual prices in the market may be much higher. As may be seen, in the case of some items, prices have risen more than 400 per cent.

TABLE 1
Rise in Prices of Essential Commodities, 1990–1999
(in Pakistan Rupees)

Items	1990/91	1994/95	1998/99
Wheat Flour (1 kg)	3.7	5.8	8.3
Gram Pulse (1 kg)	7.9	21.8	22
Tomatoes (1 kg)	12.5	18.2	21.4
Dry Onions (1 kg)	7.7	7.8	16.4
Packed Tea	20	29.1	52
Sugar (1 kg)	11.3	13.7	18.8
Beef (1 kg)	25.5	40.7	55.8
Red Chillies (1 kg)	24.4	70.1	87.4
Cooking Oil Dalda (2.5 kg)	57.7	116.8	168.1
Fresh Milk (1 liter)	7.7	12.2	17.7
Eggs (dozen)	13.3	20.6	27.1

Source: Government of Pakistan 1999a.

According to the calculations of the daily newspaper, *The News* (29 December 1996), a family of two adults and two children needs at least Rs 4549 merely to survive (for a similar calculation see *Jang*, Sunday Magazine, 3–9 August 1997), while the minimum wage has been Rs 1650 since April 1994 which covers only 40 per cent of the genuine survival requirements.

Apart from the basic costs of everyday life, it is particularly lower-middle-class families that are entangled in expensive customs and socio-cultural obligations. Dowries that are given to daughters to fullfill the expectations of future in-laws are worth several yearly incomes and place a great financial burden on families. The exchange of expensive gifts (for example, clothes) among women of the extended family, among neighbours or friends, is also a social obligation at all kinds of events like religious festivities, engagements or weddings. Furthermore, the family of the bride continues to give expensive presents to the family of the groom, on various festivals. Ceremonies like engagements and weddings have to be celebrated splendidly if the family does not want to lose their social position. It was a relief for broad sections of society when [a former] Prime Minister prohibited by law the serving of meals during wedding ceremonies. Weddings are celebrated for at least three days with several hundred guests, and the families serve expensive food if they do not want to lose their social standing.

Thus, the economic crisis and social constraints have made it increasingly difficult for the lower-middle classes to remain within their means. It is true that it is becoming more and more difficult for all sections of society to keep up their standard of living, or, as in the case of the lower classes, simply to make ends meet.[28] Yet, while there have always been working women in the upper and lower sections of society,[29] it is a relatively new phenomenon that women from the lower-middle classes are increasingly joining the labour force.

Women in (Non-)Market-Oriented Education and Training Programmes

Although, as stated by the Human Development Report for 1999, the adult literacy rate is only 25.4 per cent for women (and 55.2 per cent for men), and the 1998 Population and Housing Census gives a literacy rate of 32.6 per cent for Pakistani women above ten years of age (quoted in Government of Pakistan 1999b), more and more girls, particularly in urban areas, have gained access to formal education during the last couple of decades. According to official statistics, nearly two-thirds of all girls are enrolled in primary school, and one out of four finishes secondary school (see Table 2).

The Population Census of 1981[30] stressed the high number of educated women in the country:

> There is a large pool of educated and qualified people in our country. About one quarter of the population having matric and above qualifications are women. The number runs into almost a million (quoted from Government of Pakistan 1984).

TABLE 2

Participation Rates in Primary, Middle and Secondary School, 1998–99 (in per cent)[31]

	Both	Male	Female
1. Primary Stage (Class I-V)	77	92	62
2. Middle Stage (Class VI-VIII)	51	64	37
3. High Stage (Class IX-X)	36	45	26

Source: Government of Pakistan 1999a.

Although no up-to-date statistics are available, it can be assumed that the number of women with qualifications of matriculation (i.e. X Class) and above has, at least in the urban areas, increased considerably since the beginning of the 1980s. According to a recent report in the newspaper, *Jang* (27 November 1997),

Pakistan has 1.2 million female college graduates (BA/B.Sc.) and more than one hundred thousand female university graduates (MA/M.Sc.). *Jang* speaks here about not gainfully employed female college and university graduates in Pakistan. Although it is not clear on which data these figures are based, if women who work after finishing their education are not included, it can be assumed that the total number of college and university graduates would be slightly higher.

Indeed, getting a formal education, at least up to X Class, has become more and more important in the lower-middle classes during the last decades. Two decades ago, in 1980, only 24 per cent of urban parents wished to see their daughters educated; but according to a recent survey, 95 per cent of urban parents desire to educate their girls, and 36 per cent are keen to get them a university education. These opinions about higher education for girls are much the same across the different socio-economic classes (*Dawn*, 9 October 1999). Similarly, nearly all working women I talked to during my field research had mothers who were not educated beyond a few years of schooling, some had not been to school at all, and in all cases the mothers were significantly less qualified than their daughters. The working women had often acquired higher educational degrees than their brothers (or husbands), or they were at least equally qualified.[32]

This development toward educating girls in lower-middle-class families does not mean, however, that girls acquire the same kind of education as boys, and that they learn job-specific skills that prepare them for later employment. An education is not really considered important for preparing women for future employment and for imparting job-specific skills. Being 'educated' has rather become a social status symbol for the women and their families, and an important differentiation from the lower classes. Going to school or college does not threaten the reputation of the girl as long as she studies in gender-segregated educational institutes, and it improves her chances to find a good match in the 'marriage market' because men from lower-middle-class families do not want to marry uneducated women. For this reason, it is not common for girls to select market-oriented subjects and courses, neither in the general educational system nor in vocational training programmes. They prefer programmes that prepare them to become better homemakers by teaching them reproductive skills. In 1997, girls constituted 57.4 per cent of the matriculates in the Arts category, but only 23.9 per cent of the Science matriculates (Government of Pakistan 1999b).

The absence of job-orientation among girls can be further illustrated by looking at the subjects they choose at college level. Six out of ten female college students are enrolled in home economics, education or medicine (Figure 6).

FIGURE 6
Distribution of Female College Students among the Different Courses, 1997–98

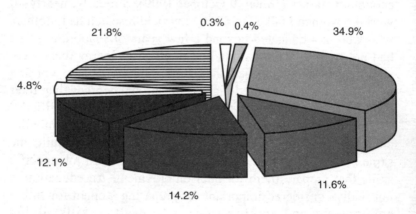

☐ Agriculture
☐ Engineering
▨ Medical
■ Home Economics
■ Education
■ Commerce
☐ Law
▤ All Others (Arts, Homeopathic, Fine Arts, Computer, etc.)

Source: Government of Pakistan 1999b.

A look at job-specific training programmes and courses at the middle level reveals a similar picture (see figure 7).

FIGURE 7

Male and Female Students in Secondary Vocational Institutions, 1997–98

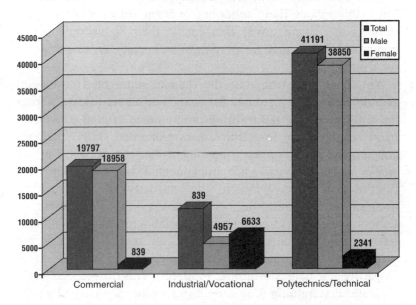

Source: Government of Pakistan 1999b.

In the secondary vocational institutions, women are concentrated in industrial homes where they learn sewing, crochet, and needlework. These skills enable women to take over more reproductive work (for example, sewing the clothes of family members), but they do not prepare them for employment in the formal sector. In commercial institutes where students are trained in electronics, typing, business skills (like accounting), in operating computers, or in driving, women are only marginally represented. The same can be said about their enrolment in Polytechnics and technical institutions. 67.6 per cent of all female students in secondary vocational institutes are concentrated in industrial homes, as against 7.9 per cent of the male students.

This gender-specific difference in the selection of courses at the middle level (and, as has been shown, also at the college level) is definitely linked to the absence of concepts of female employment among those sections of society who are the target of these educational institutes, namely, the lower-middle classes. Thus, throughout their schooling women select courses (and subjects at college level) that enable them to become better homemakers, and that are perceived by society as 'respectable' for women.

Yet, it is also true that the (gender-segregated) state-run vocational training institutes for women differ significantly from those for men, and the training programmes offered to women barely enable them to acquire market-oriented skills. Training courses and programmes for women, that run between a few weeks and three years, are implemented and coordinated by twelve ministries.[33] While the majority of the training programmes for men are coordinated by the Department of Labour, which works closely with the labour market and adjusts its programmes to the demands of the market, the training programmes for women are implemented by the Social Welfare Department (Shaheed/Mumtaz 1990: 55). This difference clearly indicates that training programmes for women are basically seen as a social issue. Shaheed/Mumtaz (1990) have pointed out that only a few of the training programmes for women are catered toward teaching them market-oriented skills. A part of the offered courses, for example, 'Household Skills', 'Repair of Domestic Appliances', 'Cooking', 'Interior Decoration', 'Housing', 'Looking after Livestock', 'Kitchen Gardening', and 'Fruit and Vegetable Preservation' just aim at improving women's skills as housewives and homemakers. Women are trained in fields like 'Handicrafts', 'Dress Making', 'Embroidery', 'Knitting', 'Traditional Skills', 'Local Crafts', and 'Sewing' that would only enable them to work in the informal sector as home-based workers or micro-entrepreneurs and in fields in which a great number of working women from the lower classes are already concentrated. Hence, while the vocational training programmes for men are directed at meeting their employment needs, the programmes for women aim at saving family income rather than enhancing employment opportunities (Kazi/Raza 1990: 6). Until the beginning of the 1980s, the Labour Department did not run a single training institute for women,[34] and in 1990, about 20,000 men were trained in more than 175 occupations, but only 176 women in ten occupations (Shaheed/Mumtaz 1990: 55). Until the mid-1990s, formal training programmes for women, run by the Labour Department in the Technical Training Centres for Women (TTCWs), had merely increased to 380 places (Government of Pakistan 1994: 118).

In addition, women do not have access to the apprenticeship system in the informal sector that runs parallel to the training programmes in the formal institutions. About 45,000 trainees annually, that is more than twice as many as those in the formal training programmes, are trained in the little craftshops and stores, particularly in the bazaars, for jobs such as hairdressers, goldsmiths, cloths sellers, or auto mechanics (Choudhary et al. 1989: 4). In contrast to the formal secondary vocational institutes, which usually demand matric certification as an entrance qualification, no formal education is required for being trained in the informal sector. Therefore, even if boys drop out of school early, they can still learn a craft and become skilled workers. Only 16 per cent of the trainees in the informal sector have completed secondary school, 33 per cent have eight years of schooling. 27 per cent of the trainees have completed primary school and 20 per cent do not have any formal education at all (Börgel 1992: 5). On-the-job training usually continues for some years, but generally trainees begin to receive a small stipend after a short while.

To sum up, it is true that there is no concept of female employment, particularly among the lower-middle classes, but this is further reinforced by the absence of possibilities for women to learn any job-specific skills. Women can only acquire skills in the formal educational institutions, but a formal degree at school or college level is of little use, because there is a mismatch between the educational system and the labour market, which does not qualify school leavers or college graduates for employment (which is one reason for the high levels of educated unemployment).[35] Similarly, the courses that are offered in the vocational training institutions for women are not only less effective than the on-the-job training in the informal sector,[36] but most courses for women do not even aim at teaching them job-specific skills.

Despite the illustrated unfavourable conditions for women regarding the acquisition of a market-oriented education, women have started to shift from non-marketable courses to training programmes that teach job-specific skills.

The Technical Training Centre for Women (TTCW), Lahore, can be named here as one example. The TTCWs are the first training institutions for women to be coordinated by the Department of Labour that aim at imparting lower-middle-class women with the middle-level job-specific skills for which there is a demand in the labour market. The first TTCW was initiated in Karachi in 1983, and three more TTCWs were set up in Lahore (1988), Quetta (1988), and Peshawar (1993). A second TTCW in Lahore was opened recently. The TTCWs were all set up as projects of bi- or multilateral development cooperation and designed as parallel institutions to the 'Technical Training Centres' for men (in 1990 there were twenty-four TTCs in the country, Shaheed/Mumtaz 1990: 55). The courses run between one and two years, and the minimum entrance qualification is completion of secondary school. The market orientation of the courses and the internships in offices and industry that are a compulsory part of the training programmes, are a novelty. When the TTCW, Lahore, was initiated in 1988, in collaboration with the Labour Department and German Technical Cooperation as a vocational training school to train women in job-specific skills, and integrate them into the labour market, there was no great demand for the offered courses. Many women wanted to enroll in the traditional fields, 'Dress Designing/Dress Making', and the course entitled 'Computer Operator', but there was a very limited interest in the other courses that were offered; namely,

'Architectural Drafting', 'Commercial Arts', 'Communication/ Electronics', 'Executive Secretary', 'Office Secretary' and 'Receptionist'. In particular, the secretarial courses did not find much acceptance because of the negative image that is attached to these occupations. The following is a revealing story. In the fall of 1992 not all women who had applied for admission in the course 'Computer Operator' could get admission (there were only sixteen seats per course and too many applicants) and some of them were offered a seat in the course 'Office Secretary'. The women were told that the contents of the courses were basically the same, the only exception being that the office secretaries learned one software programme less and were taught shorthand instead. Yet, many women refused the offer to switch to the secretarial course, and preferred not to take admission at all simply because the term 'Office Secretary' sounded less respectable to them (and probably their families) than the occupation of 'Computer Operator'.[37]

When I talked to the German team leader of the TTCW in October 1996, I was told that the situation had changed tremendously. It had become known in Lahore that the TTCW offers a good market-oriented education for nominal fees—the fees are only 20 or 30 rupees per month, and are lower than those in private institutions—and that trainees who want to work after completion of their course can easily find employment and earn a reasonable income. Now the demand for admission is great, and many families try hard, also by means of personal contacts and even intimidation, to get a seat for their daughters.

Thus, small changes in the perception of female education can be observed. Women are beginning to see their education not only as a status symbol but as a chance to learn some job-oriented skills. Many women who can be found in such market-oriented courses do not really link it to further employment, but the worsening economic conditions have brought about a reorientation in so far as women are starting to acknowledge the importance of job-specific skills. They want to learn a skill just in case they need to support their families and look for gainful employment.

NOTES

1. For other early sociological analyses of the market, see also Zelizer (1979) and DiMaggio (1977–78)
2. See the publications of Friedland/Robertson (eds.) 1990; Swedberg 1990; Zukin/DiMaggio (eds.) 1990; Martinelli/Smelser (eds.) 1990; Mingione 1991; Holton 1992; Swedberg/Granovetter (eds.) 1992; Swedberg (ed.) 1993; Hirschmann (1993); Smelser/Swedberg (eds.) 1994; Callon (ed.) 1998.
3. The term 'New Economic Sociology' was originally coined by Mark Granovetter in the mid-eighties (Swedberg 1990: 106). For a comparison of the Old and the New Economic Sociology see Granovetter (1990) and Swedberg (1990: 106f).
4. For a detailed analysis of the differences between sociological and economic analyses of the economy see Swedberg/Himmelstrand/Brulin (1990); Hirsch/Michaels/Friedmann (1990); Smelser/Swedberg (1994); Swedberg (1994).
5. Yet, on the basis of a historical analysis of nineteenth and twentieth-century Europe (Polanyi 1978), Polanyi detected a powerful counter-trend to integrate the economy once more under wider social controls. He concluded that differentiated market economies generate such extreme social and political tensions that new types of 'embedded' economies emerge. Free markets and self-sufficient economies, therefore, are seen as transitory institutions, sandwiched, so to speak, between a long historical phase of economic embeddedness, and a recent historical phase of reintegration of economic into social arrangements once more. These include welfare states in which the function of social protection re-emerges to take precedence over that of market independence (Holton 1992: 18/37; also Schrader 1995: 4f).
6. For a more detailed analysis of the 'traders' dilemma see Evers/Schrader (eds.), (1994); Evers (1994) and Schrader (1994).
7. See Pearson 1996; Dunn 1995; Lim 1990; O'Sullivan 1995 (Asia); Young 1994 (Asia); Standing 1996 (Southeast Asia); Rosa 1994 (Southeast Asia) Salaff 1990 (Southeast Asia); Dannecker 1998 (Bangladesh); Safa 1996 (Dominican Republic); Arregui/Baetz 1991 (Dominican Republic); Safa 1990 (Caribbean); Kabeer 1994 (Bangladesh); Maenner 1988 (Sri Lanka); Baylies/Wright 1993 (South Africa); Sharma 1990 (India); Joekes 1985 (Morocco); Kang 1988 (Southkorea); Lenz 1988b (Eastasia); Ecevit 1991(Turkey); Wiegersma 1994 (Nicaragua).
8. One exception is the study of women in the office sector in Mexico by Braig (1992; also 1997); further see Macleod's study (1991) of government employees in the office sector in Cairo. Macleod, however, is primarily concerned with analysing the phenomenon of reveiling among

the office workers. An older analysis of office workers in Egypt is provided by Mohsen (1985).

9. See particularly the articles in Cagatay et al. (eds.), (1995); further Elson (1993a; 1993b); Bakkar (1994); Palmer (1997); Walters (1997).

10. Extensive research on the interactions between subsistence and market production has been conducted at the Sociology of Development Research Center, Bielefeld University, Germany, since the late 1970s. For a terminological and theoretical discussion see Elwert/Wong (1981); Evers/ Schiel (1981); Otto-Walter (1981); and the articles in Smith/Wallerstein/ Evers (eds.), (1984).

11. The strong equation of female work with disgrace and a fall in social standing has also been pointed out by Shaheed (1989: 26) in her study of lower-middle-class women in Kot Lakhpat, Lahore. On this point see also Alavi (1991: 130).

12. There are good private girls' schools and colleges in the urban areas where women work as teachers. However, these private sector educational institutions cannot absorb the enormous demand for teaching posts among women. Only highly-qualified women with at least a Bachelor's or Master's degree and fluency in English can get positions in these schools, which are not well paying if one considers the qualifications of the teachers and compares their wages with those of equally-qualified women in other (male) professions in the office sector.

13. See Hafeez' study (1981: 73–159) of upper-class women in senior administrative positions that was conducted in the mid-seventies. About half of these women had lived abroad for some years for further education, a fact that already demonstrates their upper-class family background.

14. See 'Pakistan's first woman jet pilot' (The Muslim, 30 January 1992), 'PIA first woman pilot to fly airbus A-310' (The Frontier Post, 6 April 1995), and 'First woman to fly Jumbo' (Dawn, 29 October 1999); or the reports about the first women in the petroleum industry (Jang, 8 April 1997; Dawn, 9 August 1998), in horticulture (Dawn, 1 June 1996), and the first woman chief executive of a teaching hospital in Punjab (Dawn, 8 August 1998).

15. Interestingly, as among the upper (middle) classes, many members of the lower-middle classes do not consider being a pilot, a lawyer, or a computer programmer in an office to be unacceptable for women (though not as respectable as being a teacher or doctor). The reason is that these professions, in contrast to secretarial or factory work, require a high level of education. This point is also raised by Weiss (1992: 99).

16. The crude labour force participation rate is defined as the percentage of persons in the labour force in respect to the total population. The refined labour force participation rate, which is 8.4% for women in urban Pakistan, is defined as the percentage of persons in the labour force in respect to the population ten years of age and above.

17. This figure is taken from the Seventh Five-Year Plan (1988–1993).
18. In the latest Labour Force Survey, 1996–97, the occupational groups were changed. Therefore, the new occupational groups 'professionals' and 'technicians and associate professionals', which have been merged in this study into one occupational group ('professionals, technicians and associate professionals'), have been equated with the formerly existing occupational group 'professional, technical and related workers'.
19. Jumma bazaars literally mean 'Friday bazaars', because until recently the weekly public holiday was on Friday. After his election as Prime Minister in January 1997, Mr Nawaz Sharif changed the public holiday from Friday to Sunday, and now the jumma bazaars have changed into 'Sunday bazaars'.
20. It is interesting to note here that many women had started to teach in one of these schools and then, after they saw that their salary was so low and that they did not have any chances for further improvement, had switched to an office job. Out of thirteen women, five had worked as teachers earlier, and one woman had sewn clothes as a home-based worker in the informal sector.
21. For more information about women in the industrial sector, see also Weiss (1984); Hooper (1985); more up-to-date studies were not available.
22. In 1980, only 1373 women were included in the category 'office workers'; in 1990 their number was already 15,877 (INBAS 1993:27).
23. However, there is still a great dearth of trained nurses, and doctors outnumber nurses by as much as three to one. In 1997, 78,470 doctors but only 28,661 nurses were working in Pakistan (Turner 2000:1240).
24. On the process of the privatization of the economy see *Pakistan & Gulf Economist*, 21–7 December 1998; 16–22 June 1997; 19–25 May 1997; 24 March–6 April 1997; 27 April–3 May 1996.
25. Headlines in *The News* over three months indicating the price hike of basic goods in Pakistan: Packaged tea prices to be raised (4 Nov. 1996); Prices register increasing trend (13 Nov. 1996); Petrol prices go up (14 Nov. 1996); Postal rates increased (14 Nov. 1996); Surge in petrol prices to hit people (14 Nov. 1996); Records of price hike in essential items broken (15 Nov. 1996); Petrol prices raised again by 20 paisas (18 Nov. 1996); High prices of medicine (19 Nov. 1996); Gas rates up by 48pc in two years (20 Nov. 1996); Transporters raise fares on their own (26 Nov. 1996); Utility stores raise prices of 1000 items (3 Dec. 1996); Increase in transport fares (03 Dec. 1996); Transport fares to rise by 3 paisas (13 Dec. 1996); GST on many items doubled (25 Dec. 1996); Ghee prices again up by Rs 6.50 per kg (29 Dec. 1996); Gas tariff up 15 pc (31 Dec. 1996); Ghee prices raised by 60 paisas per kg (8 Jan. 1997); Petrol prices raised again (10 Jan. 1997); Prices of daily use items keep rising (11 Jan. 1997); 10 per cent rise in gas charges by March (11 Jan. 1997); Sharp reaction to price-hike in Ramazan (13 Jan. 1997);

Ghee shortage hits City, price up Rs 2.51 per kg (13 Jan. 1997); Ghee price further up (14 Jan. 1997); Ghee prices raised by another 60 paisas (15 Jan. 1997); Not by IMF advice alone (19 Jan. 1997); Rs 5 per kg raise in rice prices shocks consumers (20 Jan. 1997); Sugar price further up by Rs 1 per kg (26 Jan. 1997); Ghee prices raised by another Rs 1.50 per kilo (29 Jan. 1997).

26. The unofficial inflation rates during the last years were always above or around 20% (for 1994 see Amin 1995: 145; for 1995 see LaPorte 1996: 185; for 1996 see LaPorte 1997: 122ff.; for 1997 see Syed 1998). The Rupee stood at about Rs 25 to $US1 in mid-1995; a year later, in mid-1996, it was almost Rs 40 to $1, a devaluation of 60%. Between mid-1996 and September 1996 the Rupee was again devalued six times by the State Bank of Pakistan (LaPorte 1997: 124).

27. The disastrous effects of SAP on the Pakistani economy are being widely discussed in the local press. See The News, 11 Jan. 1997; 4 Dec. 1996; 25 Oct. 1996; 23 Nov. 1996; 19 Nov. 1996b; 11 Nov. 1996a; 2 Nov. 1996; 26 Oct. 1996; 18 Oct. 1996; The Nation, 18 Oct. 1996.

28. For articles on the worsening economic conditions affecting all sections of society, see The News, 1 June 1997a/b/c; 1 Nov. 1997 a/b/c; Pakistan & Gulf Economist, 7–13 July 1997a/b; 30 Nov.–6 Dec 1996; Jang (Sunday Magazine), 3–9 August 1997. A discussion of the impact of the mahangaai on lower-middle-class families is provided by Jang, 2 June 1998. For a detailed analysis of Pakistan's economic performance since its creation in 1947, see Hasan 1998.

29. According to Weiss' study (1992) of lower-class women in Lahore, for which the empirical data was collected in 1987, 50 per cent of the working women had started to work during the last five years. This fact indicates that women from the lower classes, too, are increasingly pushed into the market because the survival of the families depends more and more on the additional incomes of the female family members.

30. After the Population Census of 1981, which was published in 1984, a new population census was taken in the fall of 1998. The results were not published till after the completion of this study.

31. These official figures in Table 2 should be interpreted with caution. According to the United Nations Fund for Population, the school participation rates in Pakistan are much lower, namely 30% for girls (and 57% for boys) in primary school, and 23% for girls (and 46% for boys) in secondary school (The State of World Population 1998, quoted in Dawn, 5 September 1998). The report of the Human Rights Commission of Pakistan gives a primary enrolment rate for girls which is as low as 21% (Human Rights Commission of Pakistan 1999: 253).

32. During the past five years, the number of female students at the Punjab University, Lahore, has doubled (The News, 9 Nov. 1999); and less men than women have taken the BA/B.Sc. examinations of the Punjab

University (for example, in 1992), (Weiss 1994b: 426). Furthermore, female students' overall grades are higher than boys' and they top the merit lists (*The News*, 9 Nov. 1999 and 13 Nov. 1996).

33. The ministries are the following: Social Welfare Department, Small Scale Industries Corporations and Boards, Department of Labour, Department of Health, Directorates of Technical Education, Local Government and Rural Development, Establishment Division, Women's Division, Livestock and Poultry, Department of Agriculture, Department of Forestry, and Telephone and Telegraph Department (Shaheed/Mumtaz 1990: 54).

34. The numerous training programmes for women that are offered by other ministries cannot be classified as vocational/professional training programmes. Programmes that qualify school leavers with qualifications at the middle level for later employment are restricted to the Department of Labour.

35. On the mismatch between the educational system and the labour market, see Khan (1992: 275ff) and *Jang* (4 June 1997). Khan quotes a study according to which 96% of the graduates and 76% of the postgraduates worked in occupations different from their fields of specialization.

36. For a discussion of the shortcomings and structural problems of the formal vocational training system in Pakistan, see Mirza (1994b).

37. For an assessment of the TTCW, Lahore, see Mirza (1994a; 1994d).

4

FROM 'CHADDOR AUR CHARDIVARI' INTO THE MARKET: WOMEN ENTER THE OFFICE SECTOR

Andeela, Ghazal, Shagufta, Asieh: Four Case Studies

Women from the lower-middle classes who have been and are nowadays entering the office sector are not a homogenous and uniform group. They differ significantly with regard to their family background, their reasons for becoming gainfully employed, and the role their occupation plays in their lives, only to name a few examples here. On the basis of empirical findings four different types of office workers could be identified, and shall be illustrated in the following with the help of the accounts of four women, each of them representing one type of office worker.

Type One: 'Family supporter (without severe economic need)'

These women have already, prior to becoming gainfully employed, re-oriented their education from a symbolic one, i.e. from the collection of degrees in the formal educational system that have some relevance for the 'marriage market' but not much for the labour market, to a market-oriented education.

This shift is not really connected to an immediate desire for later employment but rather has to be seen in the light of the worsening economic conditions; women choose a market-oriented education so that, if worse comes to worst, they will be able to use their skills to support their families. Once having acquired market-oriented skills they decide to enter the labour market in order to maintain the living standards of their families (Andeela, Sadaf, Tasneem, Sadia).

When Andeela finished secondary school she decided to enroll in a two-year certificate course in Islamic Studies, which was offered by a local madrassa. Like all the girls who attended the course, Andeela had to live in the hostel which was attached to the madrassa. Because she started feeling homesick she broke off her studies after six months, and went back home to live with her family. She could not enroll in a college in the middle of the academic year, so she stayed home for another six months. It was her mother who recommended that she take a technical course instead of enrolling in a college. She felt that if Andeela got some technical training, she would acquire skills which could be useful in the future in case of any emerging economic problems. Andeela also felt that having a college degree would not be of any practical use and decided to enroll in the Technical Training Centre for Women, Lahore. Andeela did not want to take any of the secretarial courses offered at the centre because a secretary 'has to work closely with the boss' and 'has a lot of contact with men', and Andeela does not consider this to be a suitable job for women. So, she decided to enroll in a two-year course in 'Architectural Drafting'.

After completion of her course in the fall of 1994 she did not try to find employment because she did not have any intention to work. The perspective of working in an office was far away from her life world for several reasons. First, there were no working women in her family. Only a few girls had taught for a couple of months in schools after completing their education (mostly secondary school), just to pass the time until they got married. Second, her family background was very conservative.

All of Andeela's five brothers were studying, and the only income earner was her father, who was a government employee earning about Rs 3000. This was not enough for the whole family, but her father also owned a rickshaw and worked as a rickshaw driver in the evenings in order to make ends meet. Andeela's father had completed secondary school, while her mother had only three years of schooling to her credit. Both had married very early and were in their late thirties. The whole family, i.e. eight persons, lived in a house that, surrounded by the chardivari, consisted of a small courtyard and two rooms of about twelve square meters. Although the house was their own property—it is rather uncommon to live in rented houses—their living conditions indicated that it was difficult for them to maintain their standard of living, that they were indeed sliding down the socio-economic hierarchy. They did not possess a telephone or refrigerator, which are common in the houses of lower-middle-class families. Andeela's oldest brother, who studied at college level, was preparing for his exams privately at home in order to save college fees. However, the parents had been to Saudi Arabia to perform Haj, a trip that must have cost them at least one or two lakh rupees.

Eventually, Andeela took up a job at a salary of Rs 1600. After two years it had increased by Rs 200. Andeela is now 21 years old. She gives Rs 1000 per month to her mother to run the household and keeps the rest of her salary, Rs 800, for herself. She spends her money on her wardrobe, presents for friends and relatives and on cold drinks and snacks, which she buys when visitors drop in.

Type Two: 'Major breadwinner with severe economic need'

These office workers never thought about becoming gainfully employed and had not acquired any particular market-oriented skills. A sudden disaster and/or rapidly worsening economic conditions pushed them into the market (Sajda, Ghazal, Kishwer, Firdous, Aisha).

Ghazal is in her mid-twenties and works as a telephone operator and receptionist at a local computer company. Her parents arranged her marriage when she was still in secondary school, and after her marriage she managed to finish secondary school and then passed FA (XII Class). Her husband, who had studied up to X Class, has been a drug addict for many years, and he spends a great part of his income on drugs. The couple was supported by the in-laws until they threw them out of their house when Ghazal's daughter was four and her son was a baby. Ghazal had to earn money to make ends meet, so she started to work.

First she worked as a teacher, then as a telephone operator. Finally, she joined a company where her salary rose to Rs 3000 with paid holidays and medical leave.

Ghazal spends her entire income on the maintenance of her family, and school fees for her children, who attend the local government school. Her husband is a government employee and works at a local post office. He earns Rs 2500, as far as she knows, but he only supports her irregularly, and still spends a great part of his salary on drugs. The family live in an area that is inhabited by lower- and lower-middle-class families. Ghazal, her husband and her two children live in one small room at a monthly rent of Rs 1500. She pays Rs 500 for her children's education. Her salary is not enough to cover all expenses, so she sews shalwar-kameez for ladies and manages to earn an additional income of about Rs 1000 to 1200 per month. From that money she first bought a fan, then a second-hand refrigerator and a cupboard for which she paid in monthly installments. The room the family live in is barely furnished having only a bed, a cupboard and a mattress for the children to sleep on. Clothes are hung up on a line across the room. Since there are no chairs and table, a piece of cloth is spread out on the ground when meals are taken.

Type Three: 'Women searching for new perspectives/novelty appeal type'

These kind of office workers also have a lower-middle-class background but come from slightly better-off families. They go through some market-oriented training mainly due to their interest in a certain technical field. For them, employment is based on the novelty appeal rather than on economic need. Although they do not have to support their families, being gainfully employed helps them to acquire goods they probably could not obtain without their own income (Shagufta, Shazia, Shaheen).

Shagufta is a software developer. She did her BA, then enrolled in a one-year diploma course in Computer Science after which she started working. Shagufta's job requires teamwork—which means she must work with men. In her family, she is the first female to have entered the office sector. She is the third of seven children. Her eldest brother migrated[1] to the United States, and her elder sister is in her late twenties, single, and has studied up to X Class.

After Shagufta became gainfully employed, her sister also started to work at a non-government welfare centre for women earning Rs 2000 per month. After the centre closed down she started to design shalwar-kameez at home to sell in boutiques. Shagufta's younger sister, Ghazala, studies at the University. She is a strong supporter of veiling and wears a burqa, and more than once I witnessed discussions between her and Shagufta regarding whether women should wear the veil, work in offices, etc. Only the eldest of Shagufta's three younger brothers works. He studied up to FA, and started his own business. He makes video movies at weddings and engagements, a job that does not provide a regular income. The second brother finished college one and a half years ago, but has not found a job yet. The youngest brother still studies and has just passed his FA exam.

The family live in a township; their house is situated on a relatively broad road, is small but well-furnished and they have an air conditioner. They have a 'Western style' fitted kitchen. Shagufta stresses that she was interested in computers and wanted to work, but she also admits that when she started to work none of her brothers and sisters were gainfully employed, and her father, who had a shop in the bazaar, was the only income earner. She never had to support her family from her income, but she is well aware of the fact that due to her income she and her family possess luxury goods they could never afford otherwise. At her home she has a computer and also owns a small car. In the fall of 1997 she went to Saudi Arabia (Mecca) with her mother to perform umrah. Since her father died in the spring of 1997, her income must have become even more important for the family. The house belongs to the family, and their shop in the bazaar is rented out. Apart from Shagufta, only one sister and one brother work, their incomes are not regular and much lower than Shagufta's salary.

Type Four: 'Restarter type'

This type of office worker is still in the process of emerging. The women primarily belong to one of the other types, particularly type one or three. They stop working when they get married, however, they start working again after a while, this time (again) for financial reasons, and thus their temporary status as office workers turns into a permanent one (Asieh).

Asieh is 28 years old and works in a small advertising agency as a designer. Her elder brother encouraged her to obtain market-oriented training so that she could support herself if necessary. This type of encouragement, particularly from brothers, is rather uncommon but has to be seen against the background of their father deserting their mother.

Asieh enrolled in a two-year course in 'Commercial Arts' which was offered by the TTCW, Lahore. After completion of her course her brother encouraged her to become gainfully employed and stand on her own two feet. Asieh started to work in an advertising agency and her salary was Rs 1500. She spent her salary on her wardrobe, music tapes, gifts for friends, etc.

One year after she had started to work, she got married to her cousin. Her husband, who had only studied up to secondary school, worked as a telephone operator for a private company. Her mother-in-law was a primary school teacher at a government school and her father-in-law held a clerical position at a private company. Her sister-in-law still attended college and her brother-in-law worked as a clerk at a private office. The husband and the in-laws did not want Asieh to be a working woman so she left her job before the wedding. After getting married, Asieh started to live with her in-laws; she stayed at home and was responsible for the housework. The whole family lived in their own house located in a typical lower-middle-class residential area in the centre of the city. The three rooms of the house are well-furnished with wooden cupboards, shelves, a dining table, and a three-piece sofa set in the living room. However, a large number of these expensive items were given by Asieh's family as part of the customary *jehez* (dowry), at her wedding.

Eight months after Asieh got married her husband left his job due to a quarrel with his boss. Since they both lived in a joint family this was not an immediate catastrophe, but—apart from getting accommodation and food without having to contribute to the expenses—they did not have any money for themselves. One year after she had quit her job Asieh rejoined the advertising agency at a salary of Rs 2000 per month. Her husband found another job but earned only Rs 3000, and since they now had a baby, his income alone was not enough for all the expenses. Furthermore, he had earlier taken loans from private money lenders in order to set up his own business. The business went bankrupt, and since the interest rates of private money lenders are very high (usually 10 per cent per month) they had acquired very high debts. Thereafter her husband again left his job due to a dispute with his superiors and was again unemployed. For these reasons Asieh has continued to work. She now earns Rs 2500 and cannot think about leaving her job and staying at home as a housewife.

'I never thought that I could work with men'— Confrontation with the Male World

Venturing into the Lion's Den: The First Steps into the Office

It is common that women feel unsafe and insecure while taking the first steps into the office. They are totally inexperienced in communicating with male strangers, and in facing the world outside of their chardivari on their own. Tasneem, a draftswoman, said:

> before I started to work I never went anywhere on my own, not even to my grandmother's house [nearby]. I was always accompanied by one of my brothers or my mother (17 April 1997, p. 6).

Similarly, Ghazal recounted that:

> before I started working, I didn't know anything about this world, what happens in this world, I only knew about life at home. I was locked up in a cage. I did not go out [of the house] for months. When I needed something I got it inside the house, bangles, clothes, shoes, everything....I asked my mother-in-law and she said, 'o.k. I'll get it for you...', I did not have permission to leave the house. She [the mother-in-law] said, 'if you go outside the people will say, "this is their bahu, she is walking outside, on the streets, in the bazaar", it does not look nice'....I just stayed at home, I did not know anything about the outside world, I did not know the directions and streets, and what was happening outside (receptionist, 25 May 1997, p.10).

The women have no knowledge about the set-up in offices and the way work is done in an office environment, nor are there any working women in their families or in the neighbourhood who could serve as role models, and help them overcome their insecurities and deal with their worries and fears:

I was very afraid, I don't know why. I was so afraid that I would be alone [among men] in the office....Earlier, I only went to school, later to college, and then back home. I never experienced such a life in which you have to go to an office and work with men (Sadia, designer, 1 April 1997, p. 6ff.).

It was very strange. When I came here on my first day there were only men here. I was fearful and trembling, thinking about what might happen. During lunchtime when I was sitting at the reception they called me inside [the office]. I did not go, I was too afraid. I said that I never eat at lunch time....During the whole day I did not even drink a glass of water. On the next day my blood pressure was very low but I did not drink any water....For two months I did not even greet anybody, out of fear that if I went inside [the office] I didn't know what might happen. I felt fear, terror; at night I could not sleep....At the reception the colleagues said, 'hey', 'hello', but I never went inside [the office]. Two months passed, then one day my boss called me inside and asked me, 'why do people earn money?' I said, 'in order to make a living'. He asked me if food was not a part of that. I said, 'yes'. 'Then why don't you come here and have lunch', he asked. Then, gradually, I started to sit down with the others (Sajda, receptionist, 1 Feb. 1997, p. 9ff.).

The TTCW, Lahore, attempts to help women overcome their fears regarding work in a male-dominated office environment. Instructing women about how to behave in an office, how to talk to and work along with male colleagues and how to handle harassment and indecent behaviour from men constitutes an integral part of the training courses. Women are taken on excursions to offices to see what an office environment looks like, how the work is done there and how men and women work together. Two internships that are a compulsory part of the training courses are also to prepare women for later employment. According to the teachers of the TTCW, students' responses after the internships are overwhelmingly positive because women lose their fear of facing male strangers and working in a male-dominated office environment.

The change [from the TTCW to the office] was very frightening. First of all the teachers sent us...to do an internship for experience, so that we could build up our skills. I was very worried, 'Don't send me alone [to an office]. I can't work together with men,' I pleaded. But our teacher was very nice. She said, 'I will especially send you alone. Otherwise you won't gain confidence.' Since I had to go alone I was so worried....But the time passed nicely (Sadia, designer, 16 Dec. 1996, p. 3).

[On the first day of the internship] I was very much afraid, very, very much afraid....Our teacher accompanied us. He introduced us to each other and then he told us to get a signature from the boss. We were sitting there as quiet as mice. I was there with another girl. The other girl said, 'you ask the sir [i.e., the boss] for the signature',...and I said to her, 'you better do it'. I could not talk to him....Though our teacher was sitting there...my mother was also sitting there....So I said to her, 'you ask for it, I cannot talk to him', and she said to me, 'you ask, I cannot talk to him'. Then I said, in a whining voice,...because I knew that if I didn't get the signature our teacher would scold me, he would say, 'you got this task and why didn't you do it? Why are you afraid? When I was sitting next to you why were you afraid, did he want to eat you up?' Then I said in a tearful voice, 'I need a signature.' Our teacher quickly explained that 'she is very fearful'....But he [the boss] was very kind. He very kindly asked us to take a seat. He talked to us and I felt a bit more comfortable. Then one month passed. It passed very nicely. It was the first office experience for me. It was not so bad (Andeela, draftswoman, 2/1997, p. 7; 26 April 1997, p. 7ff.).

Apart from these attempts made by the TTCW, I never came across any educational institute or women's organization that tried to deal with the existing gap between the life world of women in the home on the one hand, and the office sector, on the other hand. The experiences at the TTCW, however, show that teaching women how to cope with a male-dominated office environment, and how to deal with men can positively influence a woman's decision to become gainfully employed in the office sector.

Another fundamental problem women are confronted with when they want to become gainfully employed is how to find a job at all. The problem women face is not the absence of vacancies but rather the way job-hunting takes place. The woman has to fix appointments with male strangers and go to offices that she does not know anything about, located in areas she is probably not familiar with.

Women are particularly afraid to work at offices that have not built up any reputation for themselves. Because of the generally low salaries in the private sector it is more profitable for men, even the ones who are not well-educated, to invest some money and start their own business. For this reason, there are countless very small offices consisting of one or two rooms that are rented in large office blocks or some backyard, in which three or four men work. Nothing is known about the background of the workers, and the office can virtually disappear overnight. Women are reluctant to contact such small offices because of their experiences with (sexual) violence toward women in male-dominated spaces. Asieh recounts the experiences she had when she first tried to find employment:

> I asked one of my friends. She had earlier worked at Rainbow Advertising and she talked to Abid Sahib. She had already left the job there. Abid Sahib said, 'OK, send her to me,' and I went there....I took a small boy [from the neighbourhood] and went there. Abid Sahib told me that there was another agency where I would get a good salary. If I wanted to go there he would send me to that place. I asked which agency this was and he said that it was in Mozang. I went there but the agency was in the boss' own house on the first floor. When I went inside I felt very strange....Because that was a house. I saw one room and there was a bed in it. And there was no woman, only two or three men and the owner. So, I became very confused. From the beginning I did not like the set-up because they all stared at me in a strange way. Then that was a flat that can be locked [from inside] like a house. I went back to Abid Sahib and said that I could not work at that place. He asked me why and I told him that I did not like the set-up. Strange people were there. This was what I felt, therefore I could not work there. If there had been another woman then maybe... (designer, 11 May 1997).

Ghazal, a receptionist, had an even worse experience when she applied for the position of a secretary. She already had a job as a telephone operator at that time but was looking for a better-paying position:

The first office was an export company; they export different kinds of food. I went for the interview but the boss wanted me to accompany him to business meetings outside the office. He even expected me to go with him to meetings taking place outside Lahore and stay in hotels overnight. The salary was high, Rs 5000, but I said that I could not stay in hotels overnight. He wanted to use me under the pretext of being in need of a secretary. He said certain things in the interview so that it was clear that he was not a good person...like 'I like you very much...', 'I would like to become your friend', 'how do you like the job and how do you like me', 'I like your eyes and lips', and I felt that he is [morally] corrupt. I said to him that I could not work there, I could not provide the services he was asking for....

The second vacancy was for a local newspaper, also as a secretary. The man was quite old, around 50 years old. He told me during the interview that, in addition to the official work, he was expecting some private friendship. 'I'll give you Rs 6000, OK, 8000, but apart from the work we should also have some fun.' I said that I was married but that did not seem to bother him. After these two experiences I gave up. I did not apply anywhere else (receptionist, 1 Dec. 1996, p. 10; 25 May 1997).

Apart from Asieh, a few other women also mentioned situations in certain office environments in which they had felt uncomfortable and unsafe, and that they had refused job offers because of this. Ghazal had applied to vacancies advertised in a newspaper, and had gone to the interviews alone. Women fear having to face situations similar to those that confronted Ghazal and Asieh, so, as a precaution, they generally do not contact offices unless there are references given by people who know the set-up of the office or people working there, and who can guarantee that they, as women, would not have to fear sexual harassment or violence.

One intermediary between women looking for jobs and potential employers is the non-governmental women's organization, Aurat Foundation. The organization offers a free employment exchange for women, although it runs on a relatively small scale. Aisha had found her job through Aurat Foundation, although most women had never heard about this employment exchange. Ms Nusrat, being responsible for the exchange, told me that she was basically trying to provide some security for women who were looking for employment:

The problem is that women very often do not contact the offices that advertise in a newspaper. They hesitate because they do not know exactly where the office is located, they do not know the people and the office environment. When they contact us and we send them to an office they feel much safer. We ask the employers who are looking for a woman to come to our office first, introduce themselves and fill out a form. Phoning us is not enough, we don't send them women on the basis of a phone call. And sometimes the interviews for jobs are conducted here.... In the beginning we phoned offices who had advertised in the newspapers and asked if they were interested in our service....Some said 'OK, send us some women', but we always demand to see the employer first. Nowadays the offices contact us themselves. They say that 'we have advertised in the newspaper but the women who applied were not up to our standards'. In fact, nobody contacted them but they do not want to admit that. Then they contact us for help....And we encourage the women to tell us whether the set-up is OK or not. If there is any bad experience we do not send women to that place again. But this rarely happens because the people who are not serious do not contact us at all (1/1997).

Another way to make job-hunting easier for women has been explored by the teachers of the TTCW in Lahore. They maintain close ties with potential employers, and send women who want to work after completion of their courses to offices they know. The teachers of the different trades offered by the TTCW always stressed that they were able to find a job for any student of their institution who had successfully finished her course. Four out of the six former

TTCW students in my sample had indeed found their jobs through the job placement of the TTCW. The other two TTCW students were Andeela, who did not wish to work at the time and Asieh, who found employment in an advertising agency near her home through a friend.

Other working women also got their jobs through personal contacts, i.e. through friends or relatives who had told them about vacancies in their own offices or at places they knew about. Only three women had found employment through newspaper ads. Two of them, Shaheen and Shagufta, who both belong to the most-skilled and best-paid women in my sample, had applied for jobs that were advertised by prestigious and well-known companies, and also Sajda, a receptionist and a colleague of Asieh, had found her job in a small advertising company through an ad in the newspaper. However, like all other women in my sample—with the exception of Ghazal's two unsuccessful attempts to find a better-paying job[2]—they were accompanied by a male or female relative, by a girl-friend or even by a child from the neighbourhood, when they went for an interview. This provided them some security in, as well as on their way to, the office.

Women also try to find employment in offices in which many employees, men and women, work, where a formalized office environment exists, and where the company is well-established and has a good name. But although they might apply at such companies, they rarely contact the organizations without reference or without knowing anything about the office environment. Leila worked part-time as an Arts' teacher at a private school. She had a Masters degree in Fine Arts and was interested in working in an advertising agency but did not know anybody working in this field who could act as a mediator for her. She was reluctant to contact advertising agencies on her own. She asked me to help her find a job so I suggested that she phone the company, and tell them that she was looking for a job. It took a long time but she finally mustered her courage and made the phone call. The person she talked to was interested and asked her to show him some samples of her work. Women miss opportunities because the gender order of society discourages them from contacting male strangers; women have to rely on mediators during their job search.

Facing the Next Hurdle: The Transportation Problem

Getting to the office and back home is a problem all women complained about. Many women felt that transport was the greatest difficulty they faced as working women. It is not considered socialy acceptable for women to ride a bicycle or drive a motorbike in Pakistani society, and cars, which women can drive, are so expensive that only families belonging to the wealthier upper and upper-middle classes can afford them. Rickshaws charge high farcs which lower-middle-class women cannot pay. Employers are commonly not concerned about how the women reach the office and rarely provide shuttle services. As a consequence, these female office workers mainly have to rely on the public transportation system. In the public buses, however, there are only two rows of seats reserved for women, and during rush hours men occupy the reserved women's seats too. For these reasons, waiting periods at the bus stops can be very long. Furthermore, working women who rely on public transportation have to walk from their home to the bus stop, wait at the bus stop for the bus, which can sometimes take up to an hour (because of their difficulties in getting a seat), and then walk from the bus stop to the office, with men staring at them or behaving indecently toward them. Nor is it uncommon for drivers and conductors in the buses to behave disrespectfully towards females (for harassment in the public transportation system see also *Dawn*, 23 Jan. 2000, 9 July 1999; *The Muslim*, 2 August 1993 and 27 March 1995).

Andeela takes one hour to reach her office by bus in the morning while it is not even a walk of 15 minutes; but since women are harassed on the streets when they are unaccompanied she can not walk to the office alone. Similarly, Ghazal complained that she could reach her office within ten minutes by motorbike but the bus took her more than one and a half hours. The transportation problem thus restricts women; they cannot work in offices which are too far away from their homes, which are located too far away from bus routes, or when they have to change the buses too often.

Another problem female office workers face on their way home, is that in winter it gets dark early and women thus run the danger of not reaching their homes before sunset. Women walking on the streets alone after dark is not approved of by society and would definitely result in harassment.

The fact that it is not considered acceptable for women to ride bicycles and motorbikes, that they have to fear harassment in public spaces, and that the public transportation system is so inefficient—particularly for female passengers—does not leave a lot of possibilities for female office workers to develop strategies that address the difficulties they face on their way to the workplace. One important strategy is to find company for trips to the office and back home.

Finding a male family member who daily accompanies a woman to her workplace—which is a time-consuming task—is not generally difficult in Pakistani society. To accompany women to the workplace, so that they will reach the office safely, is not seen as an act of generosity but is understood as the duty of men toward their female relatives.

Very few of the women interviewed travelled alone by public transportation. These were women who could not be accompanied by a male relative because there was none available to fulfill this task. Kishwer, for example, had to travel alone because her father had to work the whole day, and her two brothers were too young to escort her to the office, and then go back home, alone. Furthermore, she told me that even if there was someone available to bring her to the office in the morning, go home again and then come in the evening to pick her up, this would triple the bus fares, which she could not afford. But many of the women who had to reach the office on their own, including Kishwer, were accompanied at least as far as the bus stop in the mornings or picked up from there in the evenings.

Veiling provided the only possibility for protecting themselves from harassment in public male spaces on their way to and from work. Women commonly wore big chaddors, or, when they wore dupatte, they covered their heads also until they reached the office. Inside the office they changed the chaddors for the smaller dupatte, and they often left their heads uncovered.

The Job as Self-Fulfillment or Economic Necessity? Orientation between the (Upper) Middle and Lower Class

It has already been noted that female employment among lower-middle-class families is closely linked to economic need and results in a fall in the social standing of the respective family, viz., it does not constitute an ordinary, socially acceptable part of women's lives. The classification of the office workers into four types has indeed shown that the women's incomes constitute an important part of the household resources, or women work in order to maintain the living standard of their families. Women who work out of interest only constitute a small minority and usually belong to families situated at the upper spectrum of the lower-middle classes, and who work in relatively qualified positions with good salaries—although here, too, the financial benefits to these women and their families can not be ignored completely.[3]

Despite the fact that women primarily work for economic reasons they nevertheless clearly consider themselves to be members of the middle class. Women often made comments like 'we are middle class' or 'middle class women like us', and they indeed differ from lower-class families with regard to their living conditions, educational background and work status. As a consequence, only the women who were very needy stressed economic necessity as the reason for their employment. These women were concentrated in secretarial fields or in the kind of occupations which require a lot of public contact and which have the worst working conditions. It would be difficult to deny that they only worked in such jobs because of tremendous financial problems. For example, Firdous, who is in her mid-forties, has three children and her husband has been jobless for fifteen years. She is employed as a field worker at a market research institute, a job that requires that she go door to door to collect data for questionnaires:

> [The work is] difficult, very difficult but I have to do it out of [economic] need. And I can't see any other possibility. How could we make ends meet otherwise? I can't see any other way to make money. This is why I do this work (20 March 1997, p. 8).

But even these very needy women stress the fact that they are educated, a fact that puts them in a privileged position, because only educated women can enter the office sector. Uneducated women, on the other hand, are restricted to working in the informal sector for wages which are considerably lower than those of office workers. Sajda, a receptionist, started to work when her father died and the family lost the only breadwinner:

> I felt that, seeing all the financial problems *and being educated*, that I should work, that I should enter this [secretarial] field (1 Feb. 1997, p. 4, italics mine).

Apart from this type of worker women try to redefine their employment, not as a fall in social standing, but as an indicator of upward mobility. Questions regarding why they had started to work were often answered with: 'I was interested in working'; 'I did not want to waste my skills'; 'one should use one's qualifications'; 'my family wanted me to make progress, to move forward'; 'I felt bored at home and therefore I started to work'; 'I did not want to study further because I wanted to do something practical'. Here, the office workers take over the discourse which is more typical of upper- and upper-middle-class women who work in prestigious positions they identify with, and who connect their employment to career aspirations and self-realization. Indeed, the fact that most of the women

who have been working in the office sector for the last fifteen
years, particularly in technical occupations, are highly-educated
women who do not work out of economic need, makes it easier
for office workers from the lower-middle classes, who are now
also beginning to enter the office sector, to identify with these
women:

> I was alone in the office [i.e. the only woman sent from the TTCW
> as a trainee] but there was another woman who was my senior....She
> also worked there, as an architect, and when I saw her I felt very
> encouraged. Because she also worked in that office, and she had
> been there for some years already (Andeela, draftswoman, 26 April
> 1997, p. 8).

In order to maintain this image of upward mobility, the office
workers often tried to hide their real economic conditions. When
I asked Asieh why she had rejoined the advertising agency where
she had worked before she got married, she said, 'after getting
married I did not continue to work [because] my husband said
that I should not work. But I felt bored at home all the time and
I started to work again' (15 Jan. 1997, p. 1). Everybody in her
family were also eager to tell me exactly the same—that Asieh
worked for fun, and that money did not play any role in her
decision to become gainfully employed again. Nobody told me
that Asieh's husband had been unemployed, that she had been
pregnant at the time she started working again, that it was his
habit to leave his jobs all the time due to quarrels with his
superiors and that anyway his salary of Rs 3000 was not enough
for them to live on. In reality, money played the major role in
Asieh's decision to start working again.

Like Asieh, many office workers tried to conceal that their
fathers or brothers were unemployed, or they exaggerated the
incomes of male income earners of the family and the
educational backgrounds of their parents and siblings. This all
served to present themselves as middle-class families in which
women did not have to work for economic reasons.

Although the attempts to identify with upper- and upper-middle-class working women help the office workers to positively integrate their employment into their life world, career aspirations and self-realization through employment are nevertheless hardly compatible with their very conservative religious attitudes. Sadaf initially told me that she had been interested in working, and that her family was educated and broad-minded and did not mind her being a working woman. Later, she revealed a different attitude:

> No, no girl works out of interest, every girl who works does it because of need. These are all lies that 'yes, we work because we like our job'. If a girl needs to work then she leaves her house, otherwise Islam does not allow the woman to leave her house. She has to stay in chaddor aur chardivari....We are needy and therefore we leave the house. Apart from that there is no interest, nobody likes going to work, being pushed around in the public vans, and then people say so many [bad] things. There are so many problems that it is difficult to endure them....If you are needy, if you are very needy, then you should work. Islam has given permission to the woman when it is extremely necessary. If you are not needy then you don't have the permission, because the women are ordered to stay at home... (government employee, 19 Nov. 1996, p. 7; 17 July 1997, p. 5).

Other women expressed similar beliefs, i.e. that women are not allowed to work according to Islam, the only exception being women who are very needy. They clearly mirror the conservative religious attitude of the lower-middle classes in Pakistan, and they put women in a dilemma between their structural position on the one hand, in which they, as members of lower-middle-class families, do not want to admit that they work out of economic need, and their conservative religious beliefs on the other hand, according to which women should only work when they are needy. Only one woman, Shaheen, who worked in the best-paid and most-skilled job (in the computer branch), felt that being a working woman was not a contradiction to her religious beliefs. However, here too she thought this only permissible as long as the family did not suffer neglect—because the first and most important place of a woman was the home and not the workplace. Thus, the majority of middle-class women have not yet found a way to bridge the gap between their conservative religious attitudes and the lack of concepts for female employment on the one hand, and their actual employment in the office sector, which has already become an integral part of their lives, on the other hand. A societal change regarding the development of a professional identity among lower-middle-class working women is still in its infancy.

Reactions from the (Extended) Family and Neighbours

'It is not good to live on the daughter's income'—Breaking a Societal Taboo

To say that a family 'lives on the daughter's (or wife's) income' or that they 'eat up the money of the daughter/wife' is a strong insult among the lower-middle classes, which questions the ability of the men to support their female family members and keep them in purdah.

> ...here the people do not consider it good to eat up the earnings of the daughter. They think that she is made for the home, for the man and the home. She should stay in the chardivari, she should not come out [of the house]. If she comes out then she challenges our izzat, that 'you are men but you cannot maintain us. We are women and we are feeding you' (Andeela, draftswoman, 26 April 1997, p. 29ff.).

Many women told me that they were exposed to gossip and negative comments regarding their employment from acquaintances, people living in the mohalla, and members of the extended family, and there were no differences with regard to the educational or socio-economic background of these women, or the kind of jobs they performed. Kishwer, who belongs to a poor family, and works in a low-paying and not very prestigious secretarial job told me that the neighbours and members of the extended family worried her mother and insulted her by saying that she was eating up her daughter's income. Shagufta, one of the most-qualified and best-paid women in my sample, who belongs to a better-off family, also had to endure a lot of talk that her parents kept her in the house and did not marry her off because she was earning a good salary:

> When we hear such talk...then my mother becomes a bit angry for a moment. She says, 'leave the job, I cannot hear such things. I do not need your money.' The talk causes a lot of pain, that 'they do not get their daughters married off because they get a lot of money from them (software developer, 17 May 1997, p. 2).[4]

Three women, Tasneem, Shazia and Shaheen, told me that they were not the target of such gossip, but I was not sure if they just wanted to hide the fact that people did not approve of their being gainfully employed. Tasneem said that her neighbours and family were all very nice and did not say anything negative about her employment. But Tasneem's mother told me a very different story. 'People talk a lot', she said, 'they say that "in your house the girls now are also starting to work? You let your daughter work instead of getting her married off? You are eating up your daughter's money?" I say that..."she wanted it so much. She was very interested in having a job and therefore I supported her. I want my children to be happy and if that makes her happy then I do not object." What else can I say to the people? They talk so much and they don't give us any peace of mind. We don't say anything negative about her job but the people keep talking' (9 August 1997).

Negative comments about female office workers and their families are certainly based on their breaking the societal norm that women should stay in purdah, which is very strong among the lower-middle classes, partially because of their structural

1. Lower-middle-class residential areas (*mohalle*) in Lahore; men are seen more frequently in the lanes. A woman has come out of her house to buy vegetables from a street trader.

2. Small bazaar adjacent to the neighbourhood: women are rarely seen, that also clad in veils or *chaddors*. Men perform all tasks outside of the *chardivari*, even shopping.

3. Sadia, a designer working in her own room at Creative Designers.

4. Shaheen, working in the backroom of the computer department at Red Crescent Hospital.

5. Ghazal, working as a receptionist and telephone operator at a computer company.

6. The draftswomen, Andeela, Shazia, and Farhana, in their room at Unique Architects.

7. Interview at National Insurance with Fatima, the only female employee in her department on one of the upper floors.

8. During the work time, the female employees at National Insurance visit each other in the departments for a chat.

9. A typical working environment: men dealing with clients and occupying the front space in a room, whereas women are seated in a further corner.

position. Yet, the fact that families who invested in their daughters' education now benefit from this economically, and are better off than other families who did not consider their daughter's education to be important—at least not a market-oriented one which would enable them to find employment—also creates jealousy which finds its expression in negative comments about families 'who send their daughters to work'. Aisha, a clerical worker, is the only person in her mohalla who graduated from college. Most women and men in her area have not even completed secondary school:

> Earlier the people in our mohalla said to my mother 'why are you letting your daughter study for so long? What is the use? Marry her off.' And now they see that because of my education I earn a lot of money. Who earns Rs 4500 here [in this mohalla]? Even the men do not bring home more than Rs 2000 to 3000. And now they tell my mother, 'you were right to educate your daughter so much. Now you greatly benefit from that.' They themselves cannot do anything with their own education; they can only clean up other peoples' houses or sew clothes in their homes (1993).

Shagufta also pointed out the economic reasons for the gossip she and her family is exposed to:

> If [it were] only my brothers or my father who worked in my family then we would not be able to live under such good conditions. I and my sister work. I mean, every family member has some kind of work. For this reason we are better off and live nicely, but it is not easy [for the others] to endure this (software developer, 17 May 1997, p. 1).

The negative talk that families 'who send their daughters to work' have to endure is one more reason for the fact that women try to hide that their daughters support the families with their incomes. What is interesting here is that this also influences the way contributions from female income earners are made to the household budget. Although there are no clear patterns visible with regard to the way the office workers spend their salaries, all women, except Shaheen who belongs to a better-off family, supported their families financially.[5] All the married women, i.e. Ghazal, Firdous and Asieh, spent their whole salaries on the maintenance of their families. Another woman, Sadaf, gave her whole salary to her father. The majority of the women, however, supported their families more indirectly or sporadically, a strategy which made their real contributions immeasurable for outsiders and maintained the ideology that the male income earners still provided for their female family members, as the following examples shall illustrate.

Kishwer's father is a bus conductor who earns about Rs 100 to 150 daily. The parents and seven children live on this salary. Kishwer, the oldest child, works as a receptionist at a private hospital and earns between Rs 2000 and 2500 per month, depending on the overtime she does:

> My father had not gone to work for eight days, and we were short of money. *Ata* (flour), etc, nothing was here. I had some money and I gave them Rs 1000, 'here, buy some food'. They bought the things but they felt [bad about] it; they never ask me for money. I give it out of my own free will and then they take it. Otherwise they don't say, 'give us money; we don't have money'. They feel ashamed to ask me for money. When I see that they don't have money, I give money to my sister or brothers and tell them to buy things. It works like this and we make ends meet. I also give money to my father. He does not take it from me either, but when he has no money I give him Rs 300 or 400, 'Put this into your pockets, you should have some money with you'. Then he takes it from me (25 March 1997, p. 17).

A clear differentiation between the contributions of the male and female income earners can also be observed in Sajda's family, although here the pattern differs from that of Kishwer's case. Sajda's two brothers, the male income earners, pay all the regular expenses like utilities, food, etc., while her salary and the incomes of two sisters, goes into committees[6] in order to save up money for their dowries, and is spent on additional expenses like gifts which have to be given at weddings or engagements, or money which is also given at funerals or on other occasions.

It is very common for female office workers to spend their own money on clothes for their siblings, for food or other items for the family, for fees for their own education if they want to study further or undertake training courses. Women do not spend much money on themselves: they do not go to the cinema or to other places of entertainment; they do not visit restaurants or snack bars; they do not smoke cigarettes because that is not socially approved of in Pakistani society, their only expense is on items of personal use, such as clothes and shoes. Although women often did not want to disclose their roles as family supporters, they did not have any personal savings which indicates that their income was used to maintain themselves and their families, regardless of whether this was done directly or indirectly.

'We have to be very careful about our own behaviour'— The Social Construction of Female Office Workers as Morally Corrupt

It has already been pointed out that in Pakistani society, particularly among the lower-middle classes, criticism or gossip about a woman's character or conduct often take on sexual overtones, i.e. they often include allusions to sexual misbehaviour or sexually 'inviting' behaviour. This phenomenon is closely linked to the perception of gender relations as predominantly sexual and the lack of concepts for social interaction between the sexes, both of which are typical for purdah societies. It has further been argued that purdah is based on the assumption that external restrictions have to be imposed on unrelated men and women—particularly on women—in order to prevent extra-marital sexual relations, and that the desegregation of society and the mingling of the sexes will necessarily bring about a decay in moral standards and therefore has to be prevented.

Thus, the fact that a woman works in an office environment (an extremely gendered male space) is already seen as an indicator for the corruption of societal standards of morality. It is a common anxiety that contact with unrelated men at the workplace might result in 'love affairs' and 'love marriages', i.e. in gender relations which run utterly against the gender order of society. It is even suspected that women who leave their homes in order to work in a desegregated office environment are actually looking for opportunities to meet with men and break the purdah rules. The fact that female office workers usually do not want to admit that they work for economic reasons, but instead stress factors such as interest in their occupation or self-realization, further nourishes suspicions that the women go to offices only because they want to meet with men:

> People think badly of a girl who works in an office. They think that she goes to the office and has fun with the men, flirts with them, sits together with them. This is on their minds. 'She goes out with [male] friends. She goes to the office and she might also meet with [male] friends, move around with them.' This is the attitude (Ghazal, receptionist, 25 May 1997, p. 19).

The fear that a woman who works with men might become 'corrupted', i.e. that employment in an office might negatively affect her moral character, or that the woman might become the target of character assassination by the neighbours or members of the extended family simply because she works in a male space, are important reasons for family members not to allow their daughter, sister or wife to become gainfully employed. The following three accounts illustrate how deeply-rooted suspicions about a woman's conduct and character are reflected in the everyday life of female office workers:

> The people here talk a lot, of course. When I come home [in the evening] even half an hour late, then nobody from my family says anything. They think that there might have been an urgent matter

that kept me back or that I could not get a seat in the bus. But the neighbours see me and talk. And when they meet my mother they say, 'oh, your daughter came back very late yesterday. Did anything happen?' It is the others who create doubts [about one's moral character], not one's own family (Tasneem, draftswoman, 24 May 1997, p. 8).

My mother and father were not here for 40 days [they were performing Haj], and I continued to go to the office. At this time there were some rainfalls. My boss said, 'I will drop you in my car.' Imagine what was going on in my head: 'no sir, I cannot sit in the car because my mother and father are not at home, and if I go with you then, obviously, I have to sit in the front seat next to you. And what will the people think—that my mother and father are not at home, and the girl comes home in cars' (Andeela, draftswoman, 26 April 1997, p. 22ff.).

...my boss has offered to drop me off at my home many times but I always refused. Even when I was pregnant I went by public van. They [the colleagues] said, 'we will drop you off in the evenings' because our set-up is very friendly. But I did not go with them, because in my mohalla they would say, 'who is that guy who dropped her off in his car?' They question your character, thinking that 'this woman is [morally] not good. See, today she has come in a car, and yesterday she was sitting on a motorbike.' Everybody is alert and observes what the others do and what they do not do. For this reason I do not go anywhere. I am afraid. If I go somewhere the people in the mohalla will talk (Asieh, designer, 15 Jan. 1997, p. 15ff.).

The more contact with the public a job requires, the more irregular the working times are, and the more different work places are involved, the more a woman's character will be called into question. Firdous' job as a fieldworker for a market research institute requires extensive travel within and outside of Lahore. She often has to stay for several days in other cities and villages in order to collect data for her questionnaires. Even after thirteen years of work, her relatives still question her moral character and the decency of her job:

In our family there is no woman who works. I am the first one who left the house [in order to work]. I also had to hear the talk of relatives that this is bad work. 'She goes into the houses of other people, moves around from door to door. That is not good work.' The relatives talked so much... 'I don't know where she goes [to work], where she stays at night...she does not come home at nights'...We live in a joint family with two deveranis and one nand. When they sit together and I am not there they say that 'she leaves the house and does not come back [at night]. Who knows what kind of job that is, what she does' (20 March 1997, p. 3ff.).

Many women would never have got permission from their families to do the kind of work Firdous did—going into offices and homes of strangers, having irregular working hours, 'moving around' on the streets in areas they did not know, staying in hotels overnight, etc. Such work would have been disastrous for their reputation. Firdous is the main breadwinner in her family and she always stressed that she had to do this work because her husband did not support her financially. But she also told me that she would never allow her own daughter to do the kind of work she herself was doing because of the negative image which is attached to such an occupation. When I mentioned that there were two young, unmarried women who also worked as field workers for market research institutes and that they did not seem to mind doing such work, Firdous pointed out that these women were already in their mid-thirties but not yet married, and that the reason for their being 'old spinsters' was definitely the bad reputation connected with the kind of job they performed. She felt that, being a married woman and the only income earner, it was legitimate for her to earn money as a field worker, but this kind of work did not suit young, unmarried women.

Women try to fit their employment into the social and gender order of society by developing 'compensation strategies' through which they can indicate to their social surrounding that they have good moral characters although they do not stay in purdah but work in an extremely gendered male space. Several women told me that since they had started working they had become very careful with regard to their outward appearance. They did not use make-up and dressed simply. Women also do not go anywhere except to the office and back home. They try to come back home from the office at regular times, and not after sunset. Even Shazia, who did not have any transportation problems because she was provided with a shuttle service by her employer, refused to stay in the office to do overtime when she was once asked, because she did not feel comfortable coming home in the dark. A commonly used compensation strategy is for women to be accompanied to and from the workplace by a male relative. This is positively acknowledged by the social surroundings, because it shows that women remain protected—and supervised—in male spaces.

Opponents and Supporters in the (Nuclear) Family

Although women are commonly encouraged by their families to pursue higher education, none of the office workers were actively encouraged to use their educational qualifications and enter the labour market.[7] Several of the office workers had gone through some technical or vocational training, but even in these cases the families, and usually the women themselves, did not consider employment as the next logical step after the completion of their market-oriented training. One woman, Shazia, mentioned that she wanted to become gainfully employed and planned to enroll in a two-year vocational training programme in 'Commercial Arts'. Her parents gave her permission to take admission in the course because they were convinced that Shazia would stay at home after completing her course. When she did start working, in a prestigious organization earning a handsome salary and provided with transportation to and from work by her employer, her mother did not seem too happy.

Shazia's case indicates that the decision to enter the office sector is usually made by the women themselves and the reaction of the family members range between strong objection and object submission. Sajda decided to start working when her father died, and her elder brother, who was then the only income earner, could not provide for all eight family members. Even though her salary was crucial for the household budget, and her first job was in a gender-segregated work environment—she worked as a primary school teacher in a school near her home—she had to face severe objections from her family:

> They were very much against it. My [elder] brother said, 'you won't go to work...if you are leaving the house [to go to work] I will kill myself, I will shoot myself.' I said, 'nobody dies for another person. Tomorrow it will be you who says, "I keep on feeding you, you are a burden." I will go to work.' I did not look back if he would kill himself or not. I left the house, gave the interview and got the job (receptionist, 1 Feb. 1997, p. 4).

Women who live in families in which female employment is strongly opposed commonly tend not to become gainfully employed at all. Because she was able to push through her plan to work and support her family despite the prevalent hostility in her family toward female employment, Sajda's case constitutes an exception.

Typical answers from female workers to a question regarding how their families had reacted to their desire to become gainfully employed were: 'up to now my father hasn't said anything negative about my work'; 'the whole decision regarding the job was left to me'; 'my family did not dishearten me'; 'my family is nice, my husband does not mind it very much that I work with men.' Such comments reflect the apparent indifference of the families toward female employment, which is partially based on the fact that actively encouraging a daughter (or wife) to work would mean 'sending her out to earn money' and the fear of gossip that is attached to female employment among the lower-middle classes. The responses further indicate the difficulties the families still have in accepting that female employment is increasingly becoming an integrated part of lower-middle-class families' life world.

Interestingly, the strongest opposition to female employment is commonly raised not by the parents, but by elder brothers, who seem to be typical upholders of the gender order in society.[8] The female office workers were well aware of the fact that men (including their own brothers) are very eager to have female workers in their own offices, so that they can come into contact with and even try to flirt with them. At the same time they strongly oppose their own sisters working in an office and being exposed to unrelated males who might show the same behaviour patterns. Here, the split between gender relations within and outside the kinship system surfaces again. It not only influences the attitudes of (male) family members toward female employment, but also gender relations and behaviour patterns between men and women at the workplace (see Chapter 5).

Mothers, on the other hand, rather tend to support their daughters' desire to become gainfully employed. They even play active roles in convincing the father and the elder brothers to give the girl permission to work. When Tasneem's elder brothers were against her becoming gainfully employed and refused to give their permission, she started working without telling anybody except her mother, earning Rs 2500 per month. For two or three more months she continued telling her brothers and father that she was on an internship. Meanwhile, her mother tried to convince her father, and particularly her elder brothers, to allow Tasneem to work:

> The brothers were against her working but I said, 'OK, if she wants to work, then let her do so. We have educated her so thoroughly, sent her for further training. What is the use if she now stays at home to bake the roti and to clean up the rooms?' My sons got my point and became quiet. Nowadays nobody says a word (Tasneem's mother, 24 May 1997).

Many other women stressed the supportive behaviour of their mothers who—even though they did not actively encourage their daughters to work—at least they did not stop them from entering the office sector, and let them make the final decision about whether to become gainfully employed or not:

He [the elder brother] said that 'you should not go out and work with men...there is no need for you to go out to work.' I had completed my course but he said, 'no, forget it, there is no need [that you work].' My mother said, 'it is her own decision. If she wants to work then she can do it and if she does not want to work then she does not need to; we won't force her to go to work either (Sadia, designer, 16 December 1996, p. 5).

It is, nevertheless, crucial for all women who want to become gainfully employed, to have the permission of their parents and elder brothers (and sisters) or, when they are married, of their husbands and in-laws. Even women who are the major breadwinners in their families or contribute significantly to the household budget, as is the case with the married women (Ghazal, Firdous, Asieh), do not take the final decision to become gainfully employed by themselves. It is not considered a woman's right or her own decision to become gainfully employed; it depends on the agreement of her family. This factor makes career planning difficult—particularly for unmarried women—because the future husband and in-laws might have a negative attitude toward female employment (as is still the norm), and women always have to consider that their career may come to an end once they get married.

One strategy women and potential employers use to gain the families support for female employment in the office sector is to make the office environment transparent to the families and to personalize relations between the women's family and the (future) employer and colleagues. Family members, particularly the parents, and elder brothers, visit the office to get an impression of the set-up and to talk to the future employer. A positive impression of the working environment and the boss, and other female employees in the office, greatly reduces the negative attitude towards female employment:

(W)omen have their own constraints: transportation, the families.... So, we encourage them to bring their parents in.... Parents want to know where they would work, what the employer is all about, what the place is all about, what the atmosphere is. When we hire somebody and she says, 'I want to bring my father or mother or somebody else wants to see where I am working,' I say, 'by all means, bring them.' It helps because if their daughter is going to a place they know...they can imagine the place, they know what it looks like, when there are [a] few other women working it makes them more relaxed. And, in fact, it has helped both ways, because the women who work here are more relaxed as well (Pervaiz Sahib, architect, employer of Tasneem, 1 April 1997).

Even after the woman has started to work in an office, (male) relatives continue to drop in from time to time to talk with the woman and/or her boss:

I feel content that my family keep on coming here [to the office]. It makes them satisfied to see what kind of environment I work in. And I am also satisfied that my family knows where I am at which time, what I do and what I do not do....I often said to them, 'father, come to the office,' and he asked, 'why?' and I said, 'just like that. Drop in sometimes.' My mother also came [to the office] a few times.... They come right to my workplace. My father has met all the higher directors and talked to them (Shazia, designer, 20 April 1997, p. 14ff.).

Here, the control over a woman's action and movements is extended from the chardivari to the workplace in the sense that the family has exact knowledge about where she is sitting, the kind of work she does, etc. When Shazia was asked by her employer to make a presentation to a client she first phoned her parents and asked them if she could make the presentation, and explained where the client's place was.

Interestingly, the more institutionalized female employment becomes in a family, the less relevant the transparency of the office environment and the work seems to be. Women who had already been working for several years and had changed jobs told me that, although they were still taken to and from work by male relatives, the men had never seen the new workplace or employer.

The attitudes of the female office workers' families toward their employment puts them in a difficult position when problems at the workplace, particularly with regard to behaviour of male colleague and superiors, i.e. gender relations, emerge. When women talk about negative experiences at work or about negative aspects of the office environment, their parents or elder brothers usually recommend that they leave the job and stay at home, or they even forbid the woman from continuing to work. Women who have difficult working conditions even have to lie about the office environment and the behaviour of male colleagues in order to retain familial support for their employment:

> No, I don't tell them [the parents] anything [about the work environment]. If I tell them about my work they will never let me out of the house again because they are very izzatdar. If I came home and told them that 'my colleagues do this and that' then they would never let me do that work. I would never talk about my work at home, what happened at the workplace. On the contrary, I tell nice things, so that they don't get negative ideas....There are things we have to hide from the parents, because there are also men in the hospital who are not good. And we have to endure this because of [economic] need....I cannot say this at home. I say that the set-up is good. I endure because of [economic] need (Kishwer, receptionist, 25 March 1997, p. 9).

It is interesting to note that women do talk with their sisters and mothers about the work environment and the (male) colleagues and superiors, but not with male family members. Thus, not only familial support for female employment, but also practical advice and suggestions regarding how to deal with male colleagues and how to cope with the work environment or negative experiences do not split the families into working and non-working members but continue running along gender lines.

Skilled Workers or 'Office Decoration'? Recent Changes in the Gendered Structure of the Office Sector

Up to now the increasing market integration of lower-middle-class women into the office sector has concentrated on two different domains: 1) on technical occupations like architectural drafting, designing and computer related occupations (computer operators, software developers, hardware repairers); and 2) on secretarial jobs, for example, secretaries, receptionists and telephone operators. At first sight there do not seem to be any major differences between technical and secretarial occupations because both require a similar educational background and skill level, and are fields of employment which are commonly filled by members of the lower-middle classes. However, a closer look reveals a different picture. A fundamental distinction between secretarial and technical occupations is their conformity or non-conformity with the gender order of society. While technical occupations can be performed in accordance with purdah to a certain extent, secretarial jobs require interaction with male strangers and therefore run counter to the norms of purdah. This difference not only affects the working conditions, the gendered allocation of space and gender relations at the workplace of secretarial and technical workers (we will come back to this issue in the next chapter), it also raises the question concerning why women are increasingly entering, not only technical but also secretarial occupations, which run utterly across their own life world and why employers are exhibiting a growing demand for women to fill these positions.

When I asked women working in technical fields why they had chosen their (technical) occupation, they often stressed that it was related to the ability to perform the work in accordance with the societal norms of gender segregation, at least to a certain extent:

I selected Architectural Drafting [as a training course] because I thought that I could not work as a receptionist, I could not deal [with the male public], I could not talk...to men. I feel hesitant in the presence of men, I cannot work freely...this is why I did not select such a [secretarial] course which is not suitable for me. And our society does not make it possible for women to do such [secretarial] work (Andeela, draftswoman, 2/1997, p. 4ff).

Another crucial factor concerning the choice of a technical occupation is that, in technical fields, women are basically recruited on the basis of their qualifications, while gender plays no role, or only a minor one, when vacancies are filled.[9] There is no special need for female technical workers in the labour market, but the lack of skilled manpower at the middle range of the occupational spectrum makes it relatively easy for women to enter the field they are trained in, once they have acquired technical skills.

Integration into secretarial occupations, on the other hand, takes place differently. As Kishwer told me when I asked her why she had decided to enter the secretarial field: 'I did not choose to work as a receptionist. I did not want to do it; but I got this job and I took it' (25 March 1997, p. 4). Women who have reached a certain level in the formal educational system but have not acquired any additional skills have virtually no other option than to enter the secretarial field when they want to become gainfully employed.[10] The secretarial field is, therefore, not a conscious choice but it is the only alternative to teaching in a school, where one makes only a fraction of the salary office workers get. Despite the high figure of educated unemployment (among men) and the fact that only a formal education, but no specific additional skills, are required for many secretarial positions, women are increasingly wanted for vacancies in secretarial fields. Thus, in secretarial fields, in contrast to technical occupations, women tend to be recruited on the basis of their gender and not primarily on the basis of their skills. This trend inevitably leads to the question why there is such a growing demand from employers to recruit women for secretarial positions, although this runs across the gender order of society and there is no shortage of adequately educated men who could fill the vacancies, and who indeed did so only one decade ago.

In general, the societal perception is that women are not recruited for secretarial jobs because of their skills. Instead, they are perceived as 'showpieces' who serve to attract male clients, and who make the working atmosphere pleasant for the male staff. This perception was also unanimous among the female office workers who worked in technical fields, and it was one important reason why these women had not chosen to work in the secretarial field:

I know that in our society, particularly as far as secretaries are concerned, when women are employed then they are employed as showpieces....I want people to see my talent and not to make me a showpiece. That is the reason I did not choose the [secretarial] field (Shaheen, software developer, 6 May 1997, p. 19).

In architectural work there is izzat. It is not necessary that you come as a showpiece [to the office], that you put on make-up. There [in the secretarial jobs] it is a necessity that you come with make-up. In this architectural field it is not like this. You can not earn much money, but women get respect (Tasneem, draftswoman, 10 July 1997, p. 10).

None of the office workers in the technical occupations had permission from their families to enter the secretarial field, a fact that mirrors the hierarchy between secretarial and technical workers, the latter having better reputations and working conditions:

They [the parents] would not have allowed me to do that [i.e. to work in a secretarial field]...nobody considers that to be good. They say that, like showpieces, those women are like that. I would not have got permission for that. Now it is OK. I sit in my room and do my work. Then I go home. And they [the secretaries] have to deal with each and everyone who comes in, regardless of what he wants.... I could not do that, nor would my parents have given me permission. Nobody stopped me when I wanted to do this work, but they would not have allowed me to do that kind of [secretarial] work... (Sadia, designer, 1 April 1997, p. 3).

Ms Nusrat, coordinator of the women's employment exchange in Lahore, told me that beauty is indeed an important criteria in secretarial occupations:

Sometimes the bosses say, 'we want to have a pretty girl'. Or they do not say it, but expect it. Once, I was contacted by an office because they were looking for a secretary. So I sent two or three girls to them for an interview. Later the employer phoned me and said, 'why did you sent us such ugly girls? What did we do to you to deserve that?' I told him that we do not look at their faces but at their qualifications....Another time I was requested to send a pretty girl for a secretarial job. The girl came to my office and I said to her, 'go tomorrow morning for an interview. Then you will look fresh. And put some make-up on before you go there.' She then asked me if the make-up was a requirement for the job, but I did not tell her that I had been asked to send a pretty girl. I just told her that she would look nice if she did that, and it would make a good impression (1/1997).

Ms Abida, instructor of the secretarial courses and responsible for job placement, confirmed this, telling me that the majority of the companies who contacted the TTCW for skilled secretaries were also looking for pretty women. It was indeed a striking phenomenon that all the receptionists and secretaries I talked to and met were young, i.e. below or in their twenties and they all had a fair skin colour which is considered to be beautiful in Pakistani society. Once a TTCW trainee (secretarial course) was openly turned down in a job interview because of her dark skin colour. I have never heard of such an occurrence among technical workers, and some of the technical workers in my sample had a very dark skin complexion.

Not all employers recruit women as 'showpieces' and the employers I interviewed had credible reasons for having female secretarial workers. One employer, for example, told me that he had first employed a female technical worker but since this woman then was the only female employee in the office he felt that there should be a second woman for company. Thus, he filled the next vacancy, a secretarial position, with a woman. In a small advertising company, I was told by the employer that he had taken a women for the reception desk because he considered women to be more trustworthy. The receptionist had access to confidential information. Women, in his opinion, were not so likely to commit fraudulent acts. Such arguments, though, should not divert the attention from the fact that, keeping in mind the gender order of society both the general public as well as many employers consider women in secretarial positions to be only 'showpieces'.

In conclusion, the integration of women into the office sector does not follow a homogenous pattern but includes the recruitment of women as skilled 'human resources', the employment of women as 'showpieces', and, of course, many forms between these two extremes. Yet, the increasing employment of women as secretarial workers has not only initiated the feminization of the secretarial field; the societal perception of female office workers as 'office decoration', particularly in secretarial fields, has also caused a devaluation of secretarial occupations, because beauty and outward appearance, and not skills, are increasingly considered to be the only (or the major) entrance qualification. Despite this widespread perception, this negative stereotype cannot be confirmed here. Secretarial workers work at very different levels of skill, and international companies or big local firms often demand a college degree, fluency in the English language, and typing and computer skills from applicants for secretarial positions. Even in small offices where only formal schooling is required as entrance qualification for a secretarial position, the secretarial workers have at least an Intermediate Certificate and are thus often more qualified than technical workers (at least they have attended school for longer periods of time). Nevertheless, the stereotype of the office workers, namely of the secretarial workers as showpieces, has considerable significance for office cultures, i.e. for the working conditions of women in the office sector.

NOTES

1. Because of the economic benefits and the rise in living standards which are attached to migration, particularly among the lower-middle classes, emigration to one of the Gulf states or a Western country is still desired by many members of this section of society.

2. Later Ghazal was able to find an intermediary who helped her change her job for a better-paying position. A friend of her husband introduced her to his employer when the company he was working at had a vacancy for a position as a receptionist and telephone operator. She was selected for this vacancy and was still working at the company when I interviewed her.

3. It is worth mentioning here that the teachers of the different trades of the TTCW, Lahore, mentioned similar experiences. Trainees who are from poor families, and thus needy, and those who are not needy but want to improve the economic conditions of their families, work after the completion of their courses. Women from slightly better off families usually do not become gainfully employed.

4. In this case the problem was not actually to find a husband for Shagufta, but to find a suitable match for her elder sister, who was already in her late-twenties but not yet married. She broke off her studies after secondary school and was also a weak, frail person. Furthermore, her complexion was quite dark whereas having a fair skin colour is considered beautiful and desirable in Pakistani society. It was difficult for the family to find a marriage partner, who would be up to the standard of Shagufta's family, but it is a custom in Pakistan that the children, particularly the daughters, are married one after the other, starting with the eldest and ending with the youngest one. If, for example, a daughter is passed over because a good marriage proposal has been made to her younger sister, this will negatively affect the future marriage prospects of the elder daughter. For these reasons, Shagufta herself did not want to get married until a good marriage match had been found for her elder sister.

5. Shaheen deposited her whole salary every month and only kept a small amount for herself as pocket money. She had already bought a computer from her savings, and she was planning to save up enough money to buy a car in the future.

6. Committees are informal saving associations in which each member of a group pays the same amount of money (e.g. Rs 500, 1000) per month for a fixed period of time. The money that is collected each month is given to each member of the group in rotation. The order is decided by lot either in the beginning of the committee for all members or every month for one member who will then get the month's cash. Every person receives cash only once and for that reason the duration of the committee usually depends on the number of its members, for example, a group of 24 persons will fix the duration of the committee for two years so that every month one of the members will get the cash that has been collected. The committees enable common people to quickly disburse of a relatively large amount of money without having to pay interest rates (particularly when they are among the first ones to get the cash). Committees are a traditional and very common way of saving money, especially among women, for instance, in one mohalla, but they can also be found among employees in an office, etc. For a discussion of rotating savings and credit associations for women worldwide, see Ardener (ed.) 1995.

7. The only exceptions were Asieh, who was encouraged by her elder brother, and Shaheen, who was encouraged by her father to become gainfully employed when a job was offered to her after she had completed a training course at the TTCW in Lahore. Shaheen was convinced that her father only urged her to take the job offer because he did not believe that she would be able to work among men. He thought that this might be a good experience for her, but that she would definitely leave her job after a couple of weeks.

8. The hierarchical family structure in Pakistani society grants only elder siblings the right to give orders or pronounce prohibitions to their younger brothers and sisters and not vice versa. Even if a younger brother is against his sister becoming gainfully employed he is not really in a position to stop her from doing so.

9. There are still agencies which—on principle—do not hire women as technical workers; and in such cases gender of course plays a key role in women not being recruited.

10. It is worth mentioning here that all the women in my sample who were pushed into the labour market out of economic need worked in secretarial fields. The only exception was Firdous, whose work as a fieldworker was considered even 'worse' than that of a secretarial worker because it included irregular working times, going from door to door, and into the houses of unknown people, overnight stays out of Lahore, etc.

5

THE OFFICE SECTOR

Conceptualizing (the Multiplicity of) Office Cultures

The office sector in Pakistan consists of a wide range of office cultures;[1] accordingly, women's integration into the office sector does not follow a uniform path. On the contrary, office cultures influence the negotiation strategies employed by women in redefining gender relations at the workplace, and also the room for maneuvering in extremely gendered office spaces. First, however, the factors that facilitate the diversification of office cultures shall be discussed.[2]

Employers,[3] i.e. their life world and their view of appropriate gender relations and the (desirable) social and gender order of society have a crucial influence on office cultures. Three different types of employers—a 'Westernized type', a 'conservative type', and a 'mixed type'—can be identified.

Type One: 'The Westernized employer'

These employers have a Westernized, upper- or upper-middle-class family background, and have often studied or lived in a Western country for some years. Working with or employing women is not a new phenomenon for them; they have had female colleagues in their offices for at least 15 or 20 years. These have been highly-qualified upper- and upper-middle-class women in senior-level positions as architects, editors, designers, or even branch managers. Pervaiz Sahib, an architect, started to employ women about 10 or 15 years earlier, because there were more [female] architects available at that time. He believes there is no reason why women should not be working. Pervaiz Sahib's wife also worked in the same office as an architect—he proudly stressed this fact several times during the interview—and there was another senior female architect who had been with the company for more than ten years.

This type of employer explains the very tiny portion of middle-level female employees in contrast to the earlier absence of trained middle-level female staff. As soon as trained women, for example, women who had received market-oriented training started to enter the labour market at the beginning of the nineties, they were recruited for middle-level positions too.

Employers stress that women are recruited on the basis of their qualifications and on merit, while gender does not have any relevance in the deployment of staff. Shaheen, for instance, who was trained in 'Communications and Electronics' at the TTCW, first worked for three years at the Punjab Vocational Training Centre in Lahore after completing her course. She then applied for a job at the computer centre of a private hospital and was the first woman to be hired in the computer centre. Together with the other staff she is responsible for the computerization of all hospital medical records. I asked her employer in the computer centre, who had lived in Canada for several years, why he had employed a woman for this position and not a man. 'No, we have to focus on the requirements', he told me, 'what are the requirements…when we employ someone we do not see if it is a man or a woman….We did not consider that that person [i.e. Shaheen] is a man or woman' (Babar Sahib, 1 August 1997).

Having a mixed working environment is not considered a problem or constraint in any way for employers of the 'Westernized type'. They even have women among the highly-qualified employees who work partially outside their offices—architects who have to go to construction sites, designers who regularly visit clients—and it is not perceived inappropriate to employ women for tasks which require such kind of public exposure.[4] The transportation problem is not seen as a constraint either. Upper- and upper-middle-class working women commonly have their own cars, and the companies usually provide transportation when employees have to leave the office for work related tasks. The employers felt that it would not make any difference for them if they had to send out the driver with the office car for a male or female employee.

Zaheer Salaam, director of an advertising agency, even recruited women for sales-middle-level positions that require extensive public exposure and mobility outside the office—but he emphasized that not many women went into this field because women themselves did not want to work in sales. When I asked him for the reasons he felt that women did not enter sales because of the hot, humid, uncomfortable climatic conditions of the city. This answer brings to surface the different life worlds of these employers, on the one hand, and members of the lower-middle classes, on the other hand, and the lack of empathy 'Westernized types' of employers have with the very conservative life world of lower-middle-class women.

Type Two: 'The conservative employer'

In contrast to the 'Westernized employer', the 'conservative employer's' family background is a much more traditional one, and gender segregation and purdah are ingrained in his life world. Although he does not oppose female employment in the office sector, he nevertheless tries to provide segregated working areas for his female staff so that the integration of women in the office remains in accordance with the gender order of society and his own (conservative) life world.

Asif Sahib, the owner of a small advertising agency, and who seemed to have a conservative lower-middle-class background, faced severe opposition from his family, particularly his mother, when he wanted to employ Sadia. Both were young and unmarried. If the employee had been older—and ideally been married—nobody would have objected, but he told me that trained older women could not be found. 'Our [societal] set-up is not like this', he explained his family's worries, 'it is only for the last two years that so many women or girls have entered this occupation'.

The 'conservative type' employers do not consider work outside the office (or even contact with the public inside the office) to be appropriate for women. Therefore, women are hired for tasks in which the mingling of the sexes can be avoided to a great extent. When I asked these employers whether they considered their trade to be a good field for women, they agreed, stressing the fact that it did not require mingling with men or public exposure, that women could 'feel safe' while working in their respective fields. Employers belonging to the 'Westernized type' on the other hand—who nevertheless worked in the same fields as the 'conservative type' of employers (for example, architecture, designing, computers, etc.)—never emphasized the compatibility of women's work with the gender order of society when I raised the same question. They felt that their trade was a good field for women because it entailed mental rather than physical work; or they could not see any reason at all why their field should not be suitable for women.

Type Three: 'The mixed employer'

At first sight these employers, who commonly have a typical lower-middle-class background, seem to belong to the 'Westernized type'. They do not provide segregated working areas for women, and they also deploy women for tasks that require public contact and exposure. However, they are actually very conservative as far as their own family is concerned. Although they themselves recruit women and promote a desegregated office environment, they are not in favour of their own female family members being employed. Here, the differentiation between maharam and namaharam and the development of distinct behaviour patterns again surfaces.

Asieh, working at a small advertising agency with a desegregated set-up, pointed out what she considered the 'double standard' of her employer:

I've been working in this office for three years now but his wife has never come to the office. She does not have permission [because] if she came then the others could glance at her. He is very free with us and says, 'I am modern'. But still, he is free with others but not where his own family is concerned. In his mind there is this [concept of] purdah....In the office he builds up an intimate set-up, but this is only valid for the office; it is not valid for his household. And if there is some problem at his home, and we have to go there, then we can only enter the visitors' room, we are not allowed to go beyond that (designer, 15 January 1997, p. 16ff.).

Being conservative at home, and not allowing their wives to become gainfully employed, or even to visit the office, does not stop such employers from making amorous advances toward women in public spaces or even their own female staff. Kishwer, for example, told me about her former bosses:

There [at the old workplace] are two Hussein Sahibs. One has two daughters and one has four daughters, but still when they used to talk they always said something or the other which hurt me. For example, 'hey, what's your programme, tell me what's your programme, where would you like to go out?' these kind of things. When I left after working hours he (sic!) would say, 'come with me, I'll drop you' (receptionist, 25 March 1997, p. 6).

Asieh's boss also used to have girlfriends, and he openly brought them to the office. Once he even had an affair with one of his female employees.

Apart from the employers, the office size also facilitates the diversification of office cultures. In larger offices, the office cultures tend to be characterized by the segregation of the sexes while in smaller ones the set-up is rather de-segregated. Here, male-female interaction tends to be more informal and go beyond strictly work-related communication. Although this rule did not apply to all offices under focus, it might nevertheless indicate that in small offices, with a limited number of employees, renegotiations of gender relations, and the development of new patterns of communication between the sexes are more likely than in big offices.

Furthermore, office cultures are also influenced by the composition of the office staff. When the male staff members have a homogeneous lower-middle-class background there tends to be a very intimate set-up—not necessarily among male and female colleagues but inevitably among the male staff. Here, conversation often circles around personal matters, the language is very informal, and employees switch into their mother tongue, Punjabi, during conversation. The use of Punjabi in informal talk among men sounds very rude to outsiders, particularly women, since men use insulting language and let out streams of invective while telling jokes and talking to each other. In offices with a heterogeneous staff, the composition of the office set-up is much more formalized, simply because of the different educational and class backgrounds of the employees, and the different positions they hold in the occupational hierarchy of their organizations. Conversation remains work-related, and employees talk in the official language, Urdu, in a much more formal and polite way than when they speak in Punjabi.

National Insurance, Red Crescent Hospital, Unique Architects, Rainbow Advertising: Four Case Studies

The following analytical presentation of four case studies shall give an overview of different office cultures that develop as a corollary to women's entry into the office sector. Although the offices under study were too multi-faceted to be classified into a few types, diverse trades within the office sector, offices of different sizes and with a homogeneous as well as heterogeneous composition of their staff, and all types of employers have been covered.

Case One: National Insurance

The state-owned insurance company, 'National Insurance', has branches in all major cities in Pakistan. At the head office of National Insurance in Lahore a big room on the ground floor is divided into two equal parts by a long counter. On one side of the counter seats are placed for customers along the wall. People entering the building go directly to the counter to approach the staff. On the other side of the counter, tables are spread out irregularly at which about fifteen to twenty men sit and work. The staff have typical lower-middle-class backgrounds: many of the men wear shalwar-kameez,[5] and some of the staff look like conservative maulvis in their shalwar-kameez and long beards. Whenever customers approach the counter, one or more of the staff members get up to serve them. In the back corner, at two adjacent tables, three young women, the only female staff members on the ground floor, work. They do paperwork and are not responsible for customer service; but they go to the counter when women enter the building, which rarely happens, or when none of their male colleagues are available for customer service. Several of the remaining departments that are located on the upper floors have only male staff members; a few departments have one female employee, and in one department, two female employees work.

Until 1994, women were only recruited for the telephone exchange, an activity that does not require any direct contact with the public, and also makes possible the spatial segregation of the female employees from the male staff in the departments. The telephone exchange is located in a small room where four to six employees alternately operate the switch boards, connecting incoming phone calls with the different departments. In 1994, the members of the union decided that women could also work in other departments, 'because women are a part of our society and should, therefore, also be represented in all departments', as Ms Jamila, a telephone operator at National Insurance for more than twenty years, told me. Ms Jamila had entered National Insurance with a Master's degree, and she proudly told me that she was the first woman in her district who had ever acquired a university education. But since, at that time, women were only recruited for the telephone exchange, she had no other choice than to become a telephone operator.

The decision of the union to let female staff enter the departments was clearly attached to personal gain. It is no secret that vacancies in government service are commonly filled by the children of staff members, and through the decision to open the departments to women, the (male) employees got their sons and their daughters opportunities for job placement. About fifteen women worked in the head office of National Insurance, and at least 150–200 men. Most women had been recruited because their fathers worked at National Insurance and had been able to secure them one of the rare vacancies, and a few women had other close relatives in the company. Interestingly, most of the female employees did not have brothers who would otherwise have filled the vacant positions. They either did not have any brothers at all, or their brothers were still too young or not educated enough to fulfill the requirements of National Insurance. Several women had many sisters but only a few brothers so that the male family members, despite being gainfully employed, had not been able to financially secure the maintenance of their family.

Despite the entry of women into a few of the departments, gender segregation has widely remained intact. With one exception only, the female employees do not have any contact with the public, and the work tasks which are assigned to themic clerical work like filing, issuing and checking insurance policies, computer related chores, etc., do not require much contact with their male colleagues either. The gendered organization of space also emphasizes the segregation of the sexes at the workplace. In the few departments where more than one woman works, the female employees sit together at one or two adjacent tables. Women do not share their office desks with male colleagues; they have their own tables, and there is always adequate space between the women's and the men's workplaces. Furthermore, in the departments, which consist of one broad room each in which tables are spread out irregularly, women are usually not seated in the middle of the room, 'unprotected' from male gazes. They sit in corners, behind pillars, or in small glass boxes which are located inside some of the departments. The one-hour lunch break is also spent separately by men and women. The gendered organization of space and the allocation of work that does not require mingling with male colleagues or customers reduces male-female interaction at the workplace to a minimum. Once a union meeting was held during working hours; but even then gender segregation was maintained. The men were sitting in a broad room—one of the departments—on the first floor, and the female staff sat in a small room attached to the broad one. Through the half open door the women were listening to the speeches of the male speakers, who were standing on a stage on one side of the larger room. When some women started applauding after one speech, the others giggled, saying, 'sh, be quiet, the men can hear this outside.'

The segregation of the sexes at the workplace does not prevent a strong sexualization of gender relations, which manifests itself in women being continually stared at in all departments. 'It is a habit that the men stare; they stare a lot, and I don't like it', commented Umbreen. She sits in a glass box on the third floor, where the men sitting around the box throw furtive glances at her constantly.

Women do not even feel comfortable going to the restroom alone, which is located on the first floor and can only be accessed through a balcony. Once when standing on this balcony with a few of the female office workers I noticed that from the adjacent building two men were staring at us impertinently. Later, Tahmina and Sumeira, both of whom worked at National Insurance, told me that women did not go to the restroom alone.

Of all offices under study, National Insurance had the most segregated set-up; yet the women there were most often stared at by the male staff. It was also the only office in which all women, with only one or two exceptions, veiled their heads with their dupatte, and one woman even wore a burqa. The practice of veiling might be a reaction to gender relations and male behaviour toward women at the workplace, viz., an attempt to protect themselves in what they perceive to be a public male space.

Case Two: Red Crescent Hospital

When Shaheen started to work at Red Crescent Hospital, she was the only female employee in the computer department, whose staff consisted of about eleven persons.

The computer department is located on the first floor of the hospital. One enters a long narrow room in which about ten employees work on computers. Four workplaces are arranged on the left and right side along the walls; two other workplaces are built up along the wall opposite to the entrance. The staff is not visible to anyone entering the department because every workplace is hidden behind a partition, on which the names of the employee is written. This also means that when an employee has to be contacted, one can step behind his or her particular partition without disturbing anyone else. Behind the four workplaces another door leads into a second room. Here, several computers are installed along one wall, and there is an office desk and shelves with files and other work-related materials. The head of the computer department, Babar Sahib, usually works in this room; but staff meetings are also held here.

Everybody in the computer department is busy doing his or her work, and women do not have the impression that they are continually being stared at. The colleagues talk to each other but do so in a low voice, and their conversation remains work related. Shaheen attributes the set-up at Red Crescent Hospital to the heterogeneous backgrounds of her colleagues with respect to class, educational level, and the positions they hold, particularly to the higher proportion of educated persons among the staff, which leads to a more formalized working environment:

When you come into a room, you can judge the reputation of that place just by seeing the people.... When they talk to you they will talk in a decent way....If somebody else hears them he will say that 'these are decent people'....You cannot say that in a big organization [like Red Crescent Hospital] there are not uneducated people. They also have people who are not well educated, but they know their limits. Everybody here has a different grade, and therefore everybody remains polite....[A less educated person] will talk in a decent way because everybody's level is different and he knows that. Therefore, everybody remains decent (6 May 1997, p. 1ff).

Despite the fact that Shaheen found the set-up of Red Crescent Hospital satisfactory, she fixed her working times from 7:00 a.m. to 2:30 p.m., without a break, and with that decision very consciously avoided having lunch at her workplace. Eating during working hours indeed constituted a problem for Shaheen, because (for hygienic reasons) the staff is not allowed to eat in the computer department. Food, even when brought from home, has to be eaten in the canteen on the ground floor of the hospital. Shaheen, however, did not want to go to the canteen alone. She would have had to sit alone at a table at a public place, which is not only a meeting place for the staff of the whole hospital but also visited by (male) patients and their (male) visitors. Nor did she want to go with a male colleague; and there was no woman in her department she could ask to accompany her. Thus, she decided not to eat at all during her working hours.

When two female assistants began to work with Shaheen, she was able to ask one or the other to accompany her to the canteen whenever necessary.[6]

One of the assistants, who was in her late-twenties, married, and obviously had an upper- or upper-middle-class background, also went to the canteen alone; but for Shaheen it was still out of the question to do so. She nonetheless admitted that she had gone to the canteen with her boss a few times. He was in his mid-thirties and had lived in Canada for many years, and after working with him for more than a year, Shaheen sensed that for him it did not make any difference whether he talked to a man or a woman. She thus overcame her hesitation about meeting and talking to him in rather informal situations, such as during lunch in the canteen. Shaheen, however, did not perceive his being a 'Westernized type' of employer as exclusively positive. She felt that he lacked empathy with working women and the difficulties they have in a male-dominated working environment, and was therefore a rather 'uncaring' boss.

Case Three: Unique Architects

Six persons, three men and three women, are employed at Unique Architects, a small architectural office. The office consists of three rooms only. A young man in his early-twenties works as a receptionist and computer operator. Mr Asad Usmani, the owner of Unique Architects sits in one room and three draftswomen, Shazia, Farhana, and Andeela work in another. They are all in their early to mid-twenties. A young peon also works in the office, but he does not have any special workplace. The computer operator and receptionist, Nadeem, is responsible for dealing with visitors and clients and for work outside the office. None of the draftswomen have any contact with the public; for example, they need not go to construction sites, or work outside the office. Shazia, Farhana, and Andeela like the set-up in their office:

> We can work here with ease because we do not come into contact with anybody. Our boss gives us work and we do it. Visitors are not allowed to enter our room. Even when our Sir [i.e. the boss] is not in the office we do not let anybody into our room. There is a man outside [in the hallway] who works on the computer, and he talks to visitors and takes messages, answers the phone, etc. (Andeela, 2/1997).

An interview with Mr Asad Usmani, who is a clearly 'conservative type' of employer, brought to light that he had very consciously employed only women for the architectural drafting and allocated a separate room to them. He had set up his office three years ago, and by chance Shazia had been hired first for the architectural drafting. When he had to increase his staff, he felt it inappropriate to recruit men because then draftsmen and draftswomen would have to sit and work in close proximity to each other in the room:

> First of all, I employed Shazia, then Farhana, and finally Andeela….[When I needed a second draftswoman] I told Shazia that we needed a draftsman (sic!). You see, in Pakistan we are a very conservative society. It is not like in Western countries of Europe; it is a very conservative society. So, I told Shazia, 'we have more work, so bring some friend'—without advertising, without anything. Then we needed a third draftsman (sic!). You see, I could have employed a man also, but the problem is that if a person—a man—comes in[to] that room, there will be disturbance for the [girls]. We are Muslims and conservative, so I wanted to keep that room separate for [the] ladies. When I told them [i.e. Shazia and Farhana] that we needed another girl, they brought a third one, Andeela. So, now we have three ladies….You see, if there were a boy or man in that room…there would be rift all the time. They would be quarreling and fighting [with] each other. You see, now they are friends and working and even enjoying [themselves]… (architect, 2/97).

Mr Usmani was planning to recruit a few additional draftsmen in the near future but they would sit in a different room. When I asked him if he considered architectural drafting a good field for women, he answered, 'yes, very good; very good in the sense that they only have to sit in the office. They do not have to go outside, to the sites; they can work separately.' He thus stressed the compatibility of architectural drafting with the gender order of society. After the interview, he told me that his wife was also a working woman: she was a lecturer in a private women's college.

Despite the spatial arrangements for the female employees, lunch is taken in a mixed group. Mr Usmani goes home during the one-hour lunch break, as does the peon. Andeela, Farhana and Shazia sit around the desk in the hallway and have lunch with Nadeem. The women take turns bringing food from home, and they warm it up on a little stove. Nadeem contributes to the lunch by buying rotis for all of them daily. When Andeela, the newest employee, joined Unique Architects, she did not like to have lunch with her male colleague. However, Shazia and Farhana convinced her that it would not look nice to exclude Nadeem from their group; nor would it look nice if Andeela sat alone in another room to have lunch there. They felt that he was 'like a brother' and therefore it would not make any difference if they ate together with him.

Farhana and her fiancé also use the lunch break to secretly phone each other from time to time. Farhana's family has not allowed her to meet her fiancé before getting married to him, and of course he is not supposed to phone her at her home either. Since her boss is not in the office during the lunch break, Farhana can talk to her fiancé on the phone without intrusion.

In this small office nobody stares at the female employees or behaves in an offending manner. Nadeem is busy with his work in the hallway, and Mr Usmani sits in his own room and only comes to the draftswomen's room when there is work to discuss. Since Andeela, Farhana and Shazia sit in a separate room they do not even know when visitors or clients enter the office. They do not come into contact with any men apart from Mr Usmani, Nadeem, and the peon. None of the three cover their heads at the workplace, but when I wanted to take a photo, Andeela and Farhana quickly pulled their dupatte over their heads.

Case Four: Rainbow Advertising

Sajda has been employed at Rainbow Advertising as a receptionist for more than four years, and Asieh joined the company as an assistant designer three years ago. Sajda and Asieh are the only female employees. Apart from them, there are only a few other staff members: their employer, Mr Abid Bilal, two other assistant designers, one peon, and a typist who is employed on a part-time basis.

The office set-up is characterized by strong intimacy among the colleagues. Before the staff starts working in the mornings at 10 o'clock they first sit together, have a cup of tea and a chat. During this time, personal matters and problems are also discussed. When Asieh has a dispute with her mother-in-law or sister-in-law then this issue is raised and talked about. Sometimes Asieh enters the office in the morning and from her facial expression or her swollen cheek the others can see that she has had a dispute with her husband. Then they ask her about it and sympathize with her. Asieh's boss also talks with them when his wife and his mother quarrel; or Imraan, a trainee, keeps the others up to date about his search for a permanent job.

At Rainbow Advertising, lunch is also taken in a mixed group. Shafiq, the peon, buys food and rotis from the bazaar daily and sets the table. Then everybody sits or stands around the table and eats together. This arrangement was originally initiated by Mr Bilal, who felt that the colleagues should take their lunch jointly; and he too takes his lunch with the rest of the staff, including the peon.

Neither Asieh nor Sajda cover their heads with the dupatta in the office; they even shake hands with their colleagues.[7] Asieh explained to me that 'we do this in the office because we know each other well. This is why shaking hands is OK, but outside the office we do not shake hands with anybody.' Whenever someone can spare time during working hours he or she teaches the peon, Shafiq, how to read. Shafiq never went to school, so a few of the staff bought schoolbooks for him that he could at least learn the Urdu alphabet and reading. The women also ask their male colleagues to do personal work for them. Asieh sent her colleagues during working hours to deliver or pick up things; or to the bazaar to buy items she needed.

It was astonishing how desegregated the set-up in this office was and how familiar the men and women working there were with each other. Mr Bilal said, 'this office is not an office; it is rather like a home', a perception that is also mirrored in the use of kinship terms among some of the staff members. Although Mr Bilal is still in his thirties and thus only about ten years older than Sajda he calls her 'beta', and feels that 'Sajda has become my daughter....From the first day I felt she was like my daughter, and from the first day I liked her very much.' Some colleagues also use kinship terms and call Sajda and Asieh 'baji', while others use the term 'miss', or just address them by name.

Despite employing women and describing the office set-up as 'like a home', Mr Bilal is not in favour of female employment in his own family, and his wife is a housewife. After office hours, he gives parties for his friends in the office, which women also attend. Sajda and Asieh sometimes find empty bottles lying around from the previous night. They both know about these parties, and that their boss has affairs and girlfriends—as everybody in the office does—but for them this is acceptable as long as he behaves properly toward them. 'The colleagues are all nice', as Asieh noted. 'Our boss has affairs and girlfriends but he behaves with us. And what could we do anyway? If we say anything he will kick us out, won't he.'

The office is small and consists of three rooms only. When one enters Rainbow Advertising, one steps into a small room which serves as the reception area. Sajda sits behind a desk to receive clients or visitors, and a few chairs are placed on the other side of her desk for the latter. From the reception another door leads into a second room, which is divided by a partition. In the first part of the room a couch, some chairs and a table are placed for visitors, and in the back part of the room Mr Bilal sits behind a big desk and works on the computer. From the back part of the room, next to Mr Bilal's workplace, a door leads into the third room, in which the assistant designers and the typist work. In the beginning of my research in the fall of 1996, no particular spatial arrangements existed for female employees in that room. Three or four tables were placed there, and the staff, men and women alike, sat at their tables and worked. When in the spring of 1997 computers were purchased for the assistant designers, the workspace of the room was rearranged. Three computers were fixed for computer designing along one side of the narrow room, and behind the computers, in the back corner of the room and separated by a partition, a table and a chair were placed. The partition originally served to separate the computer section from the workplace of the typist who works at Rainbow Advertising in the evenings. Asieh, though, who had yet to learn how to operate the software programmes for designers and therefore did not do much work on the computer, started occupying that workplace during most of the day, doing there all work which had to be done manually, like cutting or pasting. She liked working behind the partition because the door leading from Mr Bilal's room to the room she worked in is made of glass, and clients visiting the office and talking to her boss in his room could peep through this glass door. Sitting behind the partition, though, Asieh remained invisible to visitors, even when they entered the room she worked in, because her workplace was located in the back corner. Furthermore, since her colleagues working on the computers could not see her either, she could stretch out during her work without hesitation. She even started to put aside her dupatta while working because it disturbed her when she had to use material like colours or glue (the dupatta is draped around the shoulders and the long, flowing lengths that hang down from each shoulder often tend to slip off). But whenever she left her workplace or when visitors entered the room she again slung her dupatta around her shoulders.

In contrast to Sajda, whose job is to receive clients and attend to the phone, Asieh's job does not involve contact with the public. Outside jobs, like deliveries or purchases, are done by the peon, and when designs have to be printed at the printing press or clients have to be visited, Mr Bilal himself takes over this work or sends one of the male assistant designers. Clients who come to the office are received by Mr Bilal himself.

A love affair between Sajda and Imraan affected the whole set-up at Rainbow Advertising. They sat together for hours, a practice that affected their work performance. As a consequence, Mr Bilal, who needed a new assistant designer on a full-time basis, recruited a new employee, Adeel, instead of offering this position to Imraan, even though he was more qualified. Furthermore, clients started to complain that the receptionist was always sitting with the same man and inquired what their relationship was. They also complained to Mr Bilal that it was difficult to phone the office because the line was always busy. Indeed, Shafiq and Adeel were also getting personal calls from women—sometimes several times per day—while people making official phone calls could not get through. Mr Bilal talked to Sajda and Imraan several times, but since they did not change their behaviour he fired Imraan and prohibited him from coming to the office to meet Sajda. Imraan continued to phone Sajda secretly, and Mr Bilal threatened to fire her too if these phone calls did not stop. However, she continued to talk to Imraan on the phone clandestinely, and whenever Mr Bilal was not in the office Imraan secretly visited the office to meet her.[8]

Inside the Office

'You always have to keep the stick in your hand'—Gender Relations at (and Beyond) the Workplace

In contrast to the diverse office cultures that are developing as a corollary to women's entry into the office sector, gender relations were more uniform across the offices under study. Male behaviour patterns toward women in (male) office space were marked by two distinct but intertwined features. First, male colleagues (with the probable exception of Westernized upper-(middle-) class employees who worked in highly-qualified positions) did not acknowledge work-related de-sexualized relationships between the sexes at the workplace. In the offices, they had, often for the first time, the chance to come into contact with unrelated women; and they took advantage of this situation by developing relationships with them (ideally sexual in nature). Second, when men were successful in their attempts to get close to a female colleague, they, at the same time, despised her for socially inappropriate behaviour; and they would never have approved of their own female relatives developing any kind of relationship with a man, or even working in the office sector at all. Here, the sexualization of gender relations in Pakistani society, and the absence of concepts for social interaction between the sexes, surfaces again. The distinction between maharam and namaharam results in the development of different gender constructs and, subsequently, of different behaviour patterns for (female) members of these categories. It is worth mentioning here that recent feminist discussions in organizational theory are increasingly criticizing the view of mainstream organizational theory that organizations are gender-neutral and asexual social phenomena. The current feminist debates are not only concerned with the relationship between sex and organization, i.e. sex as a factor that (in addition to qualification, age, and ethnic origin) influences women's access to jobs and upward mobility. Focus is also put on sexual activity in organizations, inter alia the sexualization of women, the stereotypization of women as primarily sexual beings, and the stigmatization and objectification of women's bodies (see Muller 1993). According to Ackers, 'organizations are one arena in which widely disseminated cultural images of gender are invented and reproduced' (1991: 163). Hence, the societal context, particularly the interrelationship between organizations and the gender order of society, are gaining significance in the analysis of organizations as gendered structures.[9]

Female office workers were well aware of these behaviour patterns of men at the workplace:

> Here in Pakistan the [societal] set-up is like this: when girls allow men to get close to them, then the men are very happy with these girls and it seems as if they are having a good time [together]. But at the same time, it is those very men who talk most badly about these girls...because they do not consider them to have good characters. [They say,] 'she allows us to get so close to her', although the guys have done the same thing, right? When they [i.e. the girls] smile then the guys also smile. It is the same thing. They talk so nicely with the girls, and at the same time they do not consider them [morally] good....When a guy smiles and talks [to a girl], or even has a girlfriend, nobody will say anything. And the guys know this too. And they do not consider the very girl they

have as their girlfriend to be good....They do the things they do not approve for the women in their own family. No man or guy would like for his sister or wife or daughter to develop a friendship with another man. They would never like it—but they themselves do the same eagerly. And after developing a friendship [with a woman], they tell jokes about her and ruin her reputation (Shagufta, software developer, 1 December 1996, p. 13ff.).

Common ways of achieving closer contact with female colleagues were: approaching women under the pretext of work-related issues; trying to involve them in needless small talk about personal matters, often in a low voice or when nobody else is around; inviting women for tea, lunch, etc.; offering them a lift, dirty talk and bad jokes; speaking loudly within women's earshot in order to attract their attention; or directly asking female colleagues whether they wanted to become their girlfriends. Touching women while passing things like pencils or a phone, or coming very near to women physically while passing by or talking to them, or staring at them furtively was also a common way to 'establish contact'.

Male behaviour toward women was worst among secretarial workers, due to the constant contact with the public and with (male) colleagues which are an inherent part of their occupations, and which create abundant interfaces for interaction between the sexes at work. The negative reputation of secretarial workers in comparison to technical workers, though, might be another reason for this phenomenon:

Even if they [i.e. the male colleagues] are married, they will never say that. At home they have their wife but they will make eyes at other girls. They will never look at her nicely, but in a very strange way....In our hospital there are also some men who are married, but they ask other girls to become their [girl]friends....Whether they are married or not, whether they have a daughter or sister or not, they will say that the women who come out [of the chardivari] to work are not good. They don't see her the way they see their sister or a good friend but they always see her as dirty. They just want her to become their girlfriend, so that they can enjoy themselves and can fulfill their carnal desires with her. I mean, no guy at the workplace is good; we can't trust anybody....Therefore, the woman has to remain firm, otherwise they will, slowly, slowly, extend the boundaries. Their own wives are at home; they are restricted to the house. Their sisters also remain in the house....They don't see that 'today they [i.e. the female colleagues] had to leave the house and tomorrow this can also happen to us [i.e. the women in our own family]'....They see something worthless in front of them, why shouldn't they take advantage of it (Kishwer, receptionist, 21 Nov. 1996, p. 6ff.).

The hospital Kishwer works at is characterized by a de-segregated office culture, which is also emphasized by her boss, who is a 'mixed type' of employer. I observed that communication between male and female colleagues always had some kind of flirtatious undertone.

  Men's continual attempts to gradually extend the boundaries in their daily interactions with female colleagues is a structural phenomenon all women experience as an integral part of their daily lives as office workers. The need to fix the boundaries of male-female interactions at the workplace, and not to give men the chance to extend these was, therefore, very frequently mentioned by the women:

The mahol[10] depends on yourself. After five years of [working] experience I can say that it absolutely depends on you....They [i.e. the men] do as you like. It is not true that nothing happens, but it depends on you and how you behave with the others. You must conduct yourself in such a way that they cannot do anything except work. You should be mature enough not to give them any chance. And if you have given someone the chance to get close to you once, then you cannot go back to the old relationship....If there are no obstacles on your part, then problems can emerge. Therefore, one has to remain careful....Everything depends on the girl. If she wants she can live in a very good mahol...I think that men are all the same. If they get a chance they will definitely use it. I have seen this many times (Shagufta, software developer, 1 December 1996, p. 2ff.).

I think…it depends on [the woman] herself. If you don't give them a chance they won't do anything. I never gave anyone a chance. I can't influence the people [outside of the office] when they do [bad] things on the streets but in the office I don't have problems…because I don't give them the chance to misbehave….You have to keep a stick in your hand all the time, otherwise they won't spare you…if they get a chance they won't let go (Tasneem, draftswoman, 10 Feb. 1997, p. 8).

Female office workers use different strategies to desexualize and renegotiate gender relations at their workplaces; namely, they create social distance between male and female colleagues; they develop socially obligatory relationships; they integrate male colleagues into a fictive kinship system; and they create women's spaces inside the offices.

Strategy One: 'Creating social distance'

One common strategy women employ is to restrict all conversation with male colleagues to purely work-related issues, and to be strict, even rude and scold men when they try to talk unnecessarily or come closer to them in any other way. This way women create a social distance between themselves and their male colleagues in their daily interactions with them, for example as Shaheen explained:

I do not have public contact in my job, but people who work in the hospital come to me when they have problems with the computerization [of the medical records] or any questions. When they come, then I am friendly because they want to have something explained. But when I meet them on the floor or outside of the hospital, I am no longer friendly because I am not in a formal work-related situation. I try to ignore the person, say no more than 'hey, hello' while passing by. This way I create a distance. I also talk on the telephone. That is more de-personalized than face-to-face conversation (software developer, 25 April 1997).

When employees working in other departments of the hospital enter the computer department, Shaheen does not greet or talk to them, nor does she even look in their direction. Even when male colleagues she knows enter the department she ignores them in order to demonstrate that she only establishes work-related relations. She never socializes with male colleagues, not even with those working with her in the computer department, for example, by having lunch or tea with them in the canteen, in order to avoid any unnecessary contact between her and the male staff. Shaheen, explaining her behaviour toward her male colleagues said, 'sometimes your job requires you to be very polite. But the disadvantage of being too polite is that people [i.e., the men] might misunderstand this. So you should remain balanced. If you are polite you should sometimes also be rude....If you remain polite continuously, people will try to take up close, personal contact with you.'

Keeping male-female interaction at the workplace purely work-related is nevertheless often a delicate balancing act: on the one hand, the woman must integrate into an office environment and a (male) team while remaining somewhat distant; on the other hand, she can become marginalized if she is too rude or strict with her male colleagues. Shaheen faced such a dilemma whenever there was any social gathering in her department. She could not always excuse herself from such occasions; yet she felt uncomfortable at these get-togethers, particularly when she was the only woman in her department. They brought her into situations which were not entirely work-related, and which inevitably required a certain degree of informal talk with male colleagues. In offices, on special occasions like weddings or engagements, (male) colleagues often bring sweets and snacks and also invite female colleagues to participate in a little get-together. These are friendly gestures, but—particularly in offices that are rather characterized by segregation of the sexes—they bring women into a dilemma. They want to avoid giving men the opportunity to take up personal contact with them, yet they do not want to offend the men by turning down the invitations.

Strategy Two: 'Creating socially obligatory relationships'

Another strategy of women is to embed formal working relationships into social and socially-obligatory relationships. Shazia, for instance, works in a large advertising agency, which is characterized by a rather segregated set-up. Only four or five women work in this office; and though she spends her lunch break with two other female colleagues, during work hours she sits and works together with a male colleague who is about her age. Shazia has been able to turn her formal work-related relationship with Asif into a socially obligatory one by establishing informal social relations with his family, particularly his sisters:

> We [i.e. Asif and me] are the same age; we are friends. He and his sisters have become my friends, and they keep on phoning me. They even phone me when he is not here. They also phone me at home. Sometimes they come to the office to meet me....I also phone them. Yesterday I phoned them to wish them happy Eid. He has two sisters and they have become my friends since his mother passed away....[On that day] the whole office staff went there, and I met his sisters. And since then they have become my friends. Since then I also take more care of him..., of course he is my good friend and for this reason he also cares for me (designer, 20 April 1997, p. 2).

Embedding formal work relations with male colleagues into socially obligatory ones creates social control, and thus prevents men from behaving inappropriately. It enables the development of more intimate relations between male and female colleagues, which remain maharam-like and thus de-sexualized. In Shazia's case, her colleague even became protective toward her—a behaviour that is typically shown toward female relatives—by taking over the majority of the contact with the public their jobs required. He used to talk to (male) clients allowing her to avoid public contact and exposure, although this task was officially allocated to both of them.

It was also very common that female office workers introduced their family, particularly their fathers and brothers, to their colleagues and superiors in order to personalize formal working relationships. This strategy was of course two-sided because it also helped the women's family to overcome their hesitation about the daughter/sister working in an office environment with male strangers.

Strategy Three: 'Integrating male colleagues into a (fictive) kinship system'

Furthermore, women use kinship terms to address male colleagues in order to integrate the latter into a (fictive) kinship system. It has already been pointed out that the use of kinship terms by a woman creates responsibilities for the man to respect and safeguard the woman who has indicated that she perceives him as a (fictive) family member. Fictive kinship terms, though, were only used in a few of the offices under study. In most of the offices, male colleagues and superiors were addressed by their first names, followed by the polite form of address 'sahib'. Women were called 'miss', sometimes followed by the first name. Bosses were often referred to as 'sir' or 'madam'. Subordinates were only called by their names; and after working together for a while, employees who were of a relatively equal status in the office hierarchy—men and women—also started to drop the terms 'sahib' or 'miss' and just used their first names for addressing each other. Sometimes kinship terms were only used by one of the persons, as, for instance, when Andeela, Farhana, and Shazia called their boss 'sir', while he used the terms 'beta', or 'bete' when talking to them.

One reason for the rare use of kinship terms among colleagues might be the realization that just addressing unrelated men by kinship terms does not transform the relationship into a maharam-like one, with all its social implications. Fictive kinship is common in certain socially obliging contexts, for example, among neighbours or families with close friendship ties, but using kinship terms in an office environment in order to manipulate men's conduct does not constitute a strong mechanism of social control. In her study of female factory workers in the garment industry in Bangladesh, Dannecker (1998: 142ff) comes to similar conclusions. In order to desexualize the workplace, the factory workers tried to construct fictive kinship relations with their male colleagues and superiors by addressing them as bhai or chacha. However, attempts at desexualizing male-female interaction was not accepted by male supervisors, and their behaviour toward female workers did not reflect the respect implicitly underlying (fictive) kinship:

> Why should they see us as their sisters? If they treat us as their sisters then they won't be able to enjoy themselves [with us]. They do not like this [and] if I forget this and say, 'bhai'; I mean, I call someone, [for example,] 'Hassan bhai'; then he says, 'no, don't call me "bhai", call me "Hassan".' I mean, they do not let us call them 'bhai'. In the beginning, when I was not experienced, I used to say, 'you are all my brothers, everybody.' But then I felt that nobody is anybody's brother here. Apart from the blood relationship there are no brothers. By calling strangers brothers they do not become family members. You have to keep them in their boundaries (Kishwer, receptionist, 25 March 1997, p. 7ff.).

> The...men talk in front of you very amiably and nicely, but behind your back they say bad things about the women [working in this office]....To your face they say nice things, 'yes beta, oh, for this reason you are here', 'yes beta, that is a good thing', but I have heard that behind our backs they say that 'young women are working here', 'that woman is sitting alone over there with a man',...'that woman is sitting there and drinking tea', 'this girl is talking to this man', such things. When we stand somewhere for a moment they will say, 'this girl was standing there'. They make big issues out of such small things....If they started thinking that 'these women [in the office] are also like our own daughters'—they say that in front of you; but they do not think it is the case (Sadaf, clerical worker, govt. employee, 18 July 1997, p. 4ff.).

Strategy Four: 'Creating women's spaces'

Finally, female office workers try to create spaces for themselves in the offices. This way they not only maintain physical distance between male and female colleagues, they also minimize interfaces for interaction with clients, customers, and visitors, viz., men, who are not part of the office staff.

With the above-mentioned strategies, female workers are able to prevent men from attempting to take up personal contact with them, especially in small offices. Furthermore, they are able to initiate re-negotiations of gender relations at the workplace and the development of new socially acceptable 'de-sexualized' modes of communication between the sexes. Rainbow Advertising provides one example. Their set-up is characterized by intimate but de-sexualized modes of communication among the staff members. However, these modes of communication were preceded by a long process of renegotiating gender relations at the workplace, during which time the female employees, Asieh and Sajda, created the mahol I encountered there while doing my field research. 'You build up the mahol yourself', Sajda told me. 'The mahol will become exactly the way you are yourself. You build up a good or bad mahol'. Indeed, Sajda and Asieh conducted themselves in a manner that their male colleagues never got any chance to extend the boundaries in their daily interactions with them, and no doubts were cast on their moral characters.

The de-sexualized gender relations between male and female colleagues were based on the conduct of Sajda and Asieh. 'Nobody ever misbehaved because I never allowed that to happen', Asieh told me, knowing that she and Sajda were successful in redefining gender relations at the workplace because of their own (initially) strict behaviour.

Once such negotiation processes have taken place in the offices—women have been able to renegotiate gender relations through their own conduct, and men have accepted the boundaries the women have drawn—male and female colleagues can and do become more intimate with each other. They start to talk about personal matters; and although their communication is no longer purely work-related, it remains de-sexualized. For example, men and women initially ate separately, yet after a while, when gender relations had been successfully redefined by the female employee(s), male and female colleagues formed a group during lunchtime and started to have their lunch jointly. In such set-ups, the women themselves described the mahol in terms of a family relationship: 'this has become a family system, we have become family members', said Sajda, a receptionist. 'Now it is as if they are family members, like this', said Sadia, a designer. Or 'the mahol is very good; nobody casts any doubts on anyone [regarding their moral characters]....The colleagues are all like brothers and sisters', commented Firdous, a research assistant. To sum up, gender relations are not only compared with those in a (fictive) family system; they also have strong similarities to them, and are thus maharam-like.

Treating certain colleagues as maharam-like, however, does not affect men's behaviour toward women in the office sector or in public male spaces in general. 'I don't know how they [i.e. the male colleagues] are outside [the office]. In front of us they behave', Asieh told me. And '...when a new girl comes [into the office] they will definitely try to tempt her. If I allowed them to get close to me, they would do with me what they did with the other girls who worked here. But the woman has to handle that herself. Be free but do not give anybody permission to do bad things.' Indeed, some of Asieh and Sajda's former female colleagues were not as strict as them and accepted the invitations of their boss and attended his parties in the evenings or went out with male colleagues; but 'their image was not good here', Asieh said, and thus indicated two crucial points: first, male behaviour patterns toward women in public (male) spaces might change toward individual female colleagues, but not toward women entering the office sector or public male spaces in general; second, the redefinition of gender relations to desexualized, maharam-like ones is only possible when female office workers continue to adhere to what is, in Pakistani society, particularly among the conservative lower-middle classes, considered to be socially appropriate behaviour for women.

Still, gender relations that were formerly perceived as sexual ones per se are now open to renegotiations. This not only enables the development of new, formerly unknown modes of communication between the sexes at the workplace, it also indicates how flexible the concept of purdah can be in everyday life, and how it can be accommodated to processes of societal transformation.

As Shagufta said, 'it is possible to control the mahol in offices with a few employees, but the more men there are the more difficult it becomes.' So it is that the renegotiations of gender relations, which include all male colleagues, become more and more difficult with the increasing size of an office and its staff. Shazia offers one example in her work for a large advertising company. Although she has been able to embed work relations with her immediate colleague, Asif, into a socially obligatory relationship, gender relations in the office in general, however, remain sexualized:

> I sit together with my colleague, who does the same work I do. We sit and work together for eight hours every day. He has his own computer and I have my own, but sometimes we discuss our work and we take advice from each other when we have problems. And the others take it in a wrong way. They see us talking and say, 'maybe there is something going on between them'. And when we talk we do it in a low voice so that nobody is disturbed. This is nothing unusual. Then the people say, 'why are they talking in such a low voice? Maybe they talk about something personal, maybe they even have some affair.'

As a consequence, gender segregation is usually upheld in larger offices, and communication between the sexes remains work-related. One example of the way the office size can influence renegotiations of gender relations at the workplace, is offered at the NGO where Aisha works. When there were only a handful of employees working in the office, gender relations were rather informal. Lunch was taken jointly by the office staff, and male and female colleagues were also seen in the office sitting or standing together chatting or discussing personal matters. Later, when the staff had increased to about forty persons, segregation was much more emphasized. Although several of the old staff members were still working at the office, the colleagues split into male and female groups during the lunch break; and during work not much mixing between the sexes could be observed. Referring to gender relations, one male colleague said, 'it happens all the time in the office that people talk too much. You just stand for one minute with your female colleague in the hallway and talk, and everybody will notice that and say, "see, they are talking, what are they talking about? Maybe there is something going on between them." People always talk like this and create rumours.' In this case, the increase in the number of employees made renegotiations of gender relations, and the development of intimate but de-sexualized maharam-like modes of communication between male and female colleagues, increasingly difficult. Gender relations fell back to sexualized ones, which women could only handle by maintaining segregation, and restricting all communication between the sexes to work-related issues.

Renegotiation of gender relations in the office sector is also more difficult with men who are connected to the office indirectly or temporarily; namely, clients, customers, and visitors. The shortness of the encounters, together with the lack of social control (which makes permanent office staff accountable for their behaviour, in however weak a manner) facilitate sexualized gender relations and male behaviour patterns shown toward unrelated women in public (male) spaces.

Receptionists and telephone operators complained about the numerous 'wrong calls'—as they called them. Clients and visitors who come to the office and see them working there call them later, knowing that they will attend to the phone; and they try to get them involved in conversation or invite them to meet outside the office:

I get [such] phone calls. If some customer comes [to the office], then of course he has our phone number. He sees me working here and after he has left the office he phones me, 'I liked you and I would like you to be my [girl]friend', he will say. 'Let's meet outside.' 'Have lunch with me.' 'Have dinner with me.' (Ghazal, receptionist, 25 May 1997, p. 5.)

Women also face difficulties with clients they have to deal with inside the office. Shazia and her colleagues, Shamzi and Farhat, design book covers and magazines on the computer, and sometimes clients come to their workplaces to appraise and sanction the designs they have developed:

Some clients come very close [to us]. Then we act in a disapproving manner—for example, we look at them, or stare at them, or try to give them the feeling that they should not stand here. Then they realize this themselves and retreat. And there are others who are not influenced by our behaviour, that we are staring at them or trying to indicate that they should not do that [i.e. come so close]; but our [male] executives are also caring. They react immediately and say, 'please sit down in our [visitors'] room. When they have done the work we will show it to you' (Shazia, 3 Jan. 1997, p. 7).

When women have to leave their office for work-related tasks, they again enter public (male) space in which they face the sort of gender relations as outlined above, and which they cannot renegotiate in the same way they can inside their own offices. Asieh told me that her boss once took her to the printing press. Such work is usually handled by male employees or the boss himself; but on that particular day he took her along just to show her the procedures, how scanning and printing is done, and how a printing press looks like:

There were a lot of men. They were all staring [at me] in a strange way, 'Where has this woman come from?' 'What kind of relationship does she have with this man?' [And this,] although he only took me to that place to show me how the work is done there. I did not like it. I said, 'I won't go there again; the men stare in a bad manner' (designer, 15 Jan. 1997, p. 3).

It was striking that male behaviour toward women in the
office sector was never questioned, not even by the female office
workers themselves. 'Here, everybody is nice. OK, some [male]
colleagues have their own girlfriends who also come to the
office, but that is their personal matter', commented Asieh.
However, when a woman has a boyfriend, gets male visitors or
phone calls from men at her workplace, or behaves in any
manner that could cast doubts on her moral character, then this
is not perceived as her personal matter, neither by the men nor
the women. Such behaviour indicates that this woman establishes
close contact with other men; and this is understood by male
colleagues as an 'encouragement' to extend the boundaries in
their relationship with her. Furthermore, their female colleagues
hold such women responsible for the collective behaviour men
show toward women in the office sector:

> One fish spoils the whole pond....If you behave well, then
> everybody will behave well with you and respect you. But there are
> also girls who are morally bad. I do not put the whole blame on the
> guys; some girls are not morally good. They make the [office] set-
> up dirty. If here [in this office], as an example, one woman is
> immoral, then the reputation of all girls will be spoiled—only
> because of this single woman, and although all others are [morally]
> good (Sadaf, clerical worker, govt. employee, 19 Nov. 1996, p. 2).

Here, women turn against each other, not only in cases where
women grossly violate what is perceived as (morally) proper
behaviour codes for women, but also as far as petty issues are
concerned. Once Sadaf and her colleague Rashida were talking
about another colleague of theirs, Imraana. Imraana was the
only woman in the office wearing a burqa, but she had started
to wear lipstick and make-up in the office. 'It is some women's
own fault', Sadaf complained, 'they move around like this or
take up direct contact with [male] colleagues, and then
everybody thinks that all working women are the same.'
Since male behaviour in the offices is not questioned, and
women have to define the boundaries of male-female interaction

at the workplace, and prevent men from getting the chance to extend these boundaries, harassment of female office workers is often attributed to the women themselves:

> I think that the girls themselves give the men chances....If you don't allow anybody to get close to you, nobody can do anything (Asieh, 15 Jan. 1997, p. 9).

As a consequence, women rarely admit harassment in the office sector. Shazia admitted, though reluctantly, that she had been harassed by one of the male staff members. The man had tried, by all means, to become her boyfriend; and when she made it clear that she would only establish work-related communication with him—as with all other male colleagues— he attempted to spoil her reputation in the office. He spread rumours that she would not work attentively, that her designs were not good, and that she was not talented enough for the job she was doing.

Similarly, Kishwer told me that she could not talk about the misconduct of male colleagues or clients with her boss:

> If I go to the owner and say that 'this guy has done that thing', then he won't say anything to him. He will say [to me], 'you are wrong, you must have stirred him up, and this is why he behaved this way.' He will turn against me and kick me out (receptionist, 25 March 1997, p. 8).

One employer, Asif Sahib, the owner of Creative Designers, told me that once a female employee complained about the behaviour of a male colleague. Both employees lost their jobs because, as Asif Sahib saw it, 'no one person is fully responsible for such an occurrence....As long as the woman does not give a man permission, he cannot do anything....The man only moves forward when he gets a [positive] response.'

Corners, Partitions, and Backrooms: The Gendered Organization of Space

Similar to gender relations that proved homogeneous across the office sector, the gendered organization of space in the offices was also uniform, and it unambiguously mirrored the existing gender order of Pakistani society. It emphasized the social distance between the sexes, and protected female office workers from male behaviour that is typical toward women in public male spaces. Female office workers were usually seated in corners, behind pillars or partitions, or in rooms where they were shielded from the gaze of their male colleagues as well as those of incoming customers. When men and women were not segregated physically, their workplaces were arranged in a way that they did not have to face each other, but could work with their backs to each other or side by side with their faces to the wall. Furthermore, there was usually enough space between the workplaces of male and female employees so that men and women did not have to work or pass in close proximity to one another.

Spatial provisions for women were most pronounced in offices with employers belonging to the 'conservative type'. Such spatial provisions were evident, for example, in the allocation of a separate room for the female employees. 'Women sometimes get confused when a man sits too close to them; then they cannot work well, their speed slows down', as Asif Sahib, the owner of Creative Designers, told me, and 'If you let a girl stand next to me my work speed will slow down'. Thus, Asif Sahib created enough space in his office so that men and women would be able to work comfortably. He allocated one separate room to Sadia, and clients and visitors had no access to it, nor did most of the staff:

Sadia is in our computer section. No man goes there and no man is supposed to go there either. There are only a few staff members—one sweeper, me, my elder brother, and two men who work on the computer—who enter this room. No one is supposed to go into this room....We have made this [arrangement] very consciously, and usually the room remains closed. Men sit in the office; friends come [to visit them] and sit down. And from the beginning we established such a set-up. I do not like that a girl sits in the computer room, and all the guys start coming to the office [only to glance at her] (5 April 1997, p. 15).

When a female worker, Shagufta, had to share a room with male employees, male staff from other departments of the company and friends began to visit the men working with Shagufta—only to glance at her. They even congratulated the men sitting with her because now they 'had some entertainment in the room'. Shagufta could not do much except concentrate on her work, ignore the male staff, and particularly their visitors, and remain strict when men tried to entangle her in unnecessary conversation.

Even in offices in which no special provisions are made for female employees, for example, in offices with a 'Westernized type' of employer, women try to create gender-segregated spatial arrangements for themselves. Several examples can be named here. When Tasneem started to work as a draftswoman her workplace was clearly visible to all the draftsmen working around her. A couple of weeks later, her workplace was changed to another small room where she felt protected. A female architect had her workplace in the same room; and except for the two women no one except one male architect used to work there from time to time. When a third woman, a young architect, joined the office, she chose a corner for her workplace which was advantageous for several reasons. First, colleagues peeping into that room to talk to the men working there could not see her well in the back corner. Second, the room was very narrow, and in order to reach her desk she had to pass behind the other three workplaces; but she prevented any man from passing behind her own workplace. Third, since she was sitting in a corner, she only had one male colleague nearby, instead of two. Fourth, an additional table was placed between her workplace and the one adjacent to her which increased the physical distance between her and the male colleague.

A second example of women's proactive attempts to create female spaces in the office became manifest with the placement of a partition between male and female colleagues in the computer department of Red Crescent Hospital. The female employees felt that they could thus work undisturbed, without being observed by their male colleagues.

The only exception to such a gendered organization of space was in the case of receptionists/telephone operators. These were expected to be visible to everybody, particularly clients and visitors entering the office; and their workplaces were positioned accordingly. It is interesting to note that even (some) 'conservative type' employers had female secretarial workers in their offices without perceiving this as conflicting with their own (conservative) worldview. In an interview with Asif Sahib, for instance, he stressed the importance of allocating a separate room to his female designer, Sadia. Yet, he did not consider this inconsistent with the fact that he later employed a second female employee, a receptionist, for whom of course no spatial arrangements were made. On the contrary, she sat directly behind the entrance, visible to every incoming person; and she was also the first contact person for all people visiting or phoning the office.

When I raised this issue to 'conservative type' employers who had secretarial workers in their offices or planned to recruit women for secretarial positions, I found they had either not consciously thought about this inconsistency, or they stressed the positive aspects of employing women for office jobs. When the latter was the case, they acknowledged that particular spatial arrangements are not possible for secretarial workers, but the advantages of having a woman for such positions outweighed their concerns for maintaining the gender order of society inside the offices. This point brings back to mind the observation that spatial arrangements for women in public (male) spaces in order to keep up the gender order of society are only acknowledged and upheld by men as long as they do not cause financial and/or other personal disadvantages.

Between Protection and Marginalization: The Gender-Specific Allocation of Work

The gendered organization of space observed in the office sector had its counterpart in a gender-specific allocation of work that was omnipresent in the offices under study. Women did not generally perform tasks that required contact with the public, not to even mention mobility outside the office. This way, interfaces for communication between the sexes, particularly with men who were not immediate colleagues or part of the office staff, were reduced to a minimum.

Most of the women in my sample did not have any contact with the public or contact was restricted to a limited number of the company's clients or (male) staff members from other departments. Shaheen, for example, had to deal with staff working in other departments of the hospital when they had problems with the computerization of the medical records. Shagufta computerized data for banks and private companies and sometimes had to work with the executives of the concerned institutions on a daily basis for months. Only the receptionists/telephone operators had extensive public exposure and contact.

It has already been pointed out that employers of the 'conservative type' do not allocate work to women that requires public contact and exposure. But even in offices with 'Westernized' or 'mixed types' of employers, women avoid jobs that involve customer service or require them to leave their offices for outside work. Instead, they prefer jobs in which the mingling of the sexes is minimal. Zaheer Salam, a 'Westernized type' employer, told me that he recruited men and women for tasks that require dealing with the public. For him, the qualifications of a person, not the gender, were crucial for the recruitment of staff and the assignment of tasks to them. Although a female designer, an upper-class woman with a five-year university education in Fine Arts had formerly worked for the company, and been responsible for customer service, including visiting clients in their own offices, Mr Salam concluded that most women did not want to work in fields which require such public exposure:

> When women apply here they often say, 'we do not want to do outside work but work inside [the office].' Then I ask them, 'why did you study so much? You studied Marketing [and] Sales, so why don't you go to the market?' But they say, 'no, we don't want to go outside, we want to sit in the office and work there'... (5 June 1997, p. 10).[11]

Shazia made it clear from the very start that she did not want to do any work outside the office and nobody ever asked her to do so. The designs Shazia develops have to be presented at the clients' offices, but this task is taken over by her colleague Asif. Shazia, as well as her female colleagues, Shamzi and Farhat, remain in the office the whole day. Work is allocated to them by their supervisor, who also takes back the completed work and then tells them whether corrections have to be made. Shazia only went to a client once, and before leaving her office she phoned her parents and asked for permission:

> I don't like to go out [of the office] in this way. I don't like to go to different places. From the beginning I felt that they can give me as much work as they like except for going to different places....Once I had to go, and I said that 'I won't go, I can stay here and work'; and I said that I don't have permission from my family. It is true that I do not have permission from my family, but I did not want to go either....I did not like it....If there were two or three more girls with me, then it would be different....And when I go somewhere, I do not know whether there will be girls or not. If I was the only girl I would get confused there. Therefore I do not like that [i.e. to go to different companies to visit clients] (20 April 1997, p. 4).

Even when male and female employees had the same skills and were recruited for the same positions, all tasks that had to be performed outside of the office were assigned to men. Women remained inside the office, doing exactly the same kind of work their male colleagues did. Female employees responsible for repairing computers sat in a room that not even the customers bringing the defective equipment had access to. Customers handed the computers over to men at the reception, and the male staff then forwarded the computers to the women. Male employees were also sent out to clients to check defective computer equipment, while women remained in the office and never left their workplace for such tasks.

Even when women were formally responsible for dealing with the public they, at least unofficially, handed over all work which involved contact with customers and clients to their male colleagues, and only took over such tasks temporarily when no male colleague was available.

The illustrated gender-specific allocation of work does not apply to receptionists/telephone operators, whose very work is to deal with all persons entering or phoning the office.

Advantages of Women's Deployment in the Office Sector

Experiences of Employers with Female Office Workers

The experiences of employers with female office workers in middle-level positions were overwhelmingly positive. The employers stressed that women worked harder and with more concentration than men; they were more sincere in their work; and they were very punctual. Women did not disappear for hours during work time or the lunch break (as men did); they did not get personal visitors who kept them away from their work; and they did not take many casual leaves. These qualities are in part linked to women's restricted mobility. While male employees can take their motorbikes, and leave the office for half an hour or an hour any time during the day, women cannot do the same. Any work which has to be done in public spaces is usually the responsibility of men, for example, the payments for electricity, gas, water, and telephone bills have to be deposited regularly, letters have to be posted, the motorbike has to be tuned, certain goods have to be purchased, etc. Therefore, men frequently disappear during working hours for a while or take casual leave for one day or half a day, in order to get such tasks done. Women are not responsible for this kind of work but pass it on to their brothers or other male relatives. Furthermore, it is common that men get visitors in their offices—friends or relatives who drop in for a chat—while women cannot visit each other so easily.

At least equally important was the recognition that the turnover of female staff was much lower than that of male staff. In the office sector in general, but particularly in the smaller offices, systems of internal promotion are not very distinct. Thus, men switch between companies frequently in order to improve their financial and professional standing. Women, on the other hand, have different priorities when choosing or changing a job and therefore stay in offices longer than men. Indeed, most of the women I talked to had not changed their workplace more than once, if at all.

Even marriage was not perceived as leading to a higher turnover of female employees, despite the fact that lower-middle-class women usually desire to leave their jobs after getting married. Employers of the 'Westernized type' had had highly educated upper- and upper-middle-class women working in their offices for the last 10 or 15 years, and they commonly had very qualified working women in their own families, who associate their profession with career aspirations. Since such women often have a life-long employment history, these employers assumed that the lower-middle-class women who had recently started to work in their offices would also continue to work after marriage:

> You cannot say that 'tomorrow she might get married and [for that reason] we won't employ her.' I don't think that this would be correct...You have to consider that after her marriage she might wish to continue with her job. This is also a possibility... I have observed that 80% of the working women continue to work after they get married....If we take a look at this organization, then

Shaheen has been working here for two years, but the men who were here came and left again (Babar Sahib, 1 Aug. 1997, p. 2ff.).

It is true that, contrary to these opinions of 'Westernized employers', employers who had a lower-middle-class background clearly identified female employment with economic need, and expected their female office workers to leave their jobs after marriage. Asif Sahib, for example, felt that 'you cannot say that any Pakistani girl works because of interest. Girls do not work because of interest. Out of 100 there might be 10 or 5 who work because they are interested in it. The remaining 95 have problems at home, and this is why they work....It is 100% certain that when she [i.e. Sadia, the female designer] gets married she will leave this job. She will leave, and this is one disadvantage when you take a girl. Apart from this there is no other disadvantage'. Still, these employers also acknowledged that women stayed in the offices much longer than male staff members.

Employers even made special concessions to women in order to keep them in their offices. Pervaiz Sahib, for instance, allowed his female employee, Tasneem, to leave the office half an hour before the official working hours were finished to enable her to avoid the evening rush hour and get a seat on the public bus relatively easily on her way home. One company, Ali&Ali Communications, provided transportation to and from work to the female employees, about four to five women. Zaheer Salam, the director of Ali&Ali Communications, told me that the first female employee, a telephone operator, was once harassed at the bus stop near the office. There were only two solutions to the problem: to provide transportation to the woman or give her notice. Since Mr Salam did not consider the latter alternative humane, the company started to provide shuttle services for the female employees.

The fact that women are usually not given tasks that require mingling of the sexes was not perceived as a disadvantage either. 'Conservative type' employers did not assign work to women which had to be performed outside the office or required dealing with the public. For them, such tasks were simply not part of their female employees' jobs but were to be handled by one or more of the male staff. 'Westernized employers', on the other hand, who also employed (highly-qualified) women for tasks which require dealing with the public, did not even take into consideration the fact that work which has to be performed outside the office or that includes a large amount of public contact should not be assigned to women. When I asked Pervaiz Sahib, owner of Premier Architects, whether the restricted mobility of women in public male spaces, including the transportation problem for women, was a disadvantage he answered:

> Yes, there are disadvantages, but we always feel that we need to encourage women to come to work....As a draftsperson, yes, there will be times when she might not be able to go to the sites, but that does not mean that she will not learn how to go to the sites later. As you know, my wife is an architect; she goes to all the sites... (1 April 1997).

Here again, lower-middle-class office workers benefit from the advances highly-qualified and upper-class women have made in their respective fields. Although women themselves avoid work that requires mingling of the sexes, and thus narrow their potential spectrum of activities, employers are open to assigning unconventional tasks to (lower-middle-class) women in their offices.

Changes in Office Cultures through the Entry of Women

During the time I conducted field research in Lahore, a local TV drama called 'bila unwaan' ('without name'), which very well mirrored the changes which occur in offices with all-male staff by the entry of one or more women, was broadcast on the national TV channel. The drama featured a businessman who had recently taken over a small private company and was very disappointed with his all-male staff. The employees were shown sitting together in groups in the office, chatting loudly and drinking tea, and not working properly. The outward appearance of the men was not satisfactory either. They used to come to the office unshaved, with clothes that had not been washed or ironed adequately. Furthermore, the men arrived in the office very late in the mornings, giving various excuses for their tardiness. The owner of the company tried to change the behaviour and work morale of his employees, but was unsuccessful in doing so. He, therefore, contacted a friend for advice. 'How can you call this an office?' the friend asked after inspecting the company. 'You do not even have a female secretary. Don't you know that nowadays a pretty secretary is a must in every office?' He advised the owner of the company to hire a female secretary since this would solve all the problems with his male staff. The next scene featured the newly recruited-secretary sitting on her chair in the middle of the room. She was young and pretty, well dressed, and busy working on the computer, where she speedily typed a text with her red polished fingers. The behaviour of the male employees had changed drastically from one day to the next. They had stopped chatting loudly, and everybody was sitting on their chairs, throwing furtive glances at the woman and thinking desperately about how they could initiate a conversation with her. The men started coming to the office shaved, with clean and ironed clothes, trying to make a good impression on their female colleague. Even the still unmarried owner of the company was lost in daydreaming about fictive conversation and intimate meetings with his new secretary. Before getting out of his car and into the office in the mornings, he also began to check his outfit in the mirror and to once again pass a comb through his hair.

Particularly non-'Westernized type' of employers emphasized the positive changes the recruitment of one (or more) women had brought about in their offices.[12] Ms Jamila, who had been a telephone operator for more than twenty years, was asked about how the recent entry of women into the departments had changed the office culture, she answered:

Very positively. The men have started to polish themselves up.
They have started coming to the office well-dressed, in ironed shirts
and shaved. And they are also coming on time. Furthermore, the
language in the departments has changed. It is not as rude as it was
earlier (1/1997).

The change in the use of language—often from informal Punjabi,
in which men more often use crude and dirty language, to polite
Urdu—was also stressed by other employers; for example, Asif
Sahib, as being due to the recruitment of female employees:

Many men change their language when a woman comes to the
office. And...everybody starts to come to the office well-
dressed....There is such an influence on the set-up that you won't
hear any verbal abuses, because of the woman....The jokes and fun
remain within civilized boundaries. The greatest advantage is that
the set-up becomes neat and clean....Clients don't misbehave; the
staff doesn't misbehave; and there is no loose talk (employer of
Sadia, 5 April 1997).

To sum up, the changes in office culture brought about by a
woman's integration into an office were considered an important
advantage in the employment of women as office workers.

Career Traits for Female Office Workers: Prospects and Hindrances

Since the entry of lower-middle-class women into the office
sector is a relatively new phenomenon, the prospects for female
workers in middle-level positions to achieve upward mobility
are difficult to estimate. Still, some general patterns can be
anticipated.

Across the office sector there is a considerable variation—
even among the same occupations—with regard to the salaries
of employees, their education and skill levels, their opportunities
for further upgrading their skills, and for advancement.
Particularly, larger, often foreign-owned, companies and

multinationals which offer good salaries, have their offices furnished with the latest computer software, technical equipment, air conditioners, etc., provide entitlements to annual and medical leave and some job security; but the educational backgrounds and skill levels which are required by these companies are relatively high. In small offices, on the other hand, salaries are low, technical equipment is not up-to-date, nor easily accessible; and it is common that employees do not even have a work contract. Internal promotion systems are largely absent. In order to improve oneself financially and professionally, one usually has to change the company; consequently, the turnover of the staff in the smaller offices is high. Female office workers, however, do not change their jobs often, because their job-satisfaction depends on criteria that are different from those of male office workers:

> You see, for ladies in Pakistan, considerations, especially those for taking a job, are not just monetary: atmosphere, how the boss is, if he is a gentleman or not. So, they consider more than money or salary and the like. For the men there is only salary. If he is getting Rs 3000 in one office, and somebody offers him Rs 3500, the next day he will leave the job. He will think that 'I am sustaining a loss of Rs 500 per month'. For ladies, you see, there are other problems also. They are living very close to here. They can come in five minutes by sitting in a van. You know the transport problem for ladies....[Men] can go to the other end of the city, but ladies cannot go; they cannot sit in buses for hours a day, two hours in the morning, two hours in the evening. So, this is also a consideration for ladies. It is an incentive to take a job nearby (Asad Usmani, architect, employer of Andeela, 2/1997).

Whenever female office workers were asked whether they were content with their jobs, they stressed factors like 'the mahol is very good here'; 'this office is close to my home'; 'my husband (or family) know and like the mahol'; or 'my boss is very nice'. The salary, career prospects, and opportunities to learn and further upgrade one's skills were rarely mentioned.

In some cases, women were not able to further improve themselves financially and professionally in the office they were currently working in; but despite having the opportunity to switch to another company with more promising career prospects, they remained at their old workplaces. One example is Andeela, whose salary was fixed at Rs 1600 when she started and increased by Rs 200 two years later. Andeela's salary was very low compared to other women I interviewed, like Tasneem. Both had passed the two-year course in Architectural Drafting and Tasneem's salary was Rs 3000, despite the fact that she only had a few months work experience. Apart from Andeela's low salary, there were no computers for architectural drafting. Working conditions were difficult for the draftswomen. Andeela decided to enroll in a three-month computer course in AutoCAD, which cost her Rs 7000, but she hoped that through the course, she could upgrade her skills and find a better paying job in a bigger, more prestigious company where architectural drafting was computerized. However, after the completion of her computer course, Andeela remained irresolute about changing her workplace, and decided to remain at Unique Architects. She felt that her present office was close to her home, that her boss was very nice, and that she could work with women who were also her good friends. In another office there might be many more men, and, as she said, 'in this office I get respect'. In making this decision Andeela not only lost the computer skills she had acquired during her costly course (because the absence of computers in her office did not allow her to keep in practice); she also impeded her own advancement since, apart from an annual pay raise of Rs 100 or 200, there were no prospects at Unique Architects for promotion or further upgrading her skills. Andeela's two female colleagues, Shazia and Farhana, also TTCW graduates, and with Andeela the only draftspersons at Unique Architects, had been working at Unique Architects even longer than Andeela; namely, 3.5 and 2.5 years respectively. Their salaries were also very low, Rs 2500 and Rs 1900 respectively; but Shazia and Farhana did not change their workplace for the same reasons as Andeela.

The importance women ascribed to the (good) mahol in their offices was a crucial factor preventing them from seizing opportunities which would facilitate upward mobility; for example, shifting to a more prestigious company or a better-paying position. It has already been pointed out that women create, or at least grossly influence, the office mahol through their own conduct and negotiation strategies. Once having established a good mahol they are reluctant to give up what they have worked so hard for, and join another office where renegotiations of gender relations start (again) at zero; or, as Sajda expressed it, 'if I go to a new place I won't know how the people will be. Here I have already gained the men's respect. I respect them and they respect me. That is the reason why I won't leave.'

Only two women in my sample, Shagufta and Shaheen, who both had the highest salaries and held the best positions, had consciously changed their jobs when they had the opportunity to improve themselves professionally. Shaheen had started to work at a monthly salary of Rs 2000 then, a year later, she enrolled in a one-year evening diploma course in computer science. She wanted to work in a multi-user computer environment where she would also be exposed to computer networking. Thus, when she saw a relevant vacancy at a private, well-known hospital in the local newspaper, she applied for the job. Her starting salary at the computer department of Red Crescent Hospital, was Rs 6500. Shaheen was promoted after about one year. Two (female) assistants were assigned to her. Nearly two years after Shaheen joined Red Crescent Hospital, her salary increased to Rs 11,000. Shaheen was one of the few women who acknowledged the importance of changing the workplace to achieve upward mobility:

> It is important to change the job. Although we don't know what the new office will look like, how the people will be and the mahol, we have already managed to adjust at one place, and when we change our job we have to adjust at a new place. But you can only make financial and professional progress when you change the job (software developer, 25 April 1997).

Shaheen felt that the field she had chosen, computerization of data in hospitals, was a very new field in which skilled personnel could not easily be found, and in which her career prospects were good. She was willing to leave her job if she received a better offer from another hospital.

Shaheen's example indicates that women do have opportunities to achieve upward mobility. However, their reluctance to change the office impedes advancement, and negatively affects women's wages, skill levels, job satisfaction, and their roles as office workers in general.

NOTES

1. A differentiation should be made here between 'office cultures', on the one hand, and 'gender relations' at the workplace, on the other hand. The term 'gender relations' refers to the social construction of gender, male behaviour patterns toward women at the workplace, and strategies women develop to renegotiate social relations and establish new socially acceptable patterns of communication between the sexes, as well as to maneuver in an extremely gendered office space. The term 'office cultures' refers to the concrete set-up inside the offices. These can be marked by a far-reaching segregation of the sexes regarding male-female interaction at the workplace as well as spatial arrangements for men and women, but they can also be characterized by desegregation and an astonishing intimacy among male and female colleagues. 'Gender relations' are, therefore, one important dimension of 'office cultures'.

2. On organizations as 'mini-societies that have their own distinctive patterns of culture and subculture', see Morgan (1997: 129ff.). A comprehensive review of organizational culture research is also provided by Martin/ Frost (1996).

3. In the smaller offices, the employers (or bosses) I interviewed were usually also the owners of the companies. In larger offices, when I asked the women to identify the supervisor who knew them and had probably even employed them they referred me either to the director of their company or of the department they were working in. All the employers I interviewed were men; only Shagufta's boss, the branch manager of a computer firm, was a woman; but despite my efforts she refused an interview.

4. This perception very well mirrors the life world of the more Westernized upper- and upper-middle classes, which is less pervaded by concepts of

gender segregation and purdah and the sexualization of gender relations than the life world of the lower-middle classes. However, the fact that highly-qualified women have started to work in fields which require contact with the public, and that neither they themselves nor their 'Westernized type' of employers consider their gender a constraint for their work, does not mean that lower-middle-class women would consider similar jobs as appropriate for themselves.

5. Male professionals belonging to the upper- and upper-middle classes rarely wear shalwar-kameez at the workplace but trousers and a shirt, or a suit. Women, on the other hand, wear shalwar-kameez irrespective of their class background and the position they hold at the workplace.

6. Shaheen's former boss—he had meanwhile left Red Crescent Hospital— had very consciously employed two female assistants because he had sensed that for Shaheen it was inconvenient to be the only woman in the department. Apart from the problems she had with eating at the workplace, she also felt very uncomfortable whenever there was any social gathering or informal meeting in her department. She always tried to avoid such events because there was nobody, i.e. no other woman, she could talk to.

7. This phenomenon is very uncommon, particularly among the lower-middle classes, because unrelated men and women are not supposed to have any physical contact, and shaking hands with the opposite sex is usually restricted to close relatives only.

8. Sajda was indeed fired in the beginning of 1998, a few months after the completion of my research. Imraan had meanwhile started to work as a designer for a new local newspaper, but the newspaper proved to be unsuccessful and was discontinued. He lost his job after only one month and then again tried to find employment elsewhere.

9. For further reading see Ackers, 1991; Müller 1993, 1999; and Rastetter 1994. An interesting cross-cultural analysis of organizations as 'socially constructed realities' and the way they are shaped by their societal context can be found in Morgan (1997: 119–52). A more theoretical review of approaches in organizational theory, which stress the importance of the societal context for understanding organizations is provided by Walgenbach (1995). For more comprehensive reading also see the articles in Meyer/Scott (eds.), (1992).

10. The term *mahol* refers to the behaviour of the people (here: the men) and gender relations in general in a certain (office) environment. Mahol should not be confused with an office set-up, which in this study is being used as a synonym for office cultures. Since no proper word could be found to adequately translate mahol, the term is used here in its original.

11. It is not only gender relations and male behaviour toward women in public male spaces that prevents women from choosing jobs in which they have to work outside of the office, but also the fear of gossip that

could arise when relatives or acquaintances see a female office worker, probably even with a male colleague, in public spaces. Asieh once told me that 'now my boss has also started to do interior design. And he says, "I will take you there too so that you will get some experience regarding how to do that work, how the space can be utilized." But I am afraid because if I go...and somebody sees me they will say, "she was moving around with someone in a car." Not everybody will acknowledge that I work, that this is my job, that I went outside to do some work. They will say, "God knows with whom she was moving around outside".'

12. 'Westernized employers', on the other hand, did not perceive any changes that had occurred in their offices due to the entry of women. They had had female colleagues, highly-qualified ones, for at least 15 or 20 years and were used to working with women, particularly in higher-level positions.

6

'NO CLOUDS IN THE SKY?' CHANGES IN THE LIFE WORLD OF WOMEN DUE TO EMPLOYMENT

'Since I started working, I have become very confident'—Changes in Social Identity

The continual confrontation and interaction with male strangers in extremely gendered male spaces, in public, and particularly in the workplace, inevitably bring about new behaviour patterns and changes in personal and social identity, viz., a new life style, which distinguishes the office workers from the majority of lower-middle-class women in Pakistani society.

All the women felt that their lives had changed tremendously since they had started working. Particular emphasis was placed on the enormous confidence the women had gained in interacting with male strangers and in entering male-dominated spaces. While prior to their employment, most of the office workers had never gone out alone, or spoken to strange men, they now used public transport, and went shopping alone. Shaheen summarized the changes that had occurred in her life after four years of office work, as follows:

> Now I am not as afraid of men as I was earlier. Formerly I was very much scared of men, I couldn't even talk to men. Now this is not such a problem, I can handle them. Men can be bosses but they can also be subordinates. Earlier I couldn't go to places which were male dominated, but now I can go and talk to the men (software developer, 2 Nov. 1996, p. 18).

It is true that female office workers try to create separate spaces for themselves at the workplace, and avoid mingling of the sexes as far as possible; they also integrate their daily interactions with male colleagues into their life world by referring to them as 'like family members', 'like uncles', or 'like brothers and sisters', i.e. as maharam relations. However, male and female office workers are developing new patterns of communication. These are not only enabling the establishment of a partially desegregated working environment, but are also leading to renegotiation of gender relations beyond the workplace, where male and female office workers meet as a group or, secretly, as a couple. This is occurring in Pakistani society despite the fact that gender relations are perceived by both men and women as predominantly sexual ones, that women quickly become targets of sexual harassment and assault in male spaces, and that—according to the social and gender order of society—women are supposed to stay in purdah and not interact with men; in other words, despite the fact that no societal sanctioned modes of communication exist for unrelated men and women. A slight change of gender relations is becoming visible on the horizon, which might even expand to a societal level provided that the number of (lower-middle-class) women entering the office sector, and the labour market in general, continues to rise in the future.

Apart from the confidence women gain from handling a male-dominated office environment and male-dominated spaces in public, they also experience a rise in self-esteem due to the fact that they earn and support their families financially.

It makes me happy that I contribute [financially] to the household, that I share [the responsibilities] with the others. And I stand on my own feet, I don't have to worry that I have to ask someone for Rs 10. I earn and I have money in my own pocket (Tasneem, draftswoman, 10 Feb. 1997, p. 13).

Furthermore, *gharelo* women, i.e. women who do not work or study but stay at home, often seem to live in their own sheltered world which, particularly until marriage, centres around clothes, and the latest fashion, movies and songs, and frequent visits to female relatives and girls/women living in the mohalla, where the latest gossip is exchanged. Office workers, on the other hand, seemed to be much more aware of the economic and social problems around them. 'Earlier [when I was in college] I just had to meet with my friends', Kishwer told me when I asked her about the changes which had occurred in her life after she had started to work as a receptionist. 'Now my lifestyle has changed; now all the worries have come upon me.' Several of the office workers did not even know the families living in their immediate neighbourhood. As Shaheen said, 'I don't meet anyone in the mohalla, I don't have time for that.' Many other office workers told me the same thing, indicating that their lifestyle had already changed significantly from that of non-working women in their age group.

Despite the changes in lifestyle and the new behaviour patterns women adopt while working in male spaces, which they, to a certain extent, appropriate for themselves, most office workers nevertheless expressed the desire to leave their jobs and return to the chardivari, particularly upon getting married, if it should prove economically manageable, or—as married women indicated—as soon as they could afford to drop out of the labour market financially:

> ... I'll stop work [after marriage]...if they are well off, that is, if the family I get married into, and the man earns a good living. If they can fulfill all my needs, then why should I work (Sadaf, govt. clerical worker employee, 19 Nov. 1996, p. 7).

One reason the office workers do not plan long-term employment is that they consider working in a male-dominated environment very difficult. Apart from the transportation problem, which remains a constant worry for many office workers, it is the continual renegotiations of gender relations at the workplace, the continual necessity for women to define the boundaries of their interactions with male colleagues, customers, etc., and the continual attempts of men to cross these boundaries—and not the work itself—which the office workers find very strenuous. When I asked Sadia, a designer who had already worked in a small advertising agency for about five years, whether she would recommend her occupation to other women who were interested in designing and wanted to work, she answered, 'I would say, "don't do it". It is very difficult. For a girl it is very difficult to work.' Tasneem, a draftswoman, was also disturbed by the continual effort needed to 'survive' in a male-dominated office environment. She had joined a training course in Architectural Drafting—and not a secretarial course—because she wanted to avoid contact with men at the workplace. But after she started working in an architectural office, she became disenchanted with the field she had chosen: 'I came here and found out that this is the same....These problems are also here. [If I had known that beforehand] I would not have taken the next step [and started to work]. I would have stopped after college.' Even Shagufta, a software developer and one of the highest-qualified and best-paid women in my sample, told me that if she could find a job in a female working environment she would immediately switch to that job, even at a reduced salary. Even after five years of work experience she felt that it was very difficult to work with men. But if she wanted to work in a female working environment she could only teach in a school or college. There, however, she would receive a lower salary and would not have the chance to upgrade her skills or improve her job prospects.

Another reason for the lack of interest in long-term employment is the absence of role models among the lower-middle classes, who could positively influence the development of long-term career plans. One of the very few women who expressed the desire to continue working after marriage was Umbreen, a government employee. Umbreen's elder sister, Rubeena, was married with two children, and worked as an assistant manager, earning about Rs 4500 per month.[1] Rubina clearly worked for economic reasons but Umbreen nonetheless looked up to her sister, and felt that families were much better off financially when both husband and wife worked. She wanted to try to find a husband and in-laws who would allow her to continue working after her marriage, and she was willing to refuse a good marriage match if the potential in-laws or husband insisted that she leave her job after marriage. Thus, the existence of role models can positively influence the integration of long-term employment perspectives into the office workers.

Umbreen's example already indicates another impediment to the development of long-term employment perspectives; namely, the permission women need for their employment from the future husband and in-laws. Since they usually want the daughter-in-law/wife to leave her job and stay at home after marriage, women think it inevitable that their employment will come to an end once they get married:

> I can't say yet [if I will work after marriage]. I don't think that the in-laws will give permission [to work after marriage]. Usually the people here...think that girls who work in offices are not good....I'll try not to leave the job but here...in Pakistan...you have to obey what they [the in-laws] say (Shazia, designer, 2 Jan. 1997, p. 10).

These female office workers have shown that they—belonging to very conservative families, with no experience regarding female employment in male-dominated spaces—can adjust to a male-dominated working environment; and it is very likely that the worsening economic conditions will push more and more (lower-middle-class) women into the office sector. The present economic situation will also prevent increasing numbers of office workers from the lower-middle classes from leaving their jobs after marriage, or will force them, if they stop working at the time they get married, to re-enter the labour market after a while. Despite these developments, office workers have not yet developed long-term employment perspectives. Their absence, particularly in the initial years before marriage, prevents women from improving their skills and achieving upward mobility. Over the long run this again affects their wages, career prospects, and contentment with their occupations.

The Rise of Female Office Workers in Lower-Middle-Class Families: Its Meaning for the Social (Re-)Construction of the 'Female Office Worker'

The increasing number of lower-middle-class women entering the office sector in recent years has brought about the recognition of a new type of urban (lower-middle-class) woman in Pakistani society. This is being added, though reluctantly, to the hitherto existing gender images.

Female office workers, particularly those who have to travel to their workplaces alone, are being recognized by their social surrounding as working women (but not necessarily as women working in an office). These women move alone in public (male) spaces and have a confident way of walking and addressing male strangers. They dress modestly and use little make-up. This contrasts with *gharelo* women, who tend to wear shining, rather gaudy clothes in bright colours, more jewelry and make-up.

Another significant sign of the recognition of office workers is their handbag, which *gharelo* women do not commonly possess. But how do the growing numbers of lower-middle-class female office workers, and their increasing visibility in public spaces affect their social standing?

One significant issue, which reflects the social standing of office workers among the lower-middle classes, concerns the difficulties they face in finding marriage partners. It is common that office workers do not receive marriage proposals simply because they work outside the home, in a male-dominated office environment. Working women's 'expressions of interest' to families who are looking for female marriage partners for their sons are also openly rejected. This problem is shared by secretarial and technical workers alike.

Shazia, a 23-year-old who had worked as a designer for about three years, told me that her parents were currently trying to marry her off. The marriages of her two elder sisters—who were never gainfully employed—had been arranged within their own family,[2] and the parents announced within the family that they were now looking for a marriage partner for Shazia (a common practice to attract marriage proposals). They even contacted a match-maker. In a few cases Shazia was rejected as a daughter-in-law solely because she was an office worker. Her being a designer, and not a secretarial worker, did not make much difference in the negative attitudes toward her:

> The problem is that people only later ask what kind of work I do. At first they see that I work in an office! They find out much later what kind of work I actually do....The work I do does not require much contact with men. People come and go but my work requires very little contact with men. However, just to work in an office is already a very big thing for them (20 April 1997, p. 18).

Similarly Andeela, a 21-year-old draftswoman revealed that she was rejected by families simply because she was an office worker; or potential in-laws wanted to see the office where she worked. 'Do they want to marry me or my office', she asked angrily.

Office workers with a comparatively high income felt that the trend to refuse office workers as marriage matches was changing due to worsening economic conditions. Families sent marriage proposals to well-paid working women, but these were often greedy families who were only interested in the high monthly salary which, in addition to the dowry, would flow into the household regularly. The fear of being exploited financially by future in-laws is another reason (particularly for unmarried women with higher incomes) to state on principle that they want to leave their jobs after marriage. In this way, they try to discourage such families from sending marriage proposals. One example is Shagufta, a 27-year-old, earning as much as Rs 12,000, who told me that 'women with my kind of occupation rather have the problem of facing greedy people who see how much money we earn, and who send [marriage] proposals just for that reason. Therefore, I always say that I want to leave my job after marriage.'

Because of the difficulties female office workers have in finding a marriage partner through typical arranged marriages, several unmarried women in my sample were already in their mid-twenties and older, an age at which women from the lower-middle classes (and indeed women in general) are usually already married.[3]

It has already been pointed out that, through the entry of women into the office sector, new modes of communication emerge between women and men, which also lead to the development of hitherto unknown 'de-sexualized' relationships and friendships between the sexes.[4] Yet, deviation from the conventional arranged and endogamous way of marrying is not acceptable to the conservative families of the office workers either, not only because the husband-to-be would belong to a different family, and most probably a different biradari too, but also because this would simply be considered immoral and outrageous.

When I asked Sadia (a designer, who told me that in her family there had never been a love marriage) whether her family would give her permission if she met someone in the office she wanted to marry, she answered, 'I don't know what they would say. I cannot even think about such an issue.' Andeela, who was asked the same question, gave me a similar answer:

> We cannot talk with our parents about such things. Even if we like someone and we would like to marry him we cannot say that. We can only pray to Allah that we have a good kismet. And when we have reached an age at which we feel that we want to get married we cannot say this either. We can only wait till the parents make the decision. I am talking in a low voice so that my parents cannot hear what we are talking about. Otherwise they will say, 'what kind of issues are you talking about with your guest?' (draftswoman, 29 June 1997).

Shazia told me that marriages in her family are arranged out of the family clan, but not out of their biradari. Her father is very strict about this issue, although Shazia herself does not believe in the biradari system. Shazia likes one client who regularly comes to her office but she knows that her father would never agree to let her marry this man because he belongs to a different biradari. Thus, she accepts that her parents will find a suitable marriage partner for her, and arrange her marriage.

The office workers who have already gone a step further and have secret boyfriends are also quite realistic regarding their chances of marrying that person: they are almost nil. Sajda has been a close friend of one of her male colleagues for more than two years, but she knows that her family would never agree to a marriage with him. She is actually quite disappointed about the situation she has got herself into. In her family, marriages are only arranged among relatives; there has never been a marriage outside the family, not to think about a marriage between a different biradari:

> We are not allowed to marry outside the family. That is unthinkable. Therefore, it is of no use to fall in love with someone inside or outside the office. And when you go against the will of your family, you have to totally break off relations with them. But who knows what will happen tomorrow? Maybe the man for whom I left everything, even my own family, will divorce me or marry a second wife tomorrow. And what can I do in this case? Then my family won't support me. They will say, 'you selected your husband yourself, now you have to handle the problem on your own.' Such women then go with their children to Dar-ul-Mussarat [home for battered, divorced and abandoned women], and that is no life....But we cannot stay unmarried either. We cannot live alone, and our parents [with whom we live] won't live for ever (2/1997).

These examples clearly indicate the antagonism of lower-middle-class families toward changes in life style, particularly in gender relations (even if these have already taken place in the office workers' lives). Indeed, the office workers are commonly the first ones in their families who have ever worked in a male-dominated working environment; and because of this, they are observed with great suspicion by their relatives and their social surrounding. They are the 'guinea pigs' in their families, who have to prove that contact with men at the workplace does not have any negative impact on their conduct and moral characters. They are the pioneers in their families who will decide, through their own conduct, whether the office sector will also be open to other girls in their (extended) families in the future:

I am the first one in my family who has started such a [office] job...I keep this in mind so that...the other girls [in my family] will not be stopped in the future because of negative experiences with me (Shagufta, software developer, 17 May 1997, p. 6).

But what kind of behaviour patterns can women adopt in order to initiate a positive redefinition of the currently existing (negative) image of the female office worker, by their families and social surrounding? The office workers' own opinions were quite similar on this issue:

If we leave the house in order to earn money we should not break the trust of our parents or husband. We are leaving to go to the office; therefore, we should go from the office to our home and from our home to the office, that's it (Ghazal, receptionist, 1 Dec. 1996, p. 14).

We should not have a loose character and deceive our mothers and fathers. They have trusted us and sent us outside [of the house], and the daughter should not do [morally] bad things. She should behave in a manner that her parents' izzat remains restored (Kishwer, receptionist, 24 Nov. 1996, p. 13).

We have to work here and then we go home. And [in the morning] we have to come straight here from home. We have to keep in mind that we keep up the izzat of our parents....We should not abuse the trust, izzat and freedom they have given to us (Sadaf, govt. clerical worker, 19 Nov. 1996, p. 10).

In other words, female employment in the office sector has already become a part of the women's and their families' lives, but it should not undermine the social and gender order of society.[5] Once the office workers have proved that working among men has not negatively affected their moral character and conduct, i.e. that they still adhere to the value system of the lower-middle classes, the negative attitude toward female office workers and female employment in the office sector changes:

> In the beginning they [the relatives] felt that working women are not good. Girls who move around outside are not good....But I built up my own izzat. And then they saw that nothing happened which questioned my reputation or character. I broke off my relationship with all of them and then they came to me, called me, 'come over sometimes. Why don't you come to visit us?'....They see that 'she managed the household after the death of her father'....They now see that they were wrong, that not all girls who go outside are bad....And now they call me. My cousin who earlier used to say, 'she works, what a bad thing, what a distress', now talks very nicely to me (Sajda, receptionist, 13 March 1997, p. 8ff.).

> Now none [of my relatives] says a word. They say that 'this is a nice thing, she has taken care of the household, taken care of the children.' Of all children in our family, my children go to the best school. It is an English-language school and the fees are quite high. Now they see that and they are amazed that 'she has made something out of her children' (Firdous, research assistant, 20 March 1997, p. 15).

Many women told me that the very persons who had objected to their employment in the beginning now had working women in their own families:

> Now their own daughters also work. They have seen me and now let their daughters work too. They have changed a lot in my family. When you are confident and you don't do [morally] bad things, then there are no problems. Then everyone feels attracted by you, that 'she works and we will also work' (Tasneem, draftswoman, 10 Feb. 1997, p. 14).

Shagufta told me that even those people who gossiped and talked about her negatively because she worked in an office, now came to her and asked her what kind of training she would recommend for their own daughters. 'I have really worked hard to come to this point', Shagufta said, 'I had to be very careful that nothing happened which could ruin my reputation, which could make people talk. I had to be much more careful than the women who do not work. They can afford to talk to strangers or put on a lot of make-up, but I was always very careful because I knew that people will definitely observe my behaviour.'

The prevalent antagonism among the lower-middle classes toward changes in the social and gender order of society, makes it difficult for the women to positively integrate the changes in their social identity, and the new life-style they experience after entering the office sector into their own life world, particularly into their family life and gender relations within the family. As a consequence, they construct distinct life worlds (for example, the family, the office environment), which remain disconnected from each other, and adopt different behaviour patterns and life-styles according to the respective life world. These might be socially acceptable in one life world (for example, the office), but not in another (for example, the family).

Moving between these different life worlds is often a tight-rope walk that is not easy for women to handle. One example is Andeela, in whose family, as is commonly the case among conservative Muslims, no man, not even her father or brother, sits next to her. In her office, she sits with two other females and one male colleague and has lunch with them, a situation that causes inner conflict:

> ...even my father does not sit next to me...and I cannot tell you how my father would react if he saw that a man sat near me [in the office]. It also happens sometimes that Farhana and Shazi go to say their prayers. And we are sitting next to each other...and if my father came in and saw us unexpectedly, I don't know what his reaction would be...I think he wouldn't like it, he would think, 'why is she sitting here [with him]', I think he wouldn't like it (draftswoman, 26 April 1997, p. 31).

Sajda, a receptionist who works in an office which has a largely desegregated working environment finds a similar contradiction in her daily life. The men and women working together in the office are on very informal terms with each other: they have lunch together, sit together and chat freely, and they even shake hands with each other. In her very conservative home, nobody knows about these behaviour patterns at the workplace.

Another example is Kishwer. Her family background is also a conservative lower-middle-class one. Strong gender segregation is practiced in her whole extended family, and 'love marriages' or even marriages out of ones own biradari are unthinkable. Kishwer had a boyfriend she was secretly dating. Her boyfriend worked as an operation theatre assistant in the hospital where Kishwer had been working earlier, and they had developed a friendship which had already lasted for nearly two years. They used to phone each other up several times a day at work, and Kishwer very reluctantly admitted that she was also going out with him. Sometimes, she took the afternoon off from the hospital in order to spend some hours with her boyfriend, going to a park or an ice cream parlour. She always made sure that she would reach home on time so that her family would not become suspicious. In order to find approval for their relationship at the workplace, Kishwer introduced her boyfriend to her colleagues as her fiancé. Believing that Kishwer was officially engaged, but that her parents were very conservative and did not want her to meet him before marriage—which is a common phenomenon that is meant to prevent premarital sexual relations—the colleagues tolerated and even supported her secret meetings. For instance, when someone from Kishwer's family phoned her at her workplace or came over when she was out with her boyfriend, her colleagues would say that she was busy with some work inside the hospital, and could not tend the phone or come down to the reception.

In Kishwer's case, her employment enabled her to experience a lifestyle different from that of her family or other non-working women. She was exposed to unrelated men, developed a friendship with a former colleague, and could even carve out some time and privacy for secret meetings with him. Yet, dating a man is not acceptable in Pakistani society, and women always have to bear the risk that the truth might one day surface, for example, if they are seen by relatives. In Kishwer's case, her parents later found out about her secret meetings. They were strictly against this friendship and marriage was out of the question. But since Kishwer's salary had already become a crucial part of the household budget, the parents could not do much apart from prohibiting her from further meeting with her boyfriend, and trying to control her more strictly. However, when Kishwer's younger sister was offered a job as receptionist at a private hospital, she did not get permission from her family to become gainfully employed. Here, the negative experiences with Kiṣhwer, shut the door for other girls in her family. They were not allowed to become employed in the office sector or a male-dominated work environment in general.

Furthermore, women like Kishwer commonly do not receive any sympathy from other working women, because they are the ones who are made responsible for the bad reputation of female office workers in society:

> There are also girls in our society who have ruined the reputation of all girls who work [in offices]. They talk to male strangers, sit down with them, drink tea with them, and move around [with men] here and there. So, it reflects negatively on us...these dirty fish have already made the whole pond dirty and people consider all [office workers]...dirty (Sadaf, govt. clerical worker, 17 July 1997, p. 9).

Here again it is women who are considered to be the upholders of societal standards of morality—even by women themselves. Men are not questioned when they violate the gender order of society, or when they (mis)behave in offices or in public male spaces.

Another way to accommodate the different life worlds the office workers are confronted with, is to try to reconcile them through re-veiling. Although about three to four women in my sample used to cover their heads with their dupatte in the office—the others only veiled on their way to the office and back home—two women who earlier did not cover their heads in the office started doing so. When I asked Tasneem why she had started covering her head with the dupatta after working for more than one year without doing so, she told me that she had wanted to veil for quite a while; but since she had left her head uncovered on her first working day she had hesitated, not knowing how colleagues would react. Because she really wanted to keep her head covered inside the office as well as outside, she overcame her hesitancy, and now always covers her head with a dupatta. 'We are moving further and further away from our religion', she told me, 'and I don't think that this is right.' Tasneem made this decision despite the fact that none of her female colleagues veiled. I even observed some of the obviously upper-class designers wearing sleeveless kameez; something unthinkable for women from the lower classes. Furthermore, Tasneem's veiling was rather symbolic. With the way she used her dupatta, half of her head and hair were still visible. Still, such practices of re-veiling indicate the inner conflicts office workers face and the difficulties they have in accommodating their conservative lower-middle-class life world with the public male space they work in.

(Re-)Organization of Productive and Reproductive Work

It has already been pointed out that a strict division of labour exists in families among the lower-middle classes—as across all sections of Pakistani society—which allocates all work outside the chardivari to men and all work which has to be performed inside the chardivari to women. Thus, reproductive work is considered the sole responsibility of women, the only exception being those reproductive tasks that cannot be performed inside the chardivari, like shopping. The question which arises here is how female employment in the office sector, in which the working hours stretch from morning till evening, affects the organization of reproductive work within the household.

Reproductive work is indeed being reorganized in families where one or more women enter the labour market. However, this reorganization is taking place among the female family members, while the gender-specific division of labour, which ascribes the reproductive work to women, has remained untouched. Furthermore, different patterns regarding how reproductive work is organized are developing. They are dependent upon with gendered composition of the family, i.e. the availability of other women in the household, as well as the structural position of the office workers in the family hierarchy.

Unmarried office workers have the fewest difficulties reconciling their employment with reproductive work as mothers usually take over a great part of the reproductive work once the daughter enters the labour market. Additionally, other women are commonly available in the families who perform the reproductive work and thus relieve the gainfully-employed female family members from the 'double burden' of being a working woman who is at the same time responsible for the reproductive work inside the chardivari. These are sisters who are attending school or single sisters who have already completed their education but are not gainfully employed, as well as *bhabhis* (the brothers' wives), who are traditionally responsible for most of the reproductive work once they become members of the in-laws' family. Most of the unmarried office workers told me that they did not do any housework at all on working days but that they helped the other female family members with household chores like cleaning, cooking, and washing clothes, on weekends and other holidays.

Only in cases in which female family members are few in number do unmarried office workers face difficulties reconciling their employment with reproductive work, because there are no other women in the family to take over these tasks. Andeela, who is the eldest of six children and the only daughter, has this problem: Andeela's mother is a housewife but she is frail and sickly and cannot perform much reproductive work. Since there are no other women in the family most of the reproductive work has to be performed by Andeela early in the mornings or late in the evenings when she returns from the office. Once, when her parents were away for some weeks, Andeela took responsibility for the whole household. This included the cleaning and dusting of the house, preparation of the meals, and washing and ironing the clothes of all six family members. It was considered out of question that her five brothers, who were all still students, should assist her in getting all the household chores done.

Married office workers have by far the greatest problems in coordinating their occupation with reproductive tasks because as *bahus* (daughters-in-law) they are at the bottom of the family hierarchy and are expected to do most of the reproductive work, even when there are other women (sisters-in-law, mother-in-law) in the household. As a consequence, reproductive work is hardly reorganized and women are left to manage the bulk of the reproductive work of the whole (joint) family as well as their office work.

Asieh's family consists of seven members: her mother-in-law, father-in-law, husband, one brother- and one sister-in-law, who are both still unmarried, and her baby son. Her mother-in-law is a primary school teacher in a government school nearby and her sister-in-law, who is about 20 years old, did not want to continue with her education after her FA and just stays at home. Nevertheless, being the *bahu*, Asieh is responsible for most of the reproductive work. Asieh left her job shortly before the wedding, and did not consider it too strenuous to take over all the household chores in her new home. Problems emerged, though, when her husband lost his job one year after her marriage and Asieh expressed the desire to rejoin the advertising agency she had been working for until her marriage:

> In the beginning my mother-in-law, etc. didn't like it. 'And who is going to do the housework?' The problem was not so much the job...but who will do the housework. So I said, 'don't worry, I'll do it in the evenings after coming from the office.' Then she was quiet....Actually, when I got married into this family they had in

mind that 'she will stay at home. We all leave in the morning and when we come home she will have cooked the food and done all the housework.' Here, when the bahu comes into the house everybody sees her as a servant. They do not consider her a member of the family. Before the marriage they have very high expectations....They will say, 'now she is coming and I do not have to work any longer.' The mother-in-law will say that 'the bahu is coming and I won't have any responsibilities any longer' (11 May 1997, p. 6ff.).

As a consequence, even after becoming gainfully employed again Asieh continued to do most of the reproductive work. I often visited her in the evenings and on public holidays and she was always busy with cooking, washing the dishes, cleaning the house, washing the clothes of all seven family members under a tap in the courtyard, or preparing tea and snacks for visitors who would drop in frequently. Male family members are not involved in reproductive work, and (female) domestics, when lower-middle-class families can afford them at all, are only employed for a few hours per day for household chores like sweeping the floor and courtyard, washing the clothes, and dusting. As a consequence, daily negotiation processes regarding who will do what kind of reproductive work take place among the female family members:

Most of the problems at home are between bahu, sas and nand, that is, who does which [reproductive] work. When the nand does some [reproductive] work then it will be said, 'why did the nand do this work and not the bahu?' (21 March 1997)

To conclude, reproductive work is not primarily organized according to the individual female family members' capabilities but, rather, according to their structural position in the family. Therefore, even though Asieh financially contributed to the family budget, her structural position as bahu—and not her status as a working woman and income earner—was the decisive factor for the allocation of reproductive work to her. This situation made it difficult for her to handle her job and the reproductive work:

> Working women in Pakistan have great difficulties managing the job and their household. I have so many problems. The baby is small and stays awake the whole night. After very short periods he wakes up and wants to have milk. Then I feed him and the whole night passes this way. Then I have to get up early, change the nappy, etc. I have to do everything. I do a bit of housework and then I leave for the office at about 10 o'clock. If I don't do the [house]work then the sas will talk [negatively]. When I come home [in the evenings] I directly change my clothes and start with the housework. I cook the food for dinner....These people do not see that I am also a human being, that 'we are also at home and we can also do some housework.' They don't see that I work [in an office], and they don't show any sympathy...[but] if I don't do the [house]work they won't allow me to keep my job (15 Jan. 1997, p. 5).

Although Asieh's sister-in-law did not work or study, she occupied a structurally higher position in the family and was, therefore, not expected to perform much reproductive work. She took over the easy tasks: for example, she took care of the baby during Asieh's working hours and played with him in the evenings and on weekends when Asieh was busy with reproductive work. But even this division of tasks did not always go smoothly in the structurally conflictive relationship between the sister-in-law, daughter-in-law, and mother-in-law. Once Asieh came to the office crying because she had had a dispute with her sister-in-law concerning the babysitting. 'We had a quarrel and she said, 'I can not always look after your child, I am not your servant.' 'But what shall I do? I don't know what to do, I do not have any alternatives. Maybe she thinks that I go to the office every day in order to enjoy myself. But there are no childcare facilities for working women at all. APWA [All Pakistan Women's Association] has one, but that is very far from here. How can I travel there daily? And my mother is a teacher. She cannot take care of my son.'

Indeed, the sister-in-law, supported by her mother, was not obliged to take over the babysitting of her nephew. This was seen as a generous gesture towards her brother's wife rather than her due share in the family's reproductive work. Asieh was nevertheless expected to support her family with her income and not to keep her salary to herself. The money she earned was utilized for the repayment of debts her husband had incurred when he attempted to set up a business, while her husband spent his income on the maintenance of the family. When he lost his job again, Asieh had to give a great part of her salary to her mother-in-law to cover her own, her husband's and her baby's monthly expenses. Thus, the reproductive work that Asieh performed did not exempt her from financial contributions she had to make. But neither did her salary, which went into the family budget, relieve her from the reproductive work she was expected to perform as bahu. Asieh was of course frustrated by this, feeling that, once married, women should not continue to work:

> If someone can afford that, I also say that his wife should stay at home; because otherwise the work will be doubled. For the woman it becomes very difficult...and when she lives with the in-laws it is even more difficult (11 May 1997, p. 12).

Being an office worker and, at the same time, responsible for most of the reproductive work is a double burden that all married office workers bear. In my study, older married office workers were slightly better off in comparison. They too had the sole responsibility for the reproductive work of the family, but they could delegate a part of that to their daughters. This was evident in Firdous' case and Ghazal's, whose daughter was barely eight or nine years old.

The difficulties in coordinating reproductive work with employment not only made daily life very strenuous for the married office workers, it also affected their performance at the workplace significantly. Asieh, for example, frequently reached the office late; she also often had to leave earlier or take a day off due to familial responsibilities. Whenever her baby or other family members became ill she was expected to stay at home to nurse them which meant she had to take a leave from the office. Her employer, who knew about her double burden, nevertheless admonished her several times for not sticking to the work times and he complained that she could not continue taking so many leaves and coming late so often.

Furthermore, at the time I conducted the empirical research computers were being introduced in Asieh's office. Asieh's employer had already familiarized himself with computer designing and he urged her to take up some evening courses to learn how to operate the designing packages. However, Asieh could not take his advice because she could not spare any time in the evenings. Additionally, the fees for a computer course would have been at least several thousand rupees, but Asieh was expected to contribute her salary to the household budget and only keep a small amount to herself for bus fares, lunch at the office, etc. Spending two to three monthly salaries on a computer course would not have been approved of by her family.

Since her boss could not give her designing work any longer, she slowly took over more routine work like pasting and cutting, which was actually below her skill level. Later on, shortly before I finished my research in the fall of 1997, a new male employee who was familiar with computer designing—and who stuck to the working times—was employed for a salary of Rs 3000. In other words, he received Rs 500 more than Asieh got although he was formally less qualified and experienced than her, apart from knowing how to operate a computer. He then took over most of the—now computerized—designing Asieh had done earlier.

The double burden married office workers like Asieh are confronted with is another crucial impediment for the development of long-term employment perspectives of unmarried office workers. They know that after their marriage they will not be able to change the organization of reproductive work in the household, particularly their primary responsibility as bahus for the reproductive work of the (in-laws') family. As a consequence, working women prefer to leave their jobs at the time they get married, if it is financially manageable.

NOTES

1. Initially I had interviewed both Umbreen and her sister Rubina but had not selected them for my sample.
2. Marriages are preferably arranged within the extended family, particularly among cousins. This cultural practice provides some social security for the woman because the mother-in-law-to-be is usually at the same time her aunt, and both families have already established close relations due to their kinship ties. The next preference is then to arrange the marriage outside of the extended family but inside the biradari. The great majority of office workers in my sample stated that marriages were arranged outside of the extended family but not outside of their biradari.
3. The latest age for women to get married is considered to be about 25 years. After this age finding a marriage partner becomes difficult because women are perceived to be beyond the marriageable age. This rule is less strict for women from the upper and upper-middle classes who can still find marriage matches at the age of 27 or 28. Among the lower-middle classes, however, women are usually married off earlier, i.e. the age of 22, 23, after completing their school or college education. Andeela, who is 21 years old, told me that in her family women get married at the age of 18 or 19, and the neighbours and relatives asked her parents why they continued to keep her in the house instead of marrying her off. This way of thinking mirrors the widespread attitude among the lower-middle classes that once a girl's education is completed, there is no longer any need to keep her in the house—or even to send her to work—but parents should fulfill their responsibilities and marry her off.
4. On this point see also Dannecker's study on female garment workers in Bangladesh (1998).
5. Of course, a gradual change in gender relations, and subsequently in the gender order of society takes place in the offices as well as in public male spaces in general. These changes, however, remain to a large extent outside of the immediate life world of the families of the very women who are causing them, viz., the female office workers.

7

CONCLUSION

The Emergence of Female Office Workers: 'A Trojan Horse for Pakistani Society?'

The study has analysed the inter-relationship between female employment and its societal context in urban Pakistan. It has shown that the market is embedded in society and, more importantly, also that embeddedness is gendered. The gender-specific embeddedness of female employment ('gendered embeddedness') is hereby characterized, first, by the interactions of women's work with their everyday life (including their primary responsibility for household work), and, second, by its complementarity to their life world. Therefore, an understanding of the 'women's economy' requires the contextualization of women's work in their life world. By the same token, the workplace too is culturally embedded, and it has to be analysed in its societal context.

Changes in the gendered structure of the labour market can be observed in many areas; and they are caused by all sections of Pakistani society: (Westernized) upper- and upper-middle-class women, though still heavily concentrated in a few 'female professions' (particularly teaching and medicine), are choosing new, unconventional careers like banking, journalism, and law; lower-class women, who are commonly employed as home-based piece-rate workers, are—though presently in very limited numbers—starting to leave the confines of the chardivari to work as traders at Sunday bazaars, or as hawkers in upper-(middle-)class shopping areas, where they sell items such as hair ribbons, hair-clips, or toiletries. These informal sector activities require the mingling of the sexes, and are therefore running across the purdah rules, but they are much better paying than home-based piece-rate work.

However, my hypothesis is that the most emphatic changes with regard to the gendered structure of the labour market—and the gender order of society at large—are presently being caused by the lower-middle classes. Sandwiched between the (Westernized) upper and upper-middle classes on the one hand, and the lower classes on the other hand, the lower-middle classes are a very conservative section of Pakistani society. Their life world is pervaded by purdah, the segregation of the life worlds of men and women, and the sexualization of gender relations outside the kinship system. Keeping women out of the labour market has been one important characteristic (and status symbol) of this section of society. Since the lower-middle classes have been most affected by the worsening economic conditions, women are beginning to reorient their education. Fewer and fewer women are acquiring formal degrees that have a high social value (because they constitute a crucial means of differentiating oneself from the uneducated lower classes, and improve the woman's standing in the 'marriage market') but are of not much use for later employment. Instead, they are shifting toward pursuing a market-oriented education that will open the doors to well-paying jobs. Furthermore, lower-middle-class women are increasingly entering the labour market and are starting to work in the office sector in the few middle-level occupations that are open to them, i.e. in secretarial and technical office jobs, as receptionists, secretaries, telephone operators, draftswomen, computer operators, designers, etc.

In the course of this study the interfaces and interactions between the life world and work world of lower-middle-class female office workers—or, in other words, the gendered embeddedness of female employment in the office sector—have been studied thoroughly. These women straddle between their own conservative life world, in which, due to the purdah-rules, no modes of communication exist between men and women outside of the kinship system, and the de-segregated working environment in the offices, which is an extremely gendered male space. They use many strategies, derived from their own life world, to maneuver in the office sector, to appropriate public (male) space in the offices, and to accommodate the purdah-system to the office environment. Concepts of purdah, including the sexualization of gender relations outside the kinship system, are perpetuated inside the offices, but women are also initiating the redefinition of gender relations, and new gender constructs are developing at the workplace. Formerly unknown (de-sexualized) modes of communication between male and female colleagues are emerging, and gender relations that were formerly perceived as sexual ones per se are now open to renegotiation.

It has become clear that the purdah-system—which is a central feature of the gender order of Pakistani society—is far from constituting a simplistic division between the private (female) and the public (male) sphere. Purdah is rather to be seen as a complex set of rules that governs all interactions between the sexes (Shaheed 1989: 1), in the private realm of the house as well as in the public sphere. Yet, the purdah-system is flexible and has many breaches, and purdah-rules can be redefined and adjusted to new situations. Therefore, the boundaries between male and female spaces are constantly being (re)negotiated. During the economic transformation processes, new socio-economic opportunities are being created for women, and, through their agency, women are taking advantage of these to enlarge their room for maneuver, and trying to define ways to embed these new spaces in society at large.

There is indeed a counteraction in response to the present societal transformation processes, which manifests in an Islamization process that is supported by considerable (conservative) sections of Pakistani society. According to a recent survey among the population of major cities in Pakistan, 32 per cent of the respondents—41 per cent of the men and 24 per cent of the women—were willing to accept restrictions imposed on women, as is currently done by the Taliban in Afghanistan. The figures were particularly high (namely, 41.7 per cent) in Lahore, where the empirical research was conducted, and in Islamabad (36.1 per cent). Both are cities in which women have started to participate in public life in recent years. In cities in which women remain absent from the public sphere, like Peshawar or Quetta, the figures were lower, with 16.1 per cent and 11.1 per cent respectively (*Lashker*, 18 Nov. 1997). These results indicate how deeply-split Pakistani society is regarding the current trends toward the de-segregation of public (male) spaces, including the workplace, and how much disapproval broad (conservative) sections of society are exhibiting of the societal transformation processes that are taking place, particularly the rapid changes in the gender order of society in some cities, due to women's entry into the labour market (and the public sphere in general). Here, lower-middle-class female office workers, themselves coming from very conservative sections of Pakistani society, are crucial agents of change. Their increasing presence and visibility in public (male) spaces questions, even threatens, the hitherto existing gender order of Pakistani society, or, as Tasneem said in an interview, 'during the last four or five years many changes have occurred. Earlier, women did not leave the house at all, but nowadays they have become much more visible. The transport problem has remained, but earlier we only sat on the [two] front seats [reserved for female passengers], and when these were occupied, we waited for the next bus. Nowadays, we also peep through the back door and sit down in the back [together with the male passengers] if there is no other possibility.'

Just how far lower-middle-class women's entry into the 'work world' will bring forward societal changes in gender relations will depend on future economic trends, i.e. on the number of women who will join the labour market, particularly the office sector, and actively contribute to the current transformation processes of Pakistani society. However, it seems clear that the rapid integration of lower-middle-class women into the urban labour market that can currently be detected is very likely to shake (and probably even transform) the existing gender order of society, especially by facilitating the development of new modes of communication between men and women in the office sector, as well as in public spaces in general. During recent years socio-economic changes have been accelerating, particularly in the urban areas. Women have started to work in general stores, where they are employed as saleswomen and cashiers, and where they work in various departments until closing time, late in the night. They are now employed in the fast food restaurants of multinational companies, and are recruited as bus hostesses by private travel agencies for their long-distance bus routes—all jobs that require extensive public dealing and exposure. Furthermore, many lower-middle-class married women with children are gainfully employed.

Thus, in families in which female employment was out of the question (and considered a disgrace) only a few years ago, women now have more room for maneuver. New, socially-acceptable gender images and a diversity of perspectives regarding lower-middle-class (working) women, their way of life, and life planning are emerging; and families can already be found in which one daughter strictly adheres to purdah, wears a burqa, and is not gainfully employed, while her sister decides to enroll in a market-oriented training course, and become an office worker.

To conclude, lower-middle-class office workers are active agents of change in the labour market (i.e. the office sector), in their own conservative class, and in society at large. In development sociology, market studies on working women have thus far focused on female factory workers in export-oriented industries, and on women working in the informal sector. Too little attention has been devoted to (lower-middle-class) women in the office sector. Many questions have not yet been addressed, for example: How do these women bridge the gap between their own life world and the work world, and how are their occupations embedded in their everyday life? How do the women position themselves during, and in the wake of, contradictory developments such as (also globally evolving) Islamization processes on the one hand, and economic changes on the other hand? How do they seize emerging new opportunities for themselves to renegotiate space and, through their agency, enlarge their room for maneuver? And to what extent do the office workers thereby change office cultures and gender relations at the workplace and beyond? This study begins to address these issues and thus contributes to 'engendering the embeddedness' of the market and to showing how the gendered structure of the economy is constantly being renegotiated, especially during ongoing transformation processes.

GLOSSARY*

abadi	residential area
ata	flour used for making rotis
awaaz	voice
azaan	call for prayers which is mostly made through the loudspeakers of the mosques five times a day
BA/B.Sc.	college graduation; students graduate after fourteen years of formal schooling in the Pakistani educational system
baba	old man
badmaash	scoundrel, villain
baji	elder sister
bazaar	local market
beta, bete	son, form of address which is also used for girls and women
beti	daughter
bhabhi	brother's wife
bhai	brother
bibi	polite form of address to a woman
biradari	shows the ancestry of a family; the 'Sayyeds', for example, claim to be descendants of the Prophet Muhammad (PBUH), one reason for their being strong opponents of exogamous marriages; other common castes are Rajput, Arain, Qureshi, Pathan, Sheikh, Mughal, Jat, etc.
bahu	daughter-in-law
burqa	a long, often black or brown coat that covers the whole body and often the face of the woman and is worn over the traditional shalwar-kameez
chacha	father's younger brother
chaddor	a big veil which covers the whole body of the woman

---

* All terms here have been italicized at their first occurrence in the text.

chaddor aur	
chardivari	'the veil and the four walls of the house'
chaukidar	a guard, watchman
deverani	the wife of the husband's younger brother
dholak	small drum which is played by women and girls, particularly at engagement and wedding ceremonies
dupatta	a scarf or veil which is smaller than the chaddor and which covers the upper part of the woman's body; it is worn by women in addition to the shalwar-kameez
dupatte	plural of dupatta
Eid	Muslim festival; two Eids (Eid-ul-Fitar and Eid-ul-Azha) are celebrated every year
FA/F.Sc.	Intermediate college degree which is obtained after twelve years of formal schooling
gharelo	derived from the word 'ghar' (house) and is ascribed to women—married and unmarried — who do not work or study but just stay at home
hadith	sayings of the Prophet Muhammad (PBUH)
Hafiz-e-Quran	a person who has memorized the whole Quran
Haj	the mandatory holy pilgrimage to Mecca made by Muslims
hamaam	traditional bathhouses which can be found in many Muslim societies
izzat	honour; respect
izzatdaar	respectable; honourable
jumma bazaar	Friday market; takes place on Sundays nowadays after the public holiday was changed from Friday to Sunday in the beginning of 1997
kameez	traditional long loose shirt that reaches down to the knees and is worn by men and women
khala	mother's sister
kismet	fate
lakh	one hundred thousand
larka	boy; man who is still unmarried
larki	girl; woman who is still unmarried
madrassa	religious school
mahangaai	inflation; increase in prices

maharam	men and women who are not allowed to marry each other according to Islamic law
mahol	the social side of a set-up, e.g. an office, a family, or even a society
majazi khuda	'Imaginary god', a term often used for the husband
matriculation	also 'matric'; certificate which is obtained after X Class and which is the entrance qualification for admission to colleges
maulvi	religious leader; usually in charge of a mosque
mehndi	henna; it is also the name for the first day of a wedding ceremony which only the women attend
mohalla	residential area; neighbourhood
mohalle	plural of mohalla
mullah	see 'maulvi'; in comparison to 'maulvi', 'mullah' rather carries a negative connotation
na-maharam	all men and women who are allowed to marry each other according to Islamic Law
nand	husband's sister
nazar	sight
niqab	face veil that covers the whole face, often including the eyes
nikahnama	marriage contract
PCO	Public Call Office
peon	unskilled (and often uneducated) clerical worker; 'dogsbody'
phuphi	father's sister
purdah	literally 'veil'; stands for the concept of gender segregation in Muslim (also in some Hindu) societies
rickshaw	small motorized vehicle which can transport up to three persons
roti	bread
rupee	Pakistani currency; according to official rates one US dollar is equal to approximately 51 Rupees (1/1999)
sas	mother-in-law
sahib	polite form of address to a man which follows his first name

shalwar	traditional long loose pants which are worn both by men and women
shalwar-kameez	traditional dress consisting of a shalwar and a kameez
sunna	the life and deeds of the Prophet Muhammad (PBUH)
tandoor	big ovens where rotis are baked for public sale
topi	a cap without a brim worn by Muslim men
umraah	Pilgrimage to Mecca that is not mandatory

BIBLIOGRAPHY

Abercombie, Nicholas et al. (1994). *The Penguin Dictionary of Sociology*. London, Penguin, 3rd edn.

Abu-Lughod, Lila (1993). *Writing Women's Worlds: Bedouin Stories*. Berkeley, University of California Press.

Acker, Joan (1991). 'Hierarchies, Jobs, Bodies: A Theory of Gendered Organizations'. In *The Social Construction of Gender*, eds. Judith Lorber and Susan A. Farrell, pp. 162–79. Newbury Park, California, SAGE.

Addledon, Jonathan S. (1992). *Undermining the Centre: The Gulf Migration and Pakistan*. Karachi, Oxford University Press.

Ahmed, Leila (1992). *Women and Gender in Islam: Historical Roots of a Modern Debate*. New Haven, Yale.

Akhtar, Rakhshanda (1986). 'Women, Employment Patterns and Income Generation—a Case Study of the Women of a "Kachi Abadi"'. In *Pakistan Manpower Review*, vol. 12, no. 2, pp. 58–66.

Alavi, Hamza (1991). 'Pakistani Women in a Changing Society'. In *Economy and Culture in Pakistan: Migrants and Cities in a Muslim Society*, eds. Hastings Donnan and Pnina Werbner, pp. 124–42. New York, St. Martin's Press.

Amin, Tahir (1995). 'Pakistan in 1994'. *In Asian Survey*, vol. XXXV, no. 2, pp. 140–46.

Ardener, Shirley, ed. (1995). *Money-go-rounds: the importance of rotating savings and credit associations for women*. Oxford, Berg.

Arregui, Marivi and Clara Baetz (1991). 'Free Trade Zones and Women Workers'. In *Changing Perceptions: Writing on Gender and Development*, eds. Tina Wallace and Candida March, pp. 30–38. Oxford, Oxfam.

Bakker, Isabella (1994). 'Engendering Macroeconomic Policy Reform in the Era of Global Restructuring and Adjustment'. In *The Strategic Silence: Gender and Economic Policy*, ed. ibid., pp. 1–30. Ottawa, The North-South Institute.

Balchin, Cassandra (1996). *Women, Law, and Society: An Action Manual for NGOs*. Lahore, Shirkat Gah.

Bassiri, Nasrin (1992). 'Frauen in der Islamischen Republik Iran'. In *Fatimas Töchter: Frauen im Islam*, ed. Edith Laudowicz, pp. 62–74. Köln, Papyrossa.

Bauer, Kirsten (1994). *Stichwort Frauen im Islam*. München, Wilhelm Heyne.

Baylies, Carolyn and Caroline Wright (1993). 'Female Labour in the Textile and Clothing Industry of Lesotho'. In *African Affairs*, vol. 92, pp. 577–91.

Berger, Peter and Thomas Luckmann (1979). *The Social Construction of Reality*. Middlesex, Penguin.

Block, Fred (1990). 'Political Choice and the multiple "logics" of capital'. In *Structures of Capital: The Social Organization of the Economy*, eds. Sharon Zukin and Paul DiMaggio, pp. 293–310. Cambridge, Cambridge University Press.

Börgel, Hannelore (1992). 'Bericht über Studien, Förderungs- und Projektansätze der Bi- und Multilateralen Geber in Pakistan'. Unpublished study for the German Technical Cooperation, Berlin, 27 pp.

Braig, Marianne (1992). *Mexiko - ein anderer Weg der Moderne. Weibliche Erwerbsarbeit, häusliche Dienste und Organisation des Alltags*. Köln, Böhlau.

––––––– (1997). 'Frauen in der internationalen Arbeitsteilung'. In *Begegnungen und Einmischungen. Festschrift für Renate Rott zum 60. Geburtstag*, ed. Marianne Braig et al., pp. 109–32.

Cagatay, Nilüfer et. al. (1995). 'Introduction'. In *Gender, Adjustment and Macroeconomics*, eds. ibid., pp. 1827–38. World Development (Special Issue), vol. 23, no. 11.

–––––––, eds. (1995). *Gender, Adjustment and Macroeconomics*. World Development (Special Issue), vol. 23, no. 11.

Callon, Michel, ed. (1998). *The Laws of the Market*. Oxford [et al.], Blackwell [et al.].

Cameron, John and Mohammad Irfan (1991). *Enabling people to help themselves: An Employment and Human Resource Development Strategy for Pakistan in the 1990s*. ILO-Artep.

Cebel, Malek (1995). 'Der Stoff aus dem der Schleier ist'. In *Die Zeit*, no. 9, Berlin.

Choudhary, M.A. et al. (1989). *Skill Generation and Entrepreneurship Development under 'Ostad-Shagird' System in Pakistan*. Friedrich-Ebert-Stiftung, Islamabad.

Coleman, James C. (1988). 'Social Capital and the Creation of Human Capital'. *In American Journal of Sociology*, vol. 94 (Supplement), pp. 95–120.

Dahl, Tove Stang (1997). *The Muslim Family: A Study of Women's Rights in Islam*. Oslo, Scandinavian University Press.

Dannecker, Petra (1998). 'Between Conformity and Resistance: Women Garment Workers in Bangladesh'. Unpublished Ph.D. thesis, Faculty of Sociology, Bielefeld University, Germany.

Darwisch, Khalil and Karlhans Liebl (1991). *Die 'neue' Verschleierung der arabischen Frau: eine Untersuchung zu den Gründen für die Renaissance des 'el-Hijab' in Jordanien*. Pfaffenweiler, Centaurus.

Davis, Joyce M. (1997). *Between Jihad and Salaam: Profiles in Islam*. London, MacMillan.

DiMaggio, Paul (1977-78): 'Market Structure, the Creative Process, and Popular Culture: Towards an Organizational Reinterpretation of Mass Culture Theory'. *Journal of Popular Culture*, vol. 11, pp. 436–52.

Dore, Ronald (1992). 'Goodwill and the Spirit of Market Capitalism'. In *The Sociology of Economic Life*, eds. Richard Swedberg and Mark Granovetter, pp. 159–80. Boulder/Oxford, Westview.

Dunn, Leith L. (1995). 'Free Trade Zones: Issues and Strategies'. In *A diplomacy of the oppressed: New directions in International Feminism*, ed. Georgina Ashworth, pp. 90–103. London/New Jersey, Zed Books Ltd.

Ecevit, Yildiz (1991). 'Shop floor control: the ideological construction of Turkish women factory workers'. In *Working Women: International Perspectives on Labor and Gender Ideology*, eds. Nanneke Redclift et al., pp. 56–78. London, Routledge.

Elson, Diane (1991). 'Structural Adjustment: its effect on women'. In *Changing Perceptions: Writing on Gender and Development*, eds. Tina Wallace and Candida March, pp. 39–53. Oxford, Oxfam.

——— (1993a). 'Feministische Ansätze in der Entwicklungsökonomie'. *Prokla, Zeitschrift für kritische Sozialwissenschaft*, vol. 23, no. 4, pp. 529–50.

——— (1993b). 'Gender-Aware Analysis and development economics'. *Journal of International Development*, vol. 5, no. 2, pp. 237–47.

——— (1995). 'Gender Awareness in Modeling Structural Adjustment'. In *Gender, Adjustment and Macroeconomics*, eds,

Nilüfer Cagatay et al., pp. 1851–68. World Development (Special Issue), vol. 23, no. 11.

—— and R. McGee (1995). 'Gender Equality, Bilateral Program Assistance and Structural Adjustment: Policy and Procedures'. In *Gender, Adjustment and Macroeconomics*, eds, Nilüfer Cagatay et al., pp. 1987–94. World Development (Special Issue), vol. 23, no. 11.

Elwert, Georg and Diana Wong (1981). 'Thesen zum Verhältnis von Subsistenzproduktion und Warenproduktion in der Dritten Welt.' In *Subsistenzproduktion und Akkumulation*, eds. Arbeitsgruppe Bielefelder Entwicklungssoziologen, pp. 255–78. Saarbrücken, breitenbach, 2nd edn.

Elwert, Georg (1987). 'Ausdehnung der Käuflichkeit und Einbettung der Wirtschaft'. In *Soziologie wirtschaftlichen Handelns*, ed. Klaus Heinemann, pp. 300–21. Opladen, Westdeutscher Verlag.

—— (1991). 'Gabe; Reziprozität und Warentausch. Überlegungen zu einigen Ausdrücken und Begriffen'. In *Ethnologie im Widerstreit. Kontroversen über Macht, Geschäft, Geschlecht in fremden Kulturen*, eds. Eberhard Berg et al., pp. 159–77. München, Trickster.

Elwert-Kretschmer, Karola (1985). *Haushalte zwischen Markt und Verwandtschaft. Entdörflichung und soziale Differenzierung in einem malayischen Dorf.* Saarbrücken, breitenbach.

Esser, Hartmut (1994). 'Explanatory Sociology'. In *Sociology in Germany*, ed. Bernhard Schäfers, pp. 177–90. Sociology Special Edition 3, Opladen, Leske und Budrich.

Evers, Hans-Dieter (1994). 'The traders' dilemma: a theory of the social transformation of markets and society'. In *The Moral Economy of Trade: Ethnicity and Developing Markets*, eds. Hans-Dieter Evers and Heiko Schrader, pp. 7–14. London/New York, Routledge.

—— (1995). *Globale Märkte und Soziale Transformation.* Working Paper No. 234, Sociology of Development Research Center, Bielefeld University, Germany.

—— and Tilman Schiel (1981). 'Expropriation der unmittelbaren Produzenten oder Ausdehnung der Subsistenzwirtschaft—Thesen zur bäuerlichen und städtischen Subsistenzreproduktion'. In *Subsistenzproduktion und Akkumulation*, eds. Arbeitsgruppe Bielefelder Entwicklungssoziologen, pp. 279–332. Saarbrücken, breitenbach, 2nd edn.

_____ and Heiko Schrader (1994). 'Introduction'. In *The Moral Economy of Trade: Ethnicity and Developing Markets*, eds. ibid., pp. 3–6. London/New York, Routledge.

_____ (1994). *The Moral Economy of Trade: Ethnicity and Developing Markets*. London/New York, Routledge.

Farukhi, Kemal A. (1987). 'Pakistan: The Islamic Government and Society'. In *Islam in Asia: religion, politics and society*, ed. John L. Esposito, pp. 53–96. New York, Oxford University Press.

Fazwi El-Solh, Camilla and Judy Mabro (1994). 'Islam and Muslim Women'. In *Muslim Women's Choices: Religious Belief and Social Reality*, eds. ibid., pp. 1–32. Oxford, Berg.

Fiege, Karin and Gabriele Zdunnek (1993). 'Einleitung'. In *Methoden—Hilfestellung oder Korsett? Erfahrungen mit empirischer Sozialforschung in Afrika, Asien und Lateinamerika*, eds. ibid., pp. 9–20. Saarbrücken, breitenbach.

Fischer Weltalmanach '99. Frankfurt/Main, Fischer Tachenbuch-Verlag, 1998.

French, Susan et al. (1994). 'Nursing as a career choice for women in Pakistan'. In *Journal of Advanced Nursing*, vol. 19, no. 1, pp. 140–51.

Friedland, Roger and A.F. Robertson, eds. (1990). *Beyond the Marketplace: Rethinking Economy and Society*. New York, Walter de Gruyter.

Fukuyama, Francis (1995). *Trust: The Social Virtues and the Creation of Prosperity*. New York, The Free Press.

Fuller, Graham E. (1991). *Islamic Fundamentalism in Pakistan: Its Character and Prospects*, prepared for the Under Secretary of Defense for Policy, Santa Monica, Rand.

Gerani, Shahin (1996). *Women and Fundamentalism: Islam and Christianity*. New York/London, Garland.

Göle, Nilüfer (1996). *The Forbidden Modern: Civilization and Veiling*. Michigan, Michigan University Press.

Goodwin, Jane (1995). *Price of Honor: Muslim Women lift the Veil of Silence on the Islamic World*. Boston, Little, Brown.

Government of Pakistan (1984). *Census Report of Pakistan*. Population Census Organisation, Statistics Division, Karachi.

_____ (1989a). *The Seventh Five Year Plan 1988-93*. Planning Commission, Islamabad.

_____ (1989b). *Report of the National Manpower Commission*. Planning Commission, Islamabad.

_____ (1990). *Piler Survey: Women in the Industrial Labour Force.* Statistics Division, Islamabad.

_____ (1994). *Eighth Five-Year Plan (1993-98).* Planning Commission, Islamabad.

_____ (1995a). *Labour Force Survey 1993-94.* Federal Bureau of Statistics, Statistics Division, Karachi, The Manager of Publications.

_____ (1995b). *Pakistan Statistical Yearbook 1994.* Federal Bureau of Statistics, Economic Affairs & Statistics Division, Karachi, The Manager of Publications.

_____ (1998a). *50 Years of Pakistan in Statistics. Volume II (1947-97).* Federal Bureau of Statistics, Statistics Division, March 1998.

_____ (1998b). *Labour Force Survey 1996-97.* Federal Bureau of Statistics, Statistics Division, Karachi, The Manager of Publications.

_____ (1998c). *Population and Housing Census of Pakistan 1998 (Provisional Results).* Population Census Organization, Statistics Division, July 1998.

_____ (1999a). *Economic Survey 1998-99.* Finance Division, Adviser's Wing, Islamabad.

_____ (1999b). *Pakistan Statistical Yearbook 1998-99.* Federal Bureau of Statistics, Economic Affairs & Statistics Division, Karachi, The Manager of Publications, November.

Granovetter, Mark (1992 [1985]). 'The Sociological and Economic Approaches to Labour Market Analysis: A Social Structural View'. In *The Sociology of Economic Life*, eds. Richard Swedberg and Mark Granovetter, pp. 233–64. Boulder/Oxford, Westview.

_____ (1992). 'Economic Institutions as Social Constructions: A Framework for Analysis'. *Acta Sociologica*, vol. 35, pp. 3–11.

Guenther, Ursula (1993). *Die Frau in der Revolte. Fatima Mernissis feministische Gesellschaftskritik.* Mitteilungen des Deutschen Orient-Instituts No. 46. Hamburg, Deutsches Orient-Institut.

Habermas, Juergen (1981). *Theorie des kommunikativen Handelns Vol. 1, Zur Kritik der funktionalistischen Vernunft.* Frankfurt/Main, Suhrkamp.

Haeri, Shahla (1995). 'The Politics of Dishonor: Rape and Power in Pakistan'. In *Faith & Freedom: Women's Human Rights in the Muslim World*, ed. Mahnaz Afkhami, pp. 161–74. London, I.B. Tauris.

Hafeez, Sabeeha (1981). *The Metropolitan Woman in Pakistan: Studies.* Karachi, Royal Book Company.

Hafeez, Sabeeha (1983). *Women in Industry*. Women's Division, Islamabad.

Hamilton, Gary H. and Nicole Woolsey Biggart (1992 [1988]). 'Market, Culture, and Authority: A Comparative Analysis of Management and Organization in the Far East'. In *The Sociology of Economic Life*, eds. Richard Swedberg and Mark Granovetter, pp. 181–224. Boulder/Oxford, Westview.

Harcourt, Wendy (1994). 'The globalization of the economy'. *Focus on Gender*, vol. 2, no. 3, pp. 6–14.

Hartmann, Jörg (1981). *Subsistenzkrise und Rebellion: eine Kritik der 'moral economy' bäuerlicher Gesellschaften*. Working paper No. 4, Sociology of Development Research Centre, Bielefeld University, Germany.

Hasan, Pervaiz (1998). *Pakistan's Economy at the Crossroads: Past Policies and Present Imperatives*. Karachi, Oxford University Press.

Hassan, Riffat (1987). 'Women in the Context of Change and Confrontation within Muslim Communities'. In *Women of Faith in Dialogue*. ed. Virginia R. Mollenkott, pp. 96–109. New York, Crossroads.

————— (1991a). 'Muslim Women and Post-Patriarchal Islam'. In *After Patriarchy: Feminist Transformations of the World Religions*, eds. Paula Cooley et al., pp. 39–69. Maryknoll, Orbis Books.

————— (1991b). 'The Issue of Woman-Man Equality in the Islamic Tradition'. In *Women's and Men's Liberation: Testimonies of Spirit*, eds. Leonard Grab et al., pp. 65–82. New York, Greenwood.

Heine, Ina and Peter Heine (1993). *O ihr Musliminnen...Frauen in islamischen Gesellschaften*. Freiburg, Herder.

Heller, Erdmude and Hassouna Mosbahi (1993). *Hinter den Schleiern des Islam: Erotik und Sexualität in der arabischen Kultur*. München, Beck.

Hirsch, Paul, Stuard Michaels and Ray Friedmann (1990). 'Clean Models vs. Dirty Hands: Why Economics is different from Sociology'. In *Structures of Capital: The Social Organization of the Economy*, eds. Sharon Zukin and Paul DiMaggio, pp. 39–56. Cambridge, Cambridge University Press.

Hirschman, Albert O. (1993). *Entwicklung, Markt und Moral. Abweichende Betrachtungen*. Frankfurt/Main, Fischer.

Holton, Robert J. (1992). *Economy and Society*. London & New York, Routledge.

Hoodfar, Homa (1991). 'Return to the Veil. Personal Strategy and Public Participation in Egypt'. In *Working Women. International Perspectives on Labor and Gender Ideology*, eds. Nanneke Redclift et.al., pp. 104–24. London, Routledge.

Hooper, Emma (1985). 'Women in the Urban Labour Force in Pakistan: the Case of Lahore'. 'Unpublished Ph.D. thesis, London School of Economics and Political Science, University of London.

Human Development Report 1999. United Nations Development Programme (UNDP), New York/Oxford, Oxford University Press 1999.

Human Rights Commission of Pakistan (1999). *State of Human Rights in 1998*. Lahore, Human Rights Commission of Pakistan, February 1999.

Human Rights Watch (1992). *Double Jeopardy: Police Abuse of Women in Pakistan*. Asia Watch and the Women's Right Project, USA.

———— (1999). *Crime or Custom? Violence against Women in Pakistan*. New York, Human Rights Watch.

Hussain, Maliha H. (1983). 'Women in the Urban informal Sector in Pakistan: productivity, employment, and potential for change'. Unpublished study prepared for population and Human Resources Department, The World Bank, Islamabad.

Hussain, Shazira (1991). *Pakistan mein jinsi tasheddud* (in Urdu). Lahore, Simorgh Collective.

Ibraz, Tassawar Saeed (1993). 'The Cultural Context of Women's Productive Invisibility: A Case Study of a Pakistani Village'. *Pakistan Development Review*, vol. 32, no. 1, pp. 101–25.

Institut für berufliche Bildung, Arbeitsmarkt- und Sozialpolitik (INBAS), ed. (1993). *'Labour Demand Study for PAK-German Technical Training Centre for Women at Lahore, Pakistan'*. Unpublished study, Frankfurt.

Jahangir, Asma and Hina Jilani (1990). *The Hudood Ordinances: a divine Sanction? A Research Study of the Hudood Ordinances and their Effect on the Disadvantaged Sections of Pakistani Society*. Lahore, Rhotas Books.

Jalal, Ayesha (1991). 'The Convenience of Subservience: Women and the State of Pakistan'. In *Women, Islam and the State*, ed. Deniz Kandiyoti, pp. 77–114. Philadelphia, Temple University Press.

Joekes, Susan (1985). 'Working for a lipstick? Male and female labour in the clothing industry in Morocco'. In *Women, Work, and Ideology in the Third World*, ed. Haleh Afshar, pp. 183–213. London/New York, Tavistock.

Kabeer, Naila (1994). 'Women's Labour in the Bangladesh Garment Industry: Choices and Constraints'. In *Muslim Women's Choices: Religious Belief and Social Reality*, eds. Camilla Fazwi El-Solh and Judy Mabro, pp. 164–83. Oxford, Berg.

Kandiyoti, Deniz, ed. (1991). *Women, Islam and the State*. Philadelphia, Temple University Press.

Kang, Chong-Sook (1988). 'Frauen in den selbständigen/ demokratischen Gewerkschaften in Südkorea'. *Peripherie*, no. 30/31, pp. 104–17.

Kaushik, Surenda Nath (1993). *Politics of Islamization in Pakistan: A Study of Zia Regime*. New Delhi, South Asian Publications.

Kazi, Shahnaz (1990). 'Women's Participation in the Formal Sector in Pakistan'. Lecture presented at the 'National Seminar on Women in Mainstream Development. New Directions for Policy', Islamabad, 10–12 April 1990, p. 23.

———— and Bilquees Raza (1990)/ 'The Duality of female Employment in Pakistan'. In *South Asia Bulletin*, vol. 10, no. 2, pp. 1–8.

Kebir, Sabine (1992). 'Dialektik des Schleiers. Das Beispiel Algerien'. In *Fatimas Töchter. Frauen im Islam*, ed. Edith Laudowicz, pp. 162–80, Köln, Papyrossa.

Khan, Nighat Said (1989). *Setting the Record Straight: Women Workers*. Lahore, ASR.

Khan, Shaheen (1990). 'An assessment of changes in the employment situation of Pakistani women in the informal sector'. *In Pakistan Economic and Social Science Review*, vol. 28, no. 2, pp. 137–57.

Khan, Sharukh Rafi (1992). 'Education'. In *Foundations of Pakistan's Political Economy: Towards an Agenda for the 1990s*, eds. William E. James and Subroto Roy, pp. 258–80. New Delhi, Sage.

Khatib-Chahidi, Jane (1993). 'Sexual Prohibitions, Shared Space and 'Fictive' Marriage in Shi'ite Iran'. In *Women and Space: Ground Rules and Social Maps*, ed. Shirley Ardener, pp. 112–34. Oxford, Berg, 2nd edn.

Kohli, Martin (1987). 'Ruhestand und Moralökonomie. Eine historische Skizze'. In *Soziologie wirtschaftlichen Handelns*, ed. Klaus Heinemann, pp. 391–416. Opladen, Westdeutscher Verlag.

Lachenmann, Gudrun (1993). *Selbstorganisation sozialer Sicherheit von Frauen in Entwicklungsländern*. Working paper No. 191,

Sociology of Development Research Centre, Bielefeld University, Germany.

——— (1994). *Frauen in der ländlichen Entwicklung*, lecture presented at Humboldt-University, Berlin, 16–18 June 1994.

——— (1995a). *Internationale Frauenpolitik im Kontext von Globalisierung und aktuellen Transformationsprozessen.* Working paper No. 229, Sociology of Development Research Centre, Bielefeld University, Germany.

——— (1995c). *'Methodenstreit' in der Entwicklungssoziologie.* Working paper No. 241, Sociology of Development Research Centre, Bielefeld University, Germany.

——— (1997a). *Frauen und Globalisierung: aktuelle Entwicklungen und kritische Diskurse.* Working paper No. 284, Sociology of Development Research Centre, Bielefeld University, Germany.

——— (1997b). 'Future Perspectives of Rural Women's Projects—Intervention, Interaction or Empowerment?' In *What have Women's Projects Accomplished so far?* eds. Uta Altmann and Teherani-Krönner, pp. 31–52. Berlin, Institut für Genossenschaftswesen an der Humboldt-Universität zu Berlin.

——— (1997c). 'Intervention, Interaktion, Partizipation—Zu einigen Methodenfragen der empirischen Entwicklungsforschung'. In *Entwicklung: Theorie—Empirie—Strategie*, ed. Manfred Schulz, pp. 99–114. Spektrum 45, Berliner Reihe zu Gesellschaft, Wirtschaft und Politik in Entwicklungsländern.

——— (1998). 'Strukturanpassung aus Frauensicht: Entwicklungskonzepte und Transformationsprozesse'. In *Globalisierung aus Frauensicht. Bilanzen und Visionen*, eds. Ruth Klingebiel and Shalina Randeria, pp. 294–319. Bonn, Dietz.

Lal, Jayati (1996). 'Situating Locations: The Politics of Self, Identity, and "Other" in Living and Working the Text'. In *Feminist Dilemmas in Fieldwork*, ed. Diane L. Wolf, pp. 185–215. Boulder, Colorado, Westview.

LaPorte, Robert Jr. (1996). 'Pakistan in 1995: The Continuing Crises'. *In Asian Survey*, vol. XXXVI, no. 2, pp. 179–88.

——— (1997). 'Pakistan in 1995: Starting Over Again'. *In Asian Survey*, vol. XXXVII, no. 2, pp. 118–25.

Laudowicz, Edith (1992). 'Frauen im Islam. Ein Überblick'. In *Fatimas Töchter: Frauen im Islam*, ed. ibid., pp. 7–61. Köln, Papyrossa.

Lenz, Ilse (1988a). 'Liebe, Brot und Freiheit: Zur neueren Diskussion um Subsistenzproduktion, Technik und Emanzipation in der

Frauenforschung'. *Beiträge zur feministischen Theorie und Praxis*, vol. 11, no. 21/22, pp. 167–82.

—— (1988b). 'Die Dekaden der Frauen am Fließband: Frauenarbeit und exportorientierte Industrialisierung in Ostasien'. *In Peripherie*, no. 33/34, vol. 9, pp. 171–91.

Lessinger, Johanna (1989). 'Petty Trading and Gender Segregation in Urban South Asia'. In *Women, Poverty and Ideology in Asia: Contradictory Pressures, Uneasy Solutions*, eds. Haleh Afshar and Bina Agarwal, pp. 99–127. London, MacMillan.

—— (1990). 'Work and Modesty: The Dilemma of Women Market Traders in Madras'. In *Structures and Strategies: Women, Work and Family. Women and the Household in Asia*, vol. 3, eds. Leela Dube and Ranji Palriwalla, pp. 129–50. New Delhi, Sage.

Lim, Linda Y. (1990). 'Women's Work in Export Factories: The Politics of a Cause'. In *Persistent Inequalities: Women and World Development*, ed. Irene Tinker, pp. 101–22. New York/Oxford, Oxford University Press.

Long, Norman (1989a). 'Introduction. The raison d'être for studying rural development interface'. In *Encounters at the Interface: A perspective on social discontinuities in rural development*, ed. ibid., pp. 1–10. Wageningsche Sociologische Studies 27, Wageningen, Agricultural University.

—— (1989b). 'Conclusion: Theoretical reflections on actor, structure and interface'. In *Encounters at the Interface. A perspective on social discontinuities in rural development*, ed. ibid., pp. 221–44. Wageningsche Sociologische Studies 27, Wageningen, Agricultural University.

—— (1993). 'Handlung, Struktur und Schnittstelle: Theoretische Reflexionen'. In *Entwicklungshilfe und ihre Folgen. Ergebnisse empirischer Untersuchungen in Afrika*, eds. Thomas Bierschenk and Georg Elwert, pp. 217–48. Frankfurt/New York, Campus.

—— and A. Long (1992). *Battlefields of knowledge; the interlinking of theory and practice in social research*. London, Routledge.

Macleod, Arlene Elowe (1991), *Accommodating Protest: Working Women, the New Veiling, and Change in Cairo*. New York, Columbia University Press.

Maenner, Ulrike (1988). *Sozioökonomische Effekte exportorientierter Industrialisierung. Auswirkungen einer Entwicklungsstrategie auf die Situation von Frauen in Sri Lanka*. Hamburg, Weltarchiv.

Mahmood, Sohail (1995). *Islamic Fundamentalism in Pakistan, Egypt and Iran*. Lahore/Karachi/Islamabad, Vanguard Books Ltd.

Mandelbaum, David G. (1988). *Women's Seclusion and Men's Honor: Sex Roles in North India, Bangladesh, and Pakistan*. Tucson, Arizona, University of Arizona Press.

Marker, Meher (1987a). 'Women in Purdah in Pakistan'. Unpublished manuscript, Lahore, 6 pp.

——— (1987b). 'Women, Education and Development in Pakistan'. Unpublished script presented at the 'Conference on Global Perspectives on Women's Education', Mount Holyoke College, Boston, 4–7 November 1987, 21 pp.

Martin, Joanne and Peter Frost (1996). 'The Organizational Culture War Games: A Struggle for Intellectual Dominance'. In *Handbook of Organization Studies*, eds. Clegg, Steward R, Cynthia Hardy and Walter R. Nord, pp. 599–621. London, SAGE.

Martinelli, Alberto and Neil J. Smelser, eds. (1990). *Economy and Society: Overviews in Economic Sociology*. London, Sage.

Maskiell, Michelle (1985). 'Social Change and Social Control: College-educated Punjabi Women 1913–1960'. *In Modern Asian Studies*, vol. 19, no. 1, pp. 55–83.

Maududi, Abdul A'la (1987). *Purdah and the Status of Women in Islam*. Lahore, Islamic Publications, 13th edn.

Mehdi, Rubya (1990). 'The Offence of Rape in the Islamic Law of Pakistan'. *In International Journal of the Sociology of Law*, vol. 18, no. 1, pp. 19–29.

Mernissi, Fatima (1985). *Participation of Women's Social and Human Scientific Life in the Arab World (With particular reference to Morocco)*. Division of Human Rights and Peace, UNESCO, Paris.

——— (1987). *Beyond the Veil: Male Female Dynamics in Modern Muslim Society*. London, Al Saqi Books, 2nd revised edn.

——— (1991). *Women and Islam: a historical and theological Inquiry*. Oxford, Blackwell.

Meyer, John W. and W. Richard Scott, eds. (1992). *Organizational Environments. Ritual and Rationality*. Newbury Park, California, SAGE, 2nd edn.

Mies, Maria (1991). 'Capitalist Development and Subsistence Production: Rural Women in India'. In *Women: The Last Colony*, Maria Mies, Veronika Bennholdt-Thomsen and Claudia von Werlhof, pp. 27–50. London/New Jersey, Zed Books, 2nd edn.

———— Veronika Bennholdt-Thomsen and Claudia von Werlhof (1991). *Women: The Last Colony*. London/New Jersey, Zed Books, 2nd edn.

Minai, Naila (1991). *Schwerstern unterm Halbmond. Muslimische Frauen zwischen Tradition und Emanzipation*. M–nchen, dtv.

Minces, Juliette (1992). *Verschleiert—Frauen im Islam*. Reinbeck, Rowohlt.

Mingione, Enzo (1991). *Fragmented Societies: A Sociology of Economic Life beyond the Market Paradigm*. Oxford, Basil Blackwell.

Mirza, Jasmin (1992). 'Market Integration of former Trainees of Technical Training Centre for Women (TTCW), Lahore'. Unpublished study, Lahore, November.

———— (1994a) 'Berufsausbildung für Frauen in Pakistan. Analyse eines Entwicklungsprojekts zur Förderung weiblicher Erwerbstätigkeit im gesellschaftlichen Kontext'. Unpublished M.Sc. thesis, Bielefeld University, Germany.

———— (1994b). 'Berufsausbildung in Pakistan'. *In Südasien*, vol. 13, no. 1–2, pp. 81–3.

———— (1994c). 'Männliche Festung. Frauen in Pakistan sind vom Berufsleben weitgehend ausgeschlossen'. *In der Ueberblick*, no. 2, pp. 68–71.

———— (1994d). 'Pakistan: Berufsausbildung für Frauen'. *In Südasien*, vol. 13, no. 4–5, pp. 72–5.

Moghadam, Valentine (1994). 'Introduction and Overview'. In *Gender and National Identity: Women and Politics in Muslim Societies*, ed. ibid., pp. 1–18. London/New Jersey, Zed Books.

Mohiuddin, Yasmeen (1991). 'Discrimination in the Pakistan labour market: myth and reality'. In *The Pakistan Development Review*, vol. 30, no. 4, pp. 965–82.

Mohsen, Safia K. (1985). 'New Images, Old Reflections: Working Middle-Class Women in Egypt'. In *Women and the Family in the Middle East: New Voices of Change*, ed. Elisabeth Warnock Fernea, pp. 56–71. Austin, University of Texas Press.

Morgan, Gareth (1997). *Images of Organization*. Thousand Oaks, California, SAGE, 2nd edition.

Mukhopadhyay, Swapna (1994). 'The Impact of Structural Adjustment Policies on Women: Some General Observations Relating to Conceptual Bias'. In *The Strategic Silence: Gender and Economic*

Policy, ed. Isabella Bakker, pp. 158–63. Ottawa, The North-South Institute.

Müller, Ursula (1993). 'Sexualität, Organisation und Kontrolle'. In *Transformationen im Geschlechterverhältnis: Beiträge zur industriellen und gesellschaftlichen Entwicklung*, eds. Brigitte Aulenbacher and Monika Goldmann, pp. 97–114. Frankfurt/Main, Campus.

_____ (1999). 'Geschlecht und Organisation. Traditionsreiche Debatten—aktuelle Tendenzen'. In *Transformation— Unternehmensorganisation—Geschlechterforschung*, eds. Hildegard Maria Nickel, Susanne Völker and Hasko Hüning. Opladen, Leske und Budrich.

Mumtaz, Khawar (1994). 'Identity Politics and Women: 'Fundamentalism' and Women in Pakistan'. In *Identity Politics & Women: Cultural Reassertions and Feminisms in International Perspective*, ed. Valentine M. Moghadam, 1994, pp. 228–42. Boulder, Westview.

_____ (1985). 'The Saga of Wyeth Women Workers'. *In Viewpoint*, Lahore, 28 Nov. 1985.

_____ (1986). 'Shattered Dreams, Stark Reality'. *In Viewpoint*, Lahore, 21 August 1986.

_____ (1987). 'Female Employment', *In Viewpoint*, Lahore, 5 March 1987.

Nestvogel, Renate and Heinz-Günther Klein (1986). *Women in Pakistan: General Conditions, Approaches and Proposals for the Development and Vocational Qualification of Women in the Province of Punjab*. Rossdorf, TZ-Verlagsgesellschaft.

O'Sullivan, Helene, ed. (1995). *Silk and Steel: Asian Women Workers Confront Challenges of Industrial Restructuring*. Hong Kong, Committee for Asian Women (CAW).

Otto-Walter, Renate (1981). 'Unterentwicklung und Subsistenzreproduktion - Forschungsansatz der Arbeitsgruppe Bielefelder Entwicklungssoziologen'. In *Subsistenzproduktion und Akkumulation*, eds. Arbeitsgruppe Bielefelder Entwicklungssoziologen, pp. 7–12. Saarbrücken, breitenbach, 2nd edn.

Pahnke, Donata (1992). 'Patriarchaler Fundamentalismus im Islam und Christentum'. *Beiträge zur feministischen Theorie und Praxis*, vol. 15, no. 32, pp. 9–18.

Palmer, Ingrid (1995). 'Public Finance from a Gender Perspective'. In *Gender, Adjustment and Macroeconomics*, eds. Nilüfer Cagatay et al., pp. 1981–6. World Development (Special Issue), vol. 23, no. 11.

———— (1997). 'Social and Gender Issues in Macro-Economic Policy Advice'. In *Gender and Macro Policy: Gender in Macro-Economic and Legal Policy Advice in Technical Cooperation*, ed. German Technical Cooperation, pp. 1–12. Social Policy Working Paper No. 20, Eschborn, Germany.

Papanek, Hanna (1971). 'Purdah in Pakistan: seclusion and modern occupations for women'. In *Journal of Marriage and the Family*, vol. 33, no. 3, pp. 517–30.

Pastner, Carol (1990). 'A Social Structural and Historical Analysis of Honour, Shame and Purdah in Baluchistan'. In *Pakistan: The Social Sciences' Perspective*, ed. Akbar S. Ahmed, pp. 247–59. Karachi, Oxford University Press.

Patel, Rashida (1991). *Socio-economic political status and women and law in Pakistan*. Karachi, Faiza.

Pearson, Ruth (1996). 'Industrialization and Women's Subordination: A Reappraisal'. In *Patriarchy and Economic Development: Women's Position at the End of the Twentieth Century*, ed. Valentine Moghadam, pp. 169–83. Oxford, Clarendon.

Polanyi, Karl (1978 [1944]). *The Great Transformation: Politische und ökonomische Ursprünge von Gesellschaften und Wirtschaftssystemen*. Wien, Suhrkamp.

———— (1992 [1957]). 'The Economy as Instituted Process'. In *The Sociology of Economic Life*, eds. Richard Swedberg and Mark Granovetter. Boulder/Oxford, Westview.

Rashid, Abbas (1996). 'Pakistan: The Politics of "Fundamentalism"'. In *Internal Conflicts in South Asia*, eds. Khawar Mumtaz and Kumar Rupesinge, pp. 55–80. London, Sage.

Rastetter, Daniela (1994). *Sexualität und Herrschaft in Organisationen: eine geschlechtervergleichende Analyse*. Opladen, Westdeutscher Verlag.

Reece, Debra (1996). 'Covering and Communication: The symbolism of dress among Muslim Women'. In *Howard Journal of Communications*, vol. 7, no. 1, pp. 35–52.

Reuter, Norbert (1994). 'Institutionalismus, Neo-Institutionalismus, Neue Institutionelle Ökonomie und andere "Institutionalismen". Eine Differenzierung konträrer Konzepte'. *Zeitschrift für Wirtschafts- und Sozialwissenschaften*, vol. 110, pp. 571–91.

Riesenbrodt, Martin (1990). *Fundamentalismus als Patriarchalische Protestbewegung: Amerikanische Protestanten (1910-28) und iranische Schiiten (1961-79) im Vergleich.* Tübingen, J.C.B. Mohr.

Roodet, Ruth (1999). *Women in Islam and the Middle East: A Reader.* London, I.B. Tauris & Co. Ltd.

Rosa, Kumudhini (1994). 'The conditions and organisational activities of women in Free Trade Zones: Malaysia, Philippines and Sri Lanka, 1970-1990'. In *Dignity and Daily Bread: New Forms of Economic Organising among Poor Women in the Third World and the First,* eds. Sheila Rowbotham and Swasti Mitter, pp. 73–99. New York/London, Routledge.

Sabbah, Fatna A. (1988). *Women in the Muslim Unconscious.* New York, Pergamon.

Saeed, Javaid (1994). *Islam and Modernization: A Comparative Analysis of Pakistan, Egypt, and Turkey.* Westpoint, Praeger.

Safa, Helen (1990). 'Women and Industrialisation in the Caribbean'. In *Women, Employment and the Family in the International Division of Labour,* eds. Sharon Stichter and Jane L. Parpart, pp. 72–97. London, MacMillan Press.

———— (1996). 'Gender Inequality and Women's Wage Labour: A theoretical and empirical analysis'. In *Patriarchy and Economic Development: Women's Position at the End of the Twentieth Century,* ed. Valentine Moghadam, pp. 184–219. Oxford, Clarendon.

Salaff, Janet W. (1990). 'Women, the Family, and the State: Hong Kong, Taiwan, Singapore—Newly Industrialized Countries in Asia'. In *Women, Employment and the Family in the International Division of Labour,* eds. Sharon Stichter and Jane L. Parpart, pp. 98–136. London, MacMillan Press.

Schrader, Heiko (1994). 'The Discussion of Trade in Social Science'. In *The Moral Economy of Trade. Ethnicity and Developing Markets,* eds. Hans-Dieter Evers and Heiko Schrader, pp. 27–47. London/New York, Routledge.

———— (1995). *Zur Relevanz von Polanyis Konzept der Einbettung der Wirtschaft in die Gesellschaft* Working paper No. 219, Sociology of Development Research Center, Bielefeld University, Germany.

Schuetz, Alfred and Thomas Luckmann (1979). *Strukturen der Lebenswelt.* Frankfurt/Main, Suhrkamp.

Schultz, Ulrike (1993). 'Auf Besuch bei kenianischen Frauen—
Methodische Überlegungen anläßlich zweier Forschungsaufenthalte
in Kenia'. In *Methoden - Hilfestellung oder Korsett? Erfahrungen
mit empirischer Sozialforschung in Afrika, Asien und Lateinamerika*,
eds. Karin Fiege and Gabriele Zdunnek, pp. 131–42. Saarbrücken,
breitenbach.

Shah, Nasra (1986). 'Female Employment: Trends, Structures,
Utilization and Constraints'. In *Pakistani Women: A Socioeconomic
and Demographic Profile*, ed. ibid. pp. 264–301. Pakistan Institute
of Development Economics, Islamabad.

Shaheed, Farida (1989). 'Purdah and Poverty in Pakistan'. In *Women,
Poverty and Ideology in Asia. Contradictory Pressures, Uneasy
Solutions*, eds. Haleh Afshar and Bina Agarwal, pp. 17–41. London,
MacMillan.

———— (1990). *Pakistan's Women: An Analytical Description.*
Lahore, Shirkat Gah.

———— (1995). 'Networking for Change: The Role of Women's
Groups in Initiating Dialogue on Women's Issues'. In *Faith &
Freedom: Women's Human Rights in the Muslim World*, ed. Mahnaz
Afkhani, pp. 78–103. London, I.B. Tauris.

———— and Khawar Mumtaz (undated). *Invisible Workers. Piece
Work Labour amongst Women in Lahore.* Women's Division,
Government of Pakistan, Islamabad.

———— (1987). *Women in Pakistan: Two Steps Forward, One Step
Back?* London/New Jersey, Zed Books Ltd.

———— (1990). *Women's Economic Participation in Pakistan: A
Status Report.* Unicef, Islamabad.

———— (1993). 'Target Group Study for the Technical Training Centre
for Women - Lahore'. Unpublished study, Lahore, May 1993.

Sharma, Ursula (1990). 'Public Employment and Private Relations:
Women and Work in India'. In *Women, Employment and the Family
in the International Division of Labour*, eds. Sharon Stitcher and
Jane L. Parpart, pp. 198–220. London, MacMillan Press.

Sherif, Mostafa Hashem (1987). 'What is Hijab?' *The Muslim World*,
vol. 77, no. 3–4, pp. 151–63.

Smelser, Neil. J. and Richard Swedberg, (1994). 'The Sociological
Perspective on the Economy'. In *The Handbook of Economic
Sociology*, eds. ibid., pp. 3–26. Princeton, Princeton University
Press.

_____ eds. (1994). *The Handbook of Economic Sociology*. Princeton, Princeton University Press.

Smith, Joan, Immanuel Wallerstein and Hans-Dieter Evers, eds. (1984). *Households and the World Economy*. London et.al., SAGE.

Sparr, Pamela (1994a). 'What is Structural Adjustment?' In *Mortgaging Women's Lives: Feminist Critiques of Structural Adjustment*, ed. ibid., pp. 1–12. London, Zed Books.

_____ (1994b). 'Feminist Critiques of Structural Adjustment'. In *Mortgaging Women's Lives: Feminist Critiques of Structural Adjustment*, ed. ibid., pp. 13–39. London, Zed Books.

Standing, Guy (1996). 'Cumulative Disadvantage? Women Industrial Workers in Malaysia and the Philippines'. In *Patriarchy and Economic Development: Women's Position at the End of the Twentieth Century*, ed. Valentine Moghadam, pp. 269–302. Oxford, Clarendon.

Strauss, Anselm (1987). *Qualitative Analysis for Social Scientists*. Cambridge, Cambridge University Press.

_____ (1994). *Grundlagen qualitativer Sozialforschung: Datenanalyse und Theoriebildung in der empirischen soziologischen Forschung*. München, Fink.

_____ and Juliet Corbin (1990). *Basics of Qualitative Research: Grounded Theory Procedures and Techniques*. London, SAGE.

Sudarkasa, Niara (1986). 'In a World of Women: Field Work in a Yoruba Community'. In *Women in the Field*, ed. Peggy Golde, pp. 167–94. Berkley/Los Angeles, University of California Press.

Swedberg, Richard (1990). *Economics and Sociology: On Redefining their Boundaries: Conversations with Economists and Sociologists*. Princeton, Princeton University Press.

_____ (1994). 'Markets as Social Structures'. In *The Handbook of Economic Sociology*, eds. Neil J. Smelser and Richard Swedberg, pp. 255–82. Princeton, Princeton University Press.

_____ ed. (1993). *Explorations in Economic Sociology*. New York, Russel Sage Foundation.

_____ Ulf Himmelstrand and Göran Brulin (1990) 'The Paradigm of Economic Sociology'. In *Structures of Capital: The Social Organization of the Economy*, eds. Sharon Zukin and Paul DiMaggio, pp. 57–86. Cambridge, Cambridge University Press.

_____ and Mark Granovetter, eds. (1992). *The Sociology of Economic Life*. Boulder/Oxford, Westview.

Syed, Anwar H. (1998). 'Pakistan in 1997. Nawaz Sharif's second chance to govern'. In *Asian Survey*, vol. XXXVIII, no. 2, pp. 116–25.

Thiel, Susanne (1994). 'Berufstätige Frauen in Pakistan'. In *Südasien*, vol. 14, no. 1–2, pp. 81–3.

Tirmizi, Jamshed (1989). 'The State as an Organizational Substitute for Civil Society: Some Reflections upon the Agrarian Realities of the Punjab (Pakistan)'. Unpublished Ph.D., University of Heidelberg, Germany.

Thompson, Edward P. (1971). 'The Moral Economy of the English Crowd in the 18th Century'. In *Past and Present*, vol. 50, pp. 76–136.

Turner, Barry, ed. (2000). *The Statesman's Yearbook 2000: The Politics, Cultures and Economies of the World*. London, MacMillan.

Vagt, Holger (1992). *Die Frau in Saudi-Arabien zwischen Tradition und Moderne*. Berlin, Klaus Schwarz.

Walgenbach, Peter (1995). 'Institutionalistische Ansätze in der Organisationstheorie'. In *Organisationstheorien*, ed. Alfred Kieser, pp. 269–302. Stuttgart, Kohlhammer, 2nd edn.

Walters, Bernhard (1997). 'Engendering Macroeconomics: A Reconsideration of Growth Theory'. In *Gender and Macro Policy: Gender in Macro-Economic and Legal Policy Advice in Technical Cooperation*, ed. German Technical Cooperation, pp. 48–68. Social Policy Working Paper No. 20, Eschborn, Germany.

Watson, Helen (1994). 'Women and the Veil. Personal Responses to Global Process'. In *Islam, Globalization and Postmodernity*, eds. Akbar S. Ahmed andHastings Donnan, pp. 141–59. London/New York, Routledge.

Weiss, Anita M. (1984). 'Tradition and Modernity at the Workplace: A Field Study of Women in the Pharmaceutical Industry of Lahore'. In *Women's Studies International Forum*, vol. 7, no. 4, pp. 259–64.

———— (1992). *Walls within Walls: life histories of working women in the old city of Lahore*. Boulder, Westview Press.

———— (1994a). 'Challenges for Muslim Women in a Postmodern World'. In *Islam, Globalization and Postmodernity*, eds. Akbar S. Ahmed and Hastings Donnan, pp. 127–40. London/New York, Routledge.

———— (1994b). 'The Consequences of State Policies for Women in Pakistan'. In *The Politics of social Transformation in Afghanistan,*

Iran, and Pakistan, eds. Myron Weiner and Ali Banuazizi, pp. 412–44. Syracuse, Syracuse University Press.

———— (1998) 'The gendered division of space and access in working class areas of Lahore'. In *Contemporary South Asia*, vol. 7, no. 1, pp. 71–89.

Werner, Karin (1997). *Between Westernization and the Veil: gendering in Egyptian youth cultures*. Bielefeld, transcript.

Wiegersma, Nan (1994). 'State Policy and the Restructuring of Women's Industries in Nicaragua'. In *Women in the Age of Economic Transformation*, eds. Nahid Aslanbeigui et al., pp. 192–205. London/New York, Routledge.

Wolf, Diane L. (1996). 'Situating Feminist Dilemmas in Fieldwork'. In *Feminist Dilemmas in Fieldwork*, ed. ibid., pp. 1-55. Boulder, Colorado, Westview.

Worldbank (1989). *Women in Pakistan And Economic and Social Strategy*. Country Report, Washington, D.C.

Zelizer, Viviana (1979). *Morals and Markets: The Development of Life Insurance in the United States*. New York, Columbia University Press.

———— (1988). 'Beyond the Polemics on the Market: Establishing a Theoretical and Empirical Agenda'. *Sociological Forum*, vol. 3, no. 4, pp. 614–34.

Zingel, Wolfgang-Peter (1994). 'Struktur- und Entwicklungsprobleme Asiens'. In *Handbuch der Dritten Welt, Vol. 7*, eds. Dieter Nohlen and Franz Nuscheler, pp. 14–53. Bonn, Ditz, 3rd edition.

Zuhur, Sherifa (1992). *Revealing and Reveiling: Islamist Gender Ideology in Contemporary Egypt*. Albany, State University of New York Press.

Zukin, Sharon and Paul DiMaggio, eds. (1990) *Structures of Capital: The Social Organization of the Economy*. Cambridge, Cambridge University Press.

Newspaper Articles

'Women resent transporters' misbehavior', *Dawn* [Lahore], 23 Jan. 2000.

'More violence against women reported in 1999', *Sun* [Lahore], 25 Jan. 2000.

'Eve-teasers throw acid on girl', *Dawn* [Lahore], 4 Jan. 2000.

'Mould lives according to Islam: Tarar', *The News* [Lahore], 21 Nov. 1999.

'Girls don't just wanna have fun', *The News* [Lahore], 9 Nov. 1999.

'First woman pilot to fly Jumbo', *Dawn* [Lahore], 29 Oct. 1999.

'Urban people want higher education for girls: survey', *Dawn* [Lahore], 9 Oct. 1999.

'Women's only park in a shambles', *Dawn* [Lahore], 21 Sept. 1999.

'Violence against women increases', *Dawn* [Lahore], 17 July 1999.

'Women commuters' sufferings', *Dawn* [Lahore], 9 July 1999.

'No more female administrators in education', *Dawn* [Lahore], 30 May 1999.

'New action plan for privatisation process', *Pakistan & Gulf Economist*, 21–7 Dec. 1998.

'Tarar urges women to adopt Islamic values', *The News* [Lahore], 15 Nov. 1998.

'Bazaar for craftswomen opens', *Dawn* [Lahore], 27 Oct. 1998.

'Pakistan ranks lowest among Asian states', *Dawn* [Lahore], 5 Sep. 1998.

'Islamization solution to all problems', *The Nation* [Lahore], 30 Aug. 1998.

'Breaking the curfew. Watch out! Women are in the field', *Dawn* [Lahore], 9 Aug. 1998.

'A woman as chief executive', *Dawn* [Lahore], 8 Aug. 1998.

'Population Census 1998', *The Nation* [Lahore], 9 July 1998.

'Pakistan ki aabadi 13 karor hogai izafey ke sharah mein nomaaieh kami', *Jang* [Lahore] (Urdu), 9 July 1998.

'Mahangaai ne khawateen ka gharelo budget bhi mutassir kardia', *Jang* [Lahore] (Urdu), 2 June 1998.

'Mahangaai nehin tankhaein barkaen', *Jang* [Lahore] (Urdu), 2 June 1998.

'Burqa must for girl students', *The Nation* [Lahore], 17 March 1998.

'Participation of Muslim Women in mixed gatherings', *The News* [Lahore], 16 Jan. 1998.

'Pakistan mein 12 lakh B.A. pass larkian rozgar se mahrum hein', *Jang* [Lahore] (Urdu), 27 Nov. 1997.

'Pakistan TV bans the shampoo set', *The Friday Times*, 21–7 Nov. 1997.

'Khaima numa burqa?' *Lashker* [Lahore] (Urdu), 18 Nov. 1997, evening edn.

'Gang rape ki wajuhat: beemaar zehen aur zati dushmenian', *Jang* [Lahore] (Urdu), 16 Oct. 1997.

'Mardon ki fikeraybazi pereyshan karti hai, auratein khud zimeydar hain', *Jang* [Lahore] (Urdu), 11 Aug. 1997.

'Guzara nehin hota', *Jang* [Lahore] (Urdu), Sunday Magazine, 3–9 Aug. 1997, evening edn., (by Rauf Zafar).

'The high cost of living', *Pakistan & Gulf Economist*, 7–13 July 1997b.

'Gharon mein kaam karneywali khawateen koi unkey haq me awaaz uthaneywala nehin', *Jang* [Lahore] (Urdu), 4 July 1997.

'Privatisation—at what cost?' *Pakistan & Gulf Economist*, 16–22 June 1997 (by Syed M. Aslam).

'Below Rs. 4500 you sink', *The News* [Lahore], 1 June 1997a (by Mohammad Akbar).

'Waging the struggle', *The News* [Lahore], 1 June 1997b (by Aamir Ashraf).

'The least we can do', *The News* [Lahore], 1 June 1997c (by Arif Shamin).

'Budget deficit impels govt. to expedite privatisation', *Pakistan & Gulf Economist*, 19–25 May 1997 (by Shabbir H. Kazmi).

'Lahore leads Karachi in rape, abduction', *The News* [Lahore], 22 April 1997.

'Islamic codes and conduct', *The News* [Lahore] Us-Magazine for the Young, 11 Apr. 1997.

'Acting on Quran can resolve Muslims' problems', *The News* [Lahore], 9 Apr. 1997.

'Engineering ki taleem ke leaye mazeed idarey kaaim karney ki zarurat hae', *Jang* [Lahore] (Urdu), 8 Apr. 1997.

'Will privatisation take place in 1997?' *Pakistan & Gulf Economist*, 24 Mar.–6 Apr. 1997 (by Naween A. Mangi).

'IMF conditionalities and Pakistan's economic performance', *The News* [Lahore], 11 Jan. 1997.

'Pakistan's economic enslavement', *The News* [Lahore], 29 Dec. 1996.

'Whose economic philosophy is it?' *The News* [Lahore], 4 Dec. 1996.

'Increase in Commodities Prices', *Pakistan & Gulf Economist*, 30 Nov.–6 Dec. 1996 (by M.K. Areola).

'Male's appointment in gynae ward flayed', *The News* [Lahore], 19 Nov. 1996a.

'Shoving up the economy', *The News* [Lahore], 19 Nov. 1996b.

'Fairer sex reigns supreme yet again', *The News* [Lahore], 13 Nov. 1996 (by Umaira Ansari).

'Economy comes first', *The News* [Lahore], 11 Nov. 1996a.
'Male appointed in gynaecology ward', *The News* [Lahore], 11 Nov. 1996b.
'Hazarat Fatima role model for women of all ages', *The Muslim* [Islamabad], 4 Nov. 1996 (by Nabeela Aslam).
'IMF loan at heavy cost to industry, trade and consumers', *The News* [Lahore], 2 Nov. 1996.
'And how do you manage?' *The News* [Lahore], 1 Nov. 1996a (by Mazhar Zaidi).
'Kept afloat the balloon' *The News* [Lahore], 1 Nov. 1996b.
'Where do we go from here?' *The News* [Lahore], 1 Nov. 1996c (by Farjad Nabi).
'New package in concurrence with IMF: a conspiracy against the people', *The News* [Lahore], 26 Oct. 1996.
'The demons at work', *The News* [Lahore], 25 Oct. 1996.
'The dependency syndrome', *The Nation* [Lahore], 18 Oct. 1996 (by Rashed Rahman).
'Careerwise: Women in horticulture', *Dawn* [Lahore], 1 June 1996.
'Private Sector: Greater participatory role', *Pakistan & Gulf Economist*, 27 Apr.–3 May 1996 (by Jousaf Golampota).
'Unemployment situation more serious than imagined', *The News* [Lahore], 6 Jan. 1996 (by Aftab Ahmed).
'An economic analysis of unemployment in Pakistan', *The News* [Lahore], 22 Dec. 1995.
'The unbearable harassment', *The Nation* [Lahore], 11 Nov. 1995 (by Maliha Maria).
'Purdah aurat ke leaye qila sabet hota hae', *Jang* [Lahore] (Urdu), 9 Oct. 1995.
'Mazdoor khawateen mardon se ziadah kaam karti hain', *Jang* [Lahore] (Urdu), 2 Oct. 1995.
'Pakistan. Emanzipation?' *taz* [Berlin], 15 Sep. 1995.
'The concept of pardah in Islam', *The Nation* [Lahore], 26 May 1995 (by Zaheer Hussain).
'PIA first woman pilot to fly airbus A-310', *The Frontier Post* [Lahore], 6 Apr. 1995.
'The ordeal of Eve', *The Muslim* [Islamabad], 27 Mar. 1995.
'The spectre of unemployment: change in the system needed', *Dawn* [Lahore], 6 Sep. 1994 (by Ikramul Haq).
'State of unemployment in Pakistan II', *The News* [Lahore], 25 June 1994.

'Polizeistation in Karachi nur mit Frauen besetzt', *taz* [Berlin], 3 June 1994.

'The battered half', *The Frontier Post* [Lahore], 14 March 1994.

'Undue profits for male-controlled industries', *The News* [Lahore], 28 Jan. 1994 (by Karamat Ali).

'Pakistan. Jenseits des Teppichs', *Spiegel* [Berlin], 40/1993.

'For working women transport problem becoming grave', *The Muslim* [Islamabad], 2 Aug. 1993 (by Ishtiaq Ahmed).

'Female Students to observe purdah', *The Frontier Post* [Lahore], 2 Nov. 1992 (by Mohsn Raza).

'Why worker shortage amidst massive unemployment?' *The Nation* [Lahore], 27 Sep. 1992 (by Ghani Eirable).

'Vergewaltigung und Folter in Pakistan', *taz* [Berlin], 3 June 1992.

'Pakistan's first woman jet pilot', *The Muslim* [Islamabad], 30 Jan. 1992.

'Larkion ki ziadah taadaad ko amli meidaan mein aana chahiey', *Jang* [Lahore] (Urdu), 26 Nov. 1991.

'60pc of women workers earn less than Rs 1,000', *Dawn* [Lahore], 7 Jan. 1990.

'Lahori, prices then and prices now', *Dawn* [Lahore], 29 Sep. 1989.

INDEX

BETWEEN CHADDOR AND THE MARKET

Female Office Workers in Lahore

Figure 1: Map of Pakistan

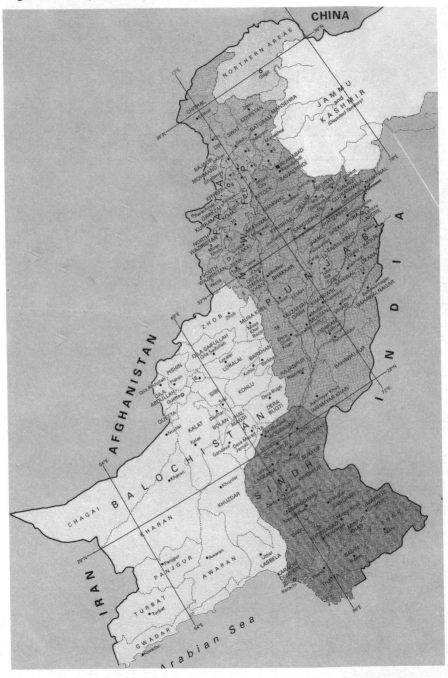